WITHDRAWN

HARVARD LIBRARY

WITHDRAWN

COLLINGWOOD AND THEOLOGICAL HERMENEUTICS

COLLINGWOOD AND THEOLOGICAL HERMENEUTICS

John P. Hogan

COLLEGE THEOLOGY SOCIETY
STUDIES IN RELIGION • 3

Lanham • New York • London

Copyright © 1989 by

The College Theology Society

University Press of America,® Inc.

4720 Boston Way
Lanham, MD 20706

3 Henrietta Street
London WC2E 8LU England

All rights reserved

Printed in the United States of America

British Cataloging in Publication Information Available

Co-published by arrangement with
The College Theology Society

Library of Congress Cataloging–in–Publication Data

Collingwood and theological hermeneutics / John P. Hogan.
p. cm.
(College Theology Society studies in religion ; 3)
"Co-published by arrangement with the College Theology Society"–
–T.p. verso.
Bibliography: p.
Includes index.
1. Hermeneutics– –History– –20th century. 2. Hermeneutics–
–Religious aspects– –Christianity– –History– –20th century.
3. History– –Philosophy– –History– –20th century. 4. Collingwood,
R.G. (Robin George), 1889–1943. I. Title. II. Series.
BD241.H624   1988   88–39924 CIP
220.6'01– –dc19
ISBN 0–8191–7247–2 (alk. paper).
ISBN 0–8191–7248–0 (pbk. : alk. paper)

All University Press of America books are produced on acid-free paper.
The paper used in this publication meets the minimum requirements of American
National Standard for Information Sciences—Permanence of Paper for Printed Library
Materials, ANSI Z39.48–1984.   ∞

TABLE OF CONTENTS

	ABBREVIATIONS	vii
	INTRODUCTION	1
I	A RAPPROCHEMENT BETWEEN PHILOSOPHY AND HISTORY	7
	Introduction	7
	The Quest for Unity	8
	Biographical Sketch	11
	The Problem of Interpretation	15
	The Hermeneutical Thread	21
	Conclusion	34
II	THE LOGIC OF QUESTION AND ANSWER	43
	Logic, Theory of Inquiry or Hermeneutic?	43
	Development of the Logic of Question and Answer	44
	Gadamer and the Logic of Question and Answer	51
	A Response to Gadamer	57
	Conclusion	64
III	THE DOCTRINE OF ABSOLUTE PRESUPPOSITIONS	71
	Introduction	71
	The Doctrine of Absolute Presuppositions	73
	An Example of the Doctrine	84
	Absolute Presuppositions and Contemporary Hermeneutics	88
	Conclusion	92
IV	THE HISTORICAL IMAGINATION	99
	Background to Theory	99
	The Historical Imagination	106
	The Criterion for Historical Truth	114
	Conclusion	116

V	HISTORICAL EVIDENCE	123
	Introduction	123
	Evidence: The Starting Point of History	126
	From Evidence to Thought: The Outside and Inside of Historical Events	133
	Conclusion	136
VI	THE RE-ENACTMENT OF PAST THOUGHT	143
	Introduction	143
	History as the Rethinking of Past Thought	145
	Event, Process and Incapsulation	152
	Re-enactment and Theological Hermeneutics	156
	Conclusion	160
VII	SOME THEOLOGICAL APPLICATIONS OF COLLINGWOOD: BULTMANN AND PANNENBERG	167
	Introduction	167
	Rudolf Bultmann	168
	Wolfhart Pannenberg	182
	Conclusion	196
	CONCLUSION	207
	SELECTED BIBLIOGRAPHY	213
	INDEX	235

ABBREVIATIONS
(of Collingwood's works)

A	*An Autobiography*
EM	*An Essay on Metaphysics*
EPM	*An Essay on Philosophical Method*
IH	*The Idea of History*
IN	*The Idea of Nature*
NL	*The New Leviathan*
PA	*The Principles of Art*
RP	*Religion and Philosophy*
SM	*Speculum Mentis*

INTRODUCTION

The question behind this book, the linkage between historical inquiry and hermeneutical reflection, surfaced some years ago while I was examining the writings of Bultmann and Gadamer. At crucial points, Collingwood's name kept appearing. My steps in pursuit of that linkage were quickened by a chance conversation with a young divinity student recently returned from Lonergan's Harvard classroom. To my passing query as to whether Lonergan ever mentioned Collingwood, he replied, "Lonergan quotes him more than the New Testament!" This not only sent me scurrying back to *Method in Theology* but also started me on a systematic trek through all of Collingwood's philosophical works.

Hermeneutics is concerned with the task of translating meaning. It seeks to bridge the cultural and temporal gaps existing between a past text or event and a present interpreter. Hermeneutical concerns have become central in theological and biblical studies and, in spite of efforts to the contrary, cannot be completely divorced from the more properly historical concern of whether and how the past can be known. This study investigates the contribution to hermeneutical theory and theological hermeneutics of R. G. Collingwood, who, as philosopher, historian, and archeologist, was singularly equipped to establish an intelligible relationship between hermeneutical consciousness and historical consciousness. It is clear from the research assembled here, the first full length treatment of Collingwood from a hermeneutical perspective, that the Oxford philosopher had a seminal influence on the development of hermeneutics in the twentieth century. That influence can readily be traced through the writings of Bultmann, Gadamer, Lonergan, and Pannenberg.

The issues at stake in the relationship between history and hermeneutics go well beyond the scholarly debate. Protestant communities have been polarized by the struggle between fundamentalists and moderates, mainly over interpretations of the Bible. Recent turmoil within American Lutheranism and the Southern Baptist Convention comes most readily to mind. Catholics, to a great extent, have been spared such turmoil. However, a kind of residual Catholic fundamentalism is already emerging concerning doctrine and morals. It could easily become an unpleasant by-product of the growing popular interest in Bible study among Catholics.

On the scholarly level the differences are not drawn so starkly. Nonetheless, in some quarters the critical-historical method becomes "an irrational, self-defeating sort of folly that spelled its own doom."[1] This extreme position is probably best exemplified in academic circles by Gerhard Maier, *The End of the Historical-Critical Method*. In other quarters, the hermeneutical approach is dismissed as a careless opening to subjectivism, relativism, or perspectivism. Hermeneutics is viewed as a new vehicle for Docetism. Although Hermes is enshrined as the messenger of the Olympian gods, he is also remembered by those sceptical about hermeneutics, as the god of cunning and fraud and the conductor of souls to Hades.

While the discussion in New Testament studies has shifted from the battle about *"geschichtlich und historisch"*[2] to a focus either on social theory or on language, story, and literary form, the history-hermeneutic debate has been left hanging. Dichotomies have emerged which separate too neatly hermeneutical concerns from historical concerns and vice versa. For example, while theologians such as Schillebeeckx, Küng, and Sobrino place considerable trust in historical method in their retrieval of the meaning of Jesus Christ, David Tracy sees it a "serious mistake to replace (the) classical Christian belief with the logically distinct one of the 'historical Jesus' (i.e. the Jesus who actually lived as reconstructed through historico-critical methods)."[3] Of course, the scholarly discussion is both nuanced and detailed and it is undeniable that there are limits to the use of strictly historical methods in dealing with scripture and doctrine. Nonetheless, necessary and helpful distinctions should not be hardened into separation and opposition. The result of such dichotomized approaches threatens to leave us, for example, with two versions of Jesus Christ, one rooted in the past—the product of historical reconstruction, and the other rooted in the present—the product of hermeneutical reflection. Have we travelled so far only to have come full circle to the Jesus of History-Christ of Faith impasse?

Roger Haight in his excellent study of liberation theology illustrates graphically the need to overcome such dichotomies in order to formulate a meaningful Christology. For Haight, Christology begins with the historical Jesus.

> The phrase, "the historical Jesus," refers to the actual, concrete, this-worldly person Jesus of Nazareth as he can be retrieved, reconstructed and known through critical historical research. This is understood as distinct from Jesus resurrected and alive but out of empirical history and no longer an actor in history like ourselves. It is also distinct from the full reality, historical and existential, that constituted the actual person of Jesus. No historically reconstructed portrait of an historical person is equivalent or adequate to his or her concrete reality. But these distinctions for the sake of clarity should not be blown up into separations and oppositions. I understand that it is Jesus who was raised, and that what little can be known of Jesus, is true to his historical actuality.[4]

Bridging the seemingly ever-widening text-context gap or what might be called the history-hermeneutic impasse is an important task for theologians. The distinctions Haight points out were designed to clarify but have hardened into obscuring oppositions.

It is the contention of this study that not only has Collingwood made a seminal contribution to the new hermeneutical approaches but that his theory of history provides deep insights into the linkage between the two interpretive operations: the hermeneutical movement from the text forward to the present and the historical movement from the text backward to the event. His understanding of history supports Pannenberg's claim that the two movements converge to form a single theme.

The arguments supporting these contentions are developed through seven chapters. The first of these surveys Collingwood's philosophy of history attempting to detect in the fabric of his reflections the hermeneutical thread. Care is taken in the first chapter not only to present Collingwood's philosophy but to develop an understanding of his thought from a hermeneutical perspective. Biographical data and the thorny questions of interpretation are addressed in the hope of dispelling any hint of a superficial appropriation of Collingwood to changing theological needs. Some years ago, Julian Hartt sarcastically criticized quick-fix appropriation with these words, ". . . Collingwood's position is deeply involved with an uncommonly sophisticated philosophical doctrine of mind; and theologians do not usually sit in on that game, though they may cozy up to apparent winners."[5] The subsequent chapters address in turn the logic of question and answer, the doctrine of absolute presuppositions, historical imagination, historical evidence, and the re-enactment theory. History as process is manifested by the "outside-inside" distinction and the incapsulation theory. These key themes are exposed as contributions, not only to a theory for the reconstruction of the past, but also for understanding that past in the present. Each chapter provokes a dialogue with leading hermeneutical, philosophical, and theological thinkers including Gadamer, Lonergan, Bultmann and the New Questers, Coreth, Stendahl, Kaufman, and Harvey. The last chapter illustrates the use and at times abuse of Collingwood's ideas by theologians. The illustrations focus on Rudolf Bultmann and Wolfhart Pannenberg.

Without claim to having settled the furor aroused by Collingwood's statement that the historian can rethink the "identical thought" of a past historical actor, the conclusion summarizes Collingwood's contribution to hermeneutics by indicating how his controversial theory of re-enactment is an apt description of what actually takes place when an interpreter attempts to understand the past by interpreting its remains in the present. Re-enactment links the historical task of reconstruction to the hermeneutical tasks of understanding and interpretation. This linkage brings us beyond the context-text dichotomy and thus Collingwood may be seen as a forerunner of the next integrative step in hermeneutics as pioneered by Gadamer. He provides clarifying insights for Gadamer's effort in that his approach more clearly articulates the relation between the interpretation of texts and the reconstruction of the historical past in the functioning of the historically effective consciousness. Collingwood's theory of history also ends up as a contribution to the unity of the theological enterprise by showing the hermeneutical dimension of biblical-historical theology and the historical dimension of systematic-hermeneutical theology.

Finally, the author wishes to acknowledge his gratitude to the Very Rev. Roger Balducelli, OSFS who directed the original research at Catholic University. Thanks should be expressed to Robert Masson, ed. *The Pedogogy of God's Image* (Chico: Scholar's Press, 1982) for permission to republish the contents of my article "The Historical Imagination and the New Hermeneutic: Collingwood and Pannenberg" as parts of Chapters IV and VII in this volume and to *The Heythrop Journal*, (1987) for permission to republish a slightly revised version of my article, "Hermeneutics and the Logic of Question and Answer: Collingwood and Gadamer," as Chapter II.

NOTES

1. Gerhard Maier, *The End of the Historical-Critical Method,* trans. Edwin W. Leverenz and Rudolph F. Norden (St. Louis: Concordia, 1977). See the forward by Eugene F. Klug, p. 9. Although Maier's target is clearly the critical-historical method, he ends up condemning a hermeneutical approach to Scripture as well.

2. Krister Stendahl, "The Bible as a Classic and the Bible as Holy Scripture," *Journal of Biblical Literature,* 103 (1984): 3.

3. David Tracy, "Review Symposium: The Analogical Imagination," *Horizons,* 8 (1981): 339.

4. Roger Haight, *An Alternative Vision: An Interpretation of Liberation Theology* (New York: Paulist, 1985), p. 314, fn. 11.

5. Julian Hartt, "Review of Faith and Reason: Essays in the Philosophy of Religion by R. G. Collingwood," *Journal of Religion,* 49 (1969): 282.

CHAPTER I

A Rapprochement Between Philosophy and History

Introduction

The difficulties of intelligently and effectively communicating the Christian faith to a world rapidly becoming more secular have made the critical historical and hermeneutical questions the storm center of theology. Twentieth century theologians as diverse as Barth, Bultmann, Lonergan, Pannenberg and Tracy have pursued a line of thought planted with the pioneering insights of Schleiermacher, Troeltsch and Dilthey and brought to flower in the "new hermeneutics" of Heidegger, Gadamer and Ricoeur.[1] The outcome of this line of thought is an altered view of theology as an inherently hermeneutical enterprise.[2] The task of interpretation was thrust upon theology as it gradually became apparent that all understanding is affected by the on-going flow of history and that past texts must be reinterpreted if they are to be meaningful in the present. This task is made possible through the medium of tradition which is the past as it brings itself to bear on the present. The gap of time cannot be eliminated; it can however be bridged. This movement from the text to the present is considered the primary task of heremeneutics. In terms of hermeneutical theology in a Christian context, this task cannot be divorced from a more properly historical concern and one which is raised in a special way due to the Christian theologian's "conscious awareness of the tradition which sustains his thought, and his explicit acknowledgement of dependence on the events which created and formed that tradition."[3] Because the Christian believes that understanding certain formative and salvific events provides access to the real meaning of human existence, both movements from text forward to the present and from the text backwards to the event need to be executed. As Pannenberg points out:

> With respect to the difference between the biblical texts and the events to which they point, we have to do with the central problem of historical study. With respect to the distance between primitive Christianity and our age, we have to do with the central problem of hermeneutic. The two are closely related and probably form a single theme.[4]

Both movements, focused by a new historical consciousness with the subsequent grasp of the historicity of all understanding, form moments on the history-hermeneutic continuum. Like theology, history itself is a hermeneutical enterprise.

While the importance of the questions raised above is obvious and the debt to the three leading theoreticians Heidegger, Gadamer and Ricoeur readily acknowledged, it is the contention of this study that the contribution of the Oxford philosopher Robin George Collingwood also deserves separate attention. Collingwood's contribution, while admittedly less direct than that of the authors named above, calls for examination precisely because he affords the possibility of linking the more properly hermeneutical questions with critical historical methodology. His importance for hermeneutical theology was first indicated by Bultmann in his Gifford Lectures in 1955. He states, "The best that is said about the problems of history is in my view, contained in the book of R. C. Collingwood, *The Idea of History* . . ."[5]

The Quest for Unity

The contemporary hermeneutics discussion, because of the broadness of its range, has served as an integrating vehicle in theology. Hermeneutics provides a platform with ample space for faith and history, systematics and scripture and theory and practice. Theoreticians attacking the hermeneutical problem of understanding have found themselves deeply immersed in questions of art, religion, history, politics and science. In short all forms of human experience are examined as mediums for unfolding meaning.[6] Hermeneutics is an integrating process. It is concerned with understanding the human in the numerous ways in which humans open themselves to be understood.

Although Collingwood does not use the word hermeneutics in its singular or plural form, he is concerned with the same need to integrate and understand human experience and knowledge. His philosophy is a hermeneutic of culture. As is evident from his writings he saw such an integration of knowledge as necessary to the very preservation of western civilization. The *rapprochement* he attempted to work out between history and philosophy was envisioned as the only way of preserving both. Collingwood's philosophy was a life-long quest of unity. His contention, often put in strident tones, was that the fragmentation of human life, a product of the Renaissance, was a disease eroding western man. Man's most basic forms of experience—art, religion, science, history and philosophy—were like a frightened horse team pulling in all different directions.[7] His life's work was concerned with the diagnosis of this fright, as well as attempting a cure. The cure he proposed was a philosophy whose central concern was the historical actions of humans, incorporating all the forms of experience in a life that is complete and undivided. As science had done so much to explain nature, Collingwood, like Dilthey, called upon philosophy to understand history. His call for a unity of experience was not, he maintained, anything new. For him it was the carrying out of the "fundamental principle" of Christianity, "that the only life worth living is the life of the whole man, every faculty of body and soul unified into a single organic system."[8] Viewed from a religious perspective, incarnation, redemption and resurrection embody the same unifying system.

The quest for the unity of knowledge is a recurrent theme expressed as we shall see in various ways, knowledge as a scale of forms, logical categories as the overlapping of knowledge, and most emphatically the *rapprochement* between philosophy and history. The task Collingwood set for himself was enormous and full success was not achieved. However his greatness may be seen in the fact that he accepted a task that was too forbidding to the great majority of English speaking philosophers of his time. His vision, similar in many ways to Hegel's, was to find its unifying thread in his concern for history as a form of knowledge which unites the other forms. Almost alone in his approach to metaphysics, religion, art and history, he preached a word not at all acceptable to the majority of his philosophical contemporaries. Although accused by many of having done away with metaphysics and religion, he saw himself as a staunch defender of both.[9]

Following a course charted by Dilthey and Croce,[10] Collingwood was interested in the process of understanding and its relation to history. He therefore dedicated himself to "a special branch of philosophical inquiry devoted to the special problems raised by historical thinking."[11] As an outstanding historian,[12] Collingwood was singularly well prepared for such a task. It was his principal concern. His understanding of the philosophy of history was not patterns, trends, cycles or predictions of the future but rather, as with Bradley,[13] Dilthey and Croce, the epistemology of historical knowing. It is in this thrust that his contribution to heremenutics may be seen. His questions were far more radical than those of traditional philosophy of history. He asked, "how is historical knowledge possible?"[14] He realized that to answer that question he had to propose a philosophy of knowledge, but one that would take into account the very historicity of mind. History is then the science of mind. It is the mind's self-knowledge and actual self-making. The historicity of mind, "for mind is what it does,"[15] long implicit in Collingwood, becomes an explicitly hermeneutical concern in *The Idea of History*. He states there that "the right way of investigating mind is by the methods of history."[16] In order for history to fulfill its proper role it must develop its own method and break free of the lifeless methods of natural science. Twentieth century philosophy in Collingwood's opinion had to construct a critique of historical reason which would do for historical studies what Kant's critique did for natural science. It was the task of history that Collingwood urged upon philosophers. The philosopher, he claimed in 1938, should "concentrate with all his might on the problem of history, at whatever cost, and so do his share in laying the foundations of the future."[17] The importance of history to philosophy as well as the close relationship of philosophy of history to the "new hermeneutic" is expressed in Collingwood's answer to the question "What is history for?"

> My answer is that history is 'for' human self-knowledge. It is generally thought to be of importance to man that he should know himself: where knowing himself means knowing not his merely personal peculiarities, the things that distinguish him from other men, what it is to be a man; secondly, knowing what it is to be the kind of man you are; and thirdly, knowing what it is to be the man *you* are and

nobody else is. Knowing yourself means knowing what you can do; and since nobody knows what he can do until he tries, the only clue to what man can do is what man has done. The value of history, then, is that it teaches us what man has done and thus what man is.;[18]

For Collingwood as for Hegel, history is the unfolding of the absolute. Ultimate reality makes itself known to us through art, religion, science and philosophy, yet always historically. All experience, all knowledge is filtered through the historicity of mind. Reality itself is a changing and growing phenomenon. Our grasp of it is never final but for Collingwood the surest handle is victory.

Biographical Sketch
The inclusion of biographical information would not be necessary in a study of most philosophers. Facts about the life of Plato or Kant contribute very little to the understanding of their thought. Not so in the case of Collingwood. Although, as we shall see, he himself played down biography as a historical or philosophical concern, his own biography does shed light on his ideas. Various historical events such as the two World Wars, as well as family background and education, played a very large role in shaping his thought. Moreover, his philosophy contains many seeming incompatibilities which as we shall see in the next section have caused great consternation in his commentators. Linked with the problem of interpretation is the question of poor health, considered by some commentators as the cause of radical changes in his philosophy. A final reason for a biographical reference is that Collingwood himself chose to write an intellectual biography in which he set out his own vision of the evolution of his thought and made some of his most provocative remarks about philosophy and history.

The principal source of Collingwood's life is, of course, *An Autobiography*.[19] This book written in 1938 traces such key themes as the logic of question and answer and metaphysics as a historical science as far back as 1917.[20] In short, in his own mind Collingwood directly related his later controversial works, *The Idea of History*, (posthumously published, 1946) *An Autobiography*, (1939), and The *Essay on Metaphysics*, (1940) to his earliest writings. *An Autobiography,* while held in esteem by some, is dismissed by Knox in what amounts to a not too well shielded accusation of insanity due to ill-health.[21]

In spite of the difficulties in interpretation, Collingwood's own life and intellectual career do run parallel and, as we shall see in the next section, permit an interpretation which bears witness to the quest for unity to which reference was made earlier in this chapter.

Collingwood was born at Cartnell Fell, near Coniston, North Lancashire, on February 22, 1889. His interests in art, archeology and the history of Roman Britain were due in no small part to the close personal and intellectual relationship he enjoyed with his father W. G. Collingwood who was friend and secretary to John Ruskin. His early education in the classics, history, archeology and science took place at home. In the opening pages of *An Autobiography* he recounts his first recollection of his chosen field, the history of thought. The overtones for an understanding of some basic hermeneutical questions are already apparent. Describing how, as a boy, he came upon an old volume which he believed must have been a compendium of Descartes' *Principia,* he writes

> . . . I already knew enough about the corresponding modern theories to appreciate the contrast which it offered. It let me into the secret which modern books had been keeping from me, that the natural sciences have a history of their own, and at any given time, have been reached not by some discovery penetrating to the truth after ages of error, but by the gradual modification of docrines previously held; and will at some future date, unless thinking stops, be themselves no less modified. I will not say that all this became clear to me at that childish age; but at least I became aware from reading this old book that science is less like a hoard of truths, ascertained piecemeal, than an organism which in the course of its history undergoes more or less continuous alteration in every part.[22]

The insights into the historical dimension of understanding revealed in this paragraph were early bolstered by that common starting place for hermeneutical reflection—art. Consorting with art and artists provided an early exposure to the openness of interpretation, characteristic of Collingwood's later approach to history. He tells us that 'no work of art' is ever finished, so that, in that sense of the phrase, there is no such thing as a 'work of art' at all."[23]

At age thirteen, the young home grown scholar went off to Rugby and later to Oxford. After the years at Rugby, "Going up to Oxford was like being let out of prison."[24] He excelled in the *literae humaniores* program and gained his first formal training in the need for and value of relating one field of study to another.[25] Along with his philosophical studies he pursued the archeological and historical interests his father had nurtured in him. He attended the lectures of the great historian and archeologist Haverfield and participated in excavations at Corbridge and Ambleside.[26]. He eventually was to become England's leading expert on Roman Britain. His interest in history and archeology were to prove most fruitful in terms of his theoretical concerns. Excavation work provided him the experimental background for his logic of question and answer apparently employed early but only articulated much later.

> For example, long practice in excavation had taught me that one condition—indeed the most important condition—of success was that the person responsible for any piece of digging, however small and however large, should know exactly why he was doing it. He must first of all decide what he wants to find out, and then decide what kind of digging will show it to him. This was the central principle of my 'logic of question and answer' as applied to archaeology.[27]

Collingwood was graduated with honors in 1912 and elected to Pembroke College as a tutor in philosophy. He almost immediately turned his attention to the study of religion and theology. This early interest is manifested by his first book published in 1916, *Religion and Philosophy*,[28] and by his involvement in a group formed by Canon B. H. Streeter which met to discuss the philosophy of religion.[29] With the exception of service with the British Admiralty Intelligence, Collingwood remained at Oxford almost until his death. From 1927 until his appointment in 1935 as the Waynefleet Professor of metaphysical philosophy, he was university lecturer in philosophy and history of Roman Britain. In 1918 he married Ethel Graham and fathered a son and a daughter. Aside from occasional trips for reasons of health, he remained at Oxford. By 1930 his health showed signs of deterioration. In 1941 illness forced his retirement. He was divroced in 1942 and married Kathleen Frances Edwardes. From this marriage a daughter was born. Collingwood died of pneumonia on January 9, 1943.[30] He was almost fifty-four.

Throughout his career Collingwood constantly placed himself against the tide. Alone among the philosophers at Oxford, he was willing to swim in the waters of systematic philosophy, metaphysics and religion. His student years saw the demise of Thomas Hill Green's school whose members had included Bradly and Bosanquet. Collingwood had obvious sympathy for their idealistic philosophy with the practical implications of its doctrine that knowing alters the known. Philosophical studies should have impact on society. In his opinion idealism, dominant at Oxford until about 1920, was taken seriously by politicians, churchmen and social reformers. However, he was not long at Oxford when this school was replaced by the realism of Cook Wilson and Prichard. For their approach he had little respect. His criticism was, to a great extent, a practical one. A school of thought which emphasized the game-like quality of philosophy and proclaimed that "knowing makes no difference to the known" could only lead to an anesthetic skepticism. In 1920, Collingwood asked the question, "Why is it that nowadays no Oxford man, unless he is either about 70 years old or else a teacher of philosophy . . . regards philosophy as anything but a futile parlour game?"[31] His rejection of realism was similar to his later disagreement with analytic philosophy taught at Oxford in the 1930's. Both approaches employing as they did a scientific method failed to take seriously enough the task of understanding the human situation. During the period after World War I with its disastrous effects hanging over Europe, Collingwood was despondent. "It seemed almost as if man's power to control 'Nature' had been increasing *pari passu* with a decrease in his power to control human affairs."[32] The same kind of harsh criticism is leveled at the prevailing philosophical-political outlook of 1938.

> I know now that the minute philosophers of my youth, for all their profession of a purely scientific detachment from practical affairs, were the propagandists of a coming Fascism. I know that Facism means the end of clear thinking and the triumph of irrationalism. I know that all my life I

have been engaged unawares in a political struggle, fighting against these things in the dark. Henceforth I shall fight in the daylight.[33]

With these words, Collingwood closed his autobiography and opened himself to attack.[34]

In spite of the difficulties of interpretation and complicated by the question of health, Collingwood's life remains an important clue for understanding his approach to philosophy and history. History provided the raw material for his questions. He refused to fall into philosophical line but rather sought to clarify in all their complexity the forms of human experience. He was open to aesthetic, political and religious experience, as well as the more contemporary concerns with perception, logical inference and ethical judgement. Although he never completed his intended system, he was always working toward such a system. The outline of the system, constructed out of a dialectical inquiry which questions and interprets all of reality while resting principally on Hegel and Croce, is not hard to see. The much more difficult question is the problem of interpretation. In spite of Collingwood's attempt to do philosophy systematically, there are points both of content and method which appear to stand in contradiction to one another. These points have caused considerable division and disagreement on the part of commentators. Two viewpoints summarize various positions, and as we shall see, correspond to different understandings of the life we have discussed: 1) the radical conversion hypothesis and 2) the dialectical interpretation. Without any claim to finality, we will examine the most important interpretations which have emerged since the publication of *The Idea of History* in 1946.

The Problem of Interpretation

The problem of interpretation has exercised many of the philosophers who have written on Collingwood.[35] Since our intent is principally to indicate his contribution to hermeneutics, we shall only outline the various approaches taken, paying particular attention to their effect, if any, on the hermeneutical dimension of Collingwood's work. What will be attempted constitutes a hermeneutic of Collingwood, a history of the history of interpretation. The themes lying behind the two positions mentioned in the preceding paragraph are Collingwood's apparent shift from an idealist to a historicist position and the more profound question of the convertibility or even identity of philosophy and history in his works.

One feature definitely stands out in the on-going interpretations: commentators have moved closer to Collingwood's own interpretation in *An Autobiography*.[36] Most recent commentaries emphasize the long developing character of a systematic approach. Collingwood himself, through the rustic metaphor of animal gestation, compares his early thoughts about history to the process of conception, birth and maturation. His ideas about history, he states, "were repeatedly written down, corrected, and rewritten; for whenever I have had a cub to lick into shape, my pen is the only tongue I have found useful."[37] However, some critics, rather than an image of birth, have seen a clear vision aborted.

In a short life Collingwood produced a long list of published works. His first book was a translation of Croce's, *The Philosophy of Giambattista Vico,* in 1913. His studies on Roman Britain alone would have assured him a place in the annals of scholarship. Philosophy, however, was his vocation and the bulk of his contribution can be read in ten books, *Religion and Philosophy* (1916); *Speculum Mentis (1924); Outlines of a Philosophy of Art* (1925); *An Essay on Philosophical Method* (1933); *The Principles of Art* (1938); *An Autobiography* (1939); *An Essay on Metaphysics* (1940); *The New Leviathan* (1942); the posthumous *The Idea of Nature* (1945); and *The Idea of History* (1946). Two other book were never published: *Truth and Contradiction* which, the author claimed, outlines his later developed logic of question and answer and was written about 1917; and *Libellus de Generatione,* a study of process or becoming, written in 1920.[38]

Collingwood's illness and early death, as well as his own claim to a long evolving process of thought, contribute to the problems of interpretation. The radical conversion or aborted vision in the midst of a brilliant career is the view advocated by T. M. Knox, Collingwood's student, friend and editor. Knox indicates that the thrust of the effort was systematic. The result, however, was a series of radically different systems.

Knox's interpretation of the development of Collingwood's thought is in direct opposition to *An Autobiography.* The crucial change is manifested, according to him, in that the later works are riddled with historicism and skepticism. He places this crucial change in the years 1936–1938. For him *An Essay on Philosophical Method* was the high point. All that came after was clearly downhill. The descent was banked only by a radical historicism.[39] This focal essay, also considered his best by Collingwood himself, had established a philosophical method along idealist's lines which supported a philosophy of pure being and clearly distinguished philosophy from history. This was most definitely a step forward according to Knox, overcoming an early skepticism illustrated in *Religion and Philosophy* which remained beyond *Speculum Mentis*. The books written after 1938, in Knox's opinion, repudiated philosophy as the science of pure being and absorbed philosophy into history.[40] Of the period from 1932–1933 on Knox states:

> What started to happen at some point during the following year was that tiny blood-vessels began to burst in the brain, with the result that the small parts of the brain affected were put out of action. It was only an intensification of this process when in 1938 he had the first of a series of strokes which eventually reduced him to helplessness . . .[41]

Knox's basic conversion thesis and conclusions have dominated Collingwood scholarship until relatively recently.[42] However his explanation for such a change is not conclusive and is not relevant philosophically. Poor health may definitely account for a deterioration in the quality of one's work but not for a shift to a different position.[43] The fallacy in Knox's argument is accented by Collingwood's own remarks. While discussing his poor health he wrote, "Whether luckily or unluckily, I have never known any illness interfere with my power of thinking and writing . . ."[44]

Knox's position has found its chief advocate in Alan Donagan. While Donagan is unable to accept the explanation of poor health or the division of works into historical and nonhistorical, he does accept the view that Collingwood's thought about the relation of philosophy to history underwent a radical change between 1936–1938.[45] In order to account for this change with its resultant skeptical and dogmatic currents, Donagan turned to *The Principles of Art* and *The New Leviathan* which expound a highly creative philosophy of mind. In 1937 Collingwood, according to Donagan, began to undermine the metaphysical position he had constructed in *An Essay on*

Philosophical Method. Nonetheless, the reasons justifying the radical conversion theory are mysterious. Donagan makes two final attempts at explaining the historicist thrust of the later Collingwood. The first makes the point that Collingwood's absorption in historical work during 1935–1936 might have prompted his identification of history with philosophy. The second point links Collingwood's commitment to metaphysics, a discipline under critical attack, to "Ayer's view that the propositions of traditional metaphysics are unverifiable."[46] How might metaphysics be vindicated in the face of Ayer's critique? The propositions taken to be unverifiable were not propositons, but rather absolute presuppositions, allowing for no test of verification. The task of metaphysics, as proposed in *An Essay on Metaphysics*, therefore is precisely to examine "what absolute presuppositions have been held, by whom, and why; and prima facie, these questions are historical."[47] Thus, according to Donagan, metaphysics becomes a historical science partly, at least, in order to save it from total annihilation.

While the radical conversion interpretation, as we have pointed out, has been the received understanding of Collingwood, two more recent studies by Louis O. Mink and Lionel Rubinoff place themselves against this current.

Louis O. Mink argues that Collingwood's entire work "was a continuous examination of the possibility and nature of dialectical thinking (and that, quite consistently, the apparent changes in his view are themselves dialectical transformations)."[48] In agreement with Knox and Donagan, he dismisses *Religion and Philosophy* as an early attempt at a system which failed. It failed because the idea of system had not yet been linked with the idea of dialectic. That linkage occurred in *Speculum Mentis* and is the source of Collingwood's later and more subtle dialectic. According to Mink, *An Essay on Philosophical Method* is a dialectical logic "produced by reflection on the kind of thinking exemplified but not discussed ('shown' but not 'said') in *Speculum Mentis*."[49] Mink goes on to interpret this dialectical pattern by means of an analysis of the theory of imagination in *The Principles of Art* and the philosophy of mind in *The New Leviathan*. He, like Donagan, stresses the later works.

> There is much to be explicated and assessed in this philosophy of mind; the point of present relevance is that its

development between 1933 and 1941 is a smoothly continuous and internally consistant fulfillment of the program of the *Essay on Philosophical Method*. It is Collingwood's theory of the dialectical nature of mind, as it reveals itself through action and imagination and is reflected upon in ethics, aesthetics and logic.[50]

For Mink, the moment of tergiversation came not in midcareer but very early, between *Religion and Philosophy* and *Speculum Mentis*. In the former, for example, religion, philosophy and theology are identical. They were considered instances of scientific thought. In *Speculum Mentis* they are distinguished but placed as part of a series in which each form of experience is viewed as making explicit what is only implicit in the forms below it. The logic of implicit and explicit provides the structure of a scale of forms important for many central Collingwoodian themes, the relation of thought and action, the inside and outside of historical events, and "of the series of mental functions whose relations constitute the dialectic of mind."[51] Collingwood's philosophy is dialectical in Mink's interpretation in that his later philosophy makes explicit what was only implicit in his earlier thought.

An approach similar to that of Mink's in that it interprets Collingwood dialectically appears in the full-scale treatment by Lionel Rubinoff. This analysis is especially pertinent since it deals explicitly with the main goal of Collingwood's philosophy as stated in *An Autobiography*, "a *rapprochement* between philosophy and history."[52] Rubinoff's treatment is to a great extent a defense of Collingwood's own interpretation. He argues against the radical conversion hypothesis that Collingwood's thought is systematic, and in agreement with Mink, that the later philosophy should be understood as dialectically growing out of the early thought. Although the later philosophy placed heavy emphasis on history, at no point did Collingwood fail to grant due autonomy to philosophy.[53]

Rubinoff differs with Mink in that for him *Speculum Mentis* is the core book and provides the programatic projection for a system. He also stresses the importance of religion and brings *Religion and Philosophy* to the center of Collingwood's philosophy.[54] *Speculum Mentis* organized the various forms of experience art, religion, science, history and philosophy into a dialectical scale of forms. The logical principles of these overlapping forms are later worked out in *An Essay on Philosophical Method.*[55]

Aware of the difficulties raised by the so-called reform of metaphysics proposed in *An Essay on Metaphysics,* Rubinoff responds to criticism that Collingwood had succumbed to historicism. If Collingwood can in any way be identified with historicism it can only be, according to Rubinoff, with a "transcendental historicism" which indicates that truth, while grounded in history, is not totally historical in character.

> That is to say, although it is only through the historical process that truth brings itself into existence, and only through historical thinking that it reveals itself to thought, what is revealed at any given time in history is nevertheless absolute and trans-historical, a permanent aspect of the self-completing and infinite "absolute" standpoint or concrete universal, whose final revelation once achieved, would coincide with the end of all time.[56]

In this stance, opposed to the relativism of radical historicism, Collingwood is placed along with Hegel, Husserl, Rickert, the early Heidegger, and Cassirer.[57] His metaphysics is compared to Husserl's phenomenology. Both recognize the historicity of thought while "both proceed from a firm commitment to the need for a transcendental philosophy of spirit or mind."[58] According to Rubinoff, both Husserl and Collingwood were attempting to unveil the transcendental structures of mind. Metaphysics in the sense common to both is not concerned with the abstract study of being but is rather "an inquiry into the process whereby being constitutes itself within the life of mind."[59] Collingwood's contribution to philosophy owes much to the fact that he was able to show not only the role of philosophy in this process but also the role of art, religion, science and especially history.

The dialectical process continues building on all the forms of experience until human presuppositions coincide with the absolute standpoint. This signals the end of presuppositions but also the end of history. Only at that point will alienation from the self be fully overcome and dependence on presuppositions abolished.[60] For the expression of such a moment, Collingwood, in his "drama of absolute mind," returns to the Christian religious-eschatological language of incarnation fall and redemption.[61]

While difficulties remain with all of the received interpretations of Collingwood, the dialectical inquiry, historicity of thought and his reflections on historical understanding point up his relevance to the discussion of hermeneutics. In spite of the various interpretations from historicist to idealist, Collingwood's contribution cuts across philosopnical lines. While rejecting his idealist context, Lonergan acknowledges that "what Collingwood taught about the historical imagination, historical evidence and the logic of question and answer"[62] remains focal to the historical-hermeneutical questions. The approach employed in this study will not constitute a new interpretation. To a large extent, it will draw on *An Autobiography* and Rubinoff's essay. Collingwood's own interpretation is a direct contradiction of the radical conversion hypothesis and dwells at length on significant questions for history and hermeneutics. He traces his central methodological tools, such as the logic of question and answer, the overlap of classes, and metaphysics as the study of absolute presuppositions back as early as World War I. All of these are related to the study of history. Rubinoff's work is an elaborate explanation supporting this approach using the notion of philosophy as a dialectical scale of forms, each form involving errors, but gradually raising themselves to truth.

The Hermeneutical Thread

Building on the dialectical interpretation we will now attempt to search out the hermeneutical thread in the carpet of Collingwood's philosophy. Or, to use another metaphor, we attempt to tie together the various strands of thought from the hermeneutical perspective. This will be undertaken by way of surveying the philosophical works in order to isolate those elements which are pertinent to hermeneutical theory. Subsequent chapters will flesh out in detail Collingwood's contribution.

Philosophy of history was a core concern of Collingwood during his whole career. For him, however, philosophy of history was not concerned with patterns, trends, or explanation theories. It was rather a critical endeavor, a hermeneutic. The historicity of mind, found early in his works provides the hermeneutical opening. The questions he raised are the radical, critical, hermeneutical questions.

What is history? What is history for? How do we know what happened in the past? What does it mean to admit the historicity of understanding? These, according to Collingwood, are the questions which the philosopher of history should be asking. It is Collingwood's responses to these questions which have influenced historians, biblical scholars and theologians. However, for the most part discussion and use of Collingwood is limited to two books, *An Autobiography* and *The Idea of History*. The result is an understanding less than complete, as it is bounced between idealist and historicist interpretations. Our contention is that if we perceive the hermeneutical thread throughout his work we shall accomplish two things: first, we shall acquire a tool for the interpretation of Collingwood's own work; second, we shall make explicit his contribution to contemporary hermeneutical theory.

Before pursuing our introductory survey, some remarks on hermeneutical theory are in order. Hermeneutical theory has moved beyond methodology whether historical, linguistic or psychological, understood in the manner of Schleiermacher or Dilthey toward an ontologically based examination of the process of understanding itself. Hans-Georg Gadamer's work *Truth and Method* documents this development. The heremeneutical experience, understanding, is that which takes place whenever one bridges the temporal gap between the interpreter and the subject matter, as conceived by the author or artist, and expressed in a text or a work of art. Hermeneutics no longer establishes rules for understanding. It rather exposes the structure of understanding itself which happens within a tradition. Commenting on the above views of Gadamer, Kimmerle states:

> ... the improper ontological presupposition of the hermeneutic theories normative until now are exposed. Hermeneutics again becomes universal, but in a sense reverse to Schleiermacher: it does not lead to the abolition of all immediate understanding because this understanding has always to be realized consciously and artfully, but rather it offers the conceptual manifestation of that which always happens in understanding, and which a more rigorously scientific understanding cannot transcend either. This *ontological* turn of hermeneutics leads to abolition of herme-

neutics as a special art or methodology. The theory of understanding becomes a central philosophical problem.[63]

Heavily indebted to Heidegger, Gadamer asserts that understanding is a historically operative process taking place in a "historically operative consciousness" in which the horizon of the past merges with that of the present. Understanding, and therefore interpretation, is possible only within a tradition. The very "prejudices" of one's tradition, according to Gadamer, making understanding possible. For him, language is the pivotal "prejudice" which provides the medium in which understanding can happen. Language is the locus where past and present merge.[64]

While Gadamer seems only directly dependent on Collingwood for the logic of question and answer,[65] his overall hermeneutical theory, as we shall see, has close parallels with Collingwood's theory of history. The differences of course are great, especially the centrality of language in Gadamer as the place where understanding and indeed being itself happens. For Collingwood, the wider notion of history as human action suffices to provide that place. Nonetheless, Gadamer's approach, employing various metaphors to describe the hermeneutical experience as an interaction between present "prejudices" and the subject matter of the text,[66] raises in a new way Collingwood's understanding of the philosophy of history.

Philosophical reflection on history for Collingwood is precisely the raising of the hermeneutical question. Is historical knowledge possible? His response, which has been appropriated by many proponents of the new hermeneutical options,[67] is that the past can only be known by re-experiencing it in some manner. Like the central axioms of contemporary hermeneutical theory, Collingwood's understanding of historical knowledge is dialectical, centered on imagination and oriented to the present. Although it does not emphasize the linquisticality of understanding, such presuppositions or prejudices are focal. History is an inquiry into the meaning of human actions that have been done in the past. It is constructed by interpreting evidence found in the present and is undertaken for human self-knowledge.[68] Collingwood's idea of history involves a hermeneutic where understanding, interpretation, translation and even explanation come together. History is hermeneutical in its object which is thought, in its method which is interpretation of evidence and in its value which is human self-knowledge.

> Historical knowledge is the knowledge of what mind has done in the past, and at the same time it is the re-doing of this, the perpetuation of past acts in the present. Its object is therefore not a mere object, something outside the mind which knows it; it is an activity of thought, which can be known only in so far as the knowing mind reenacts it and knows itself as so doing. To the historian, the activities whose history he is studying are not spectacles to be watched, but experiences to be lived through in his own mind; they are objective, or known to him, only because they are also subjective, or activities of his own.[69]

This quote indicates in a summary fashion the significance of Collingwood for contemporary hermeneutics. He admits to no "hard" historical facts isolated from interpretation. History studies "facts" but only as they are made known in human action. The meaning of such action is grasped through the prism of human understanding. What the historian seeks is the "inside" of an event or thought. Historical method consists in the reconstruction or re-enactment of past thoughts which are woven together by interpolation, inference and imaginative reconstruction. Human actions, the externalization of thoughts, are the processive unfolding of mind. History is the tracing of that continuous process. The past is significant because it remains integral to the present and incapsulated in it.[70]

These ideas, although only explicitly spelled out in Collingwood's later writings, were long unfolding. As Mink indicates, history as the "concrete universal" and the overall notion of historical consciousness form the link between the early and later Collingwood.[71] The thread of hermeneutics starts at the beginning in *Religion and Philosophy* published in 1916. Here religion is identified with philosophy but understood very definitely as an interpretation of the world. It is not simply ritual or conduct; it is a "creed or theology and at the same time a cosmology or philosophical theory of the world."[72] History as the science of human nature, the "inside" and "outside" of events, the logic of question and answer, and history as the reenactment of past thought in the present, are all implicitly introduced in this work and applied to historical theology.

> It profits nothing to catalogue the heresies of early Christianity and get them off by heart, unless one enters with some degree of sympathy into the problems which men wish to solve, and tries to comprehend the motives which led them to offer their various answers. But this sympathy and understanding are purely religious, theological, philosophical; to understand a heresy one must appreciate the difficulty which led to it; and that difficulty, however expressed, is always a philosophical difficulty. The merely external history of dogma killeth; it is the internal—the entering into the development of thought—that maketh alive.[73]

The same process of seeking motives and intentions, and reconstructing thoughts is applied to the ⁀ ⁀ly of Jesus. In terms that must be considered somewhat prophetic since they were written before 1916, Collingwood emphasized that the historical Jesus would never solve the problem of the meaning of Christianity, since Jesus never was a historical fact pure and simple. Jesus "held definite beliefs about God and himself and the world; his interest was not historical but theological."[74] This was also true of his followers. Historical theology must gain access to that living faith and not rest content with the mere repetition of formulas. It must seek meaning and ascertain whether that meaning constituted a satisfactory theology.

> Then we should be in a position to understand from within the new doctrines of Jesus and really to place ourselves at the fountainhead of the faith. To speak of studying the mind of Jesus from within may seem presumptuous, but no other method is of the slightest value.[75]

In his brief treatment of Jesus, Collingwood separates himself from the then current interpretations. He opposes both historical positivism and historical skepticism. Neither the bare fact of Christ's existence nor a Christ myth would be of much help to the believer.

> It is easy to say that the Christ myth embodies facts about God's nature which, once known, are known whether they are learnt from one source or from another. That is by no means the whole truth. The life of Christ gives us, conspicuously, two other things. It gives us an example of how a human life may satisfy the highest possible standards; and it puts us in contact with the personality of the man who lived in that life.[76]

In order for the example to have value, it must be historical. It is the historical life of Jesus which guarantees that perfection is possible for humans, but grasping that perfection has to do first of all with grappling with the thoughts expressed in the actions of Jesus. History and philosophical and theological reflection are necessary to one another as fact to interpretation. Indeed a controversial conclusion of this first book is that history and philosophy are identified.[77]

These early concerns, with their overtones for hermeneutics, continued with Collingwood's subsequent writings. A more dialetical overtone became apparent with the address he delivered at the Ruskin centenary in 1919. Emphasizing the Hegelian bent of Ruskin's work and referring to him as philosophically "the best equipped mind of his generation,"[78] Collingwood interprets Ruskin in terms strikingly similiar to his own later logic of question and answer and to the theory of absolute presuppositions. Ruskin's "rings of thought" are principles which are central and incontrovertible. They form the nucleus of a person's thinking and constitute the ultimate horizon for understanding. "You may think of them as a kind of ring of solid thought—something infinitely tough and hard and resistent—to which everything the man does is attached."[79] Not only does the theory of absolute presuppositions come to be introduced, but also a view of philosophy as historical and dialectical which refuses to separate one aspect of life from another. Collingwood's assessment of Ruskin's thought sound much like his later appraisal of his own philosophy.[80]

It was not long before Collingwood altered his position. By 1921, he could not completely accept Croce's identification of philosophy and history. More importantly for our concern, he again stressed their profound interdependence. To separate them is only to make them lifeless monsters. When they are cross-fertilized, history becomes the history of the human spirit in its outer secular building up of laws and institutions in which philosophy can flourish; and philosophy becomes the ongoing process of raising and solving "the endless intellectual problems whose succession forms the inner side of this secular struggle."[81]

In 1924, Collingwood published his *Speculum Mentis*. Here he set out systematically his map of knowledge and the forms of experience—art, religion, science, history and philosophy. Each is a different map but charts the same territory, human experience. Each provides a way of understanding life. Although at this point philosophy has priority, no form of experience is absolutized. The project of *Speculum Mentis* may be viewed as a hermeneutic of culture from various perspectives. It is in this work that Collingwood speaks of the object of history as the "concrete universal" which means that "history is the knowledge of an infinite whole whose parts, respecting the plan of the whole in their structure, are only known by reference to their context."[82] Since the context is never completely known, the part is never grasped as it actually is. History is, in its essence, universal history, although that universality is never fully achieved. Nevertheless the concrete universal, that is, the universal grasped in individual being or history, however imperfectly, pervades all of Collingwood's works.

The logic of history as the logic of the concrete universal and its relation to the historical consciousness also makes an impact on historical methodology. The attempt to overcome what Collingwood was later to name rather disdainfully "scissors and paste" history is already apparent in *Speculum Mentis*.

> Over this field, the historian is absolutely free to range in whatever direction he will, limited not by his 'authorities' but only by his own pleasure. For the maturity of historical thought is the explicit consciousness of the truth that what matters is not an historian's sources but the use he makes of them.[83]

In this central work, Collingwood gives his first articulated but brief introduction to "knowledge as question and answer." He presents a taste of what receives a fuller but not exhaustive treatment much later in *An Autobiography*.[84] Concerning this dialectical inquiry, Collingwood informed his readers that "questioning is the cutting edge of knowledge; assertion is the dead weight behind the edge that gives it driving force . . . Information may be the body of knowledge, but questioning is its soul."[85] Building on Plato's dialogue of the soul with itself, the dialectic of question and answer as a hermeneutical tool is introduced.

After the publication of *Speculum Mentis,* the turn to hermeneutical thinking becomes clearer. The phenomenology of all the forms of knowing outlined in this work opens the way to the historicity of the thinking process itself. The philosophy of history is understood as "the study of historical thinking."[86] The roles of imagination, language and history receive attention in *Outlines of a Philosophy of Art.* The philosopher is part of the historical process he is studying. An important task for him, therefore, is to understand how he, as a historical product, is both a participator in and spectator of that process. Using this clue, not unlike Gadamer's "effective historical consciousness," Collingwood adds "he (the philosopher) is able to reinterpret that process itself, and to see in every phase of it a nisus toward self-consciousness."[87] The inquirer is actually achieving consciousness of the spirt since, like Hegel, Collingwood maintained that history is the outpouring of spirit. Knowledge and action come together. In knowing history we know ourselves. By knowing ourselves, we create ourselves by creating an intelligible world of spirit.

The essays which close out the 1920's, the early Collingwood according to Knox, deal directly with critical, scientific history. In "The Limits of Historical Knowledge",[88] the importance of historical evidence, so integral to the later works, is emphasized. "The Philosophy of History" of 1930 presents a sketch of the ideas developed later in *The Idea of History.* The historian's pursuit ultimately concerns the present rather than the past. While giving a prime place to data as evidence, he emphasizes the interlocking of data and interpretation. The closing paragraph provides a preview of what was to come.

> Finally, since the past in itself is nothing, the knowledge of the past in itself is not, and cannot be, the historian's goal. His goal, as the goal of a thinking being, is knowledge of the present; to that everything must return, round that

everything must revolve. But, as historian, he is concerned with one special aspect of the present—how it came to be what it is. In that sense, the past is an aspect or function of the present; and that is how it must always appear to the historian who reflects intelligently on his own work, or, in other words, attempts a philosophy of history.[89]

The early period, as is made abundantly clear from the above, contained at least seminally, the notions of historicity of mind and understanding, the logic of question and answer and absolute presuppositions The close of this period, accompanied by the onslaught of illness and also by something of a moratorium on writing between 1930 and 1932, is, in the opinion of those interpreters who see two Collingwoods, a turning point.[90] Accordingly they, and T. M. Knox in particular, claim that it is with *An Essay on Philosophical Method*, published in 1933, that the real Collingwood emerges. Here philosophy as a separate discipline is championed. The waves of skepticism, dogmatism and historicism are left behind, and the autonomy of philosophy in the guise of idealism and traditional metaphysics brings calm to the stormy sea of his thought. However, even in this work, the historical and hermeneutical linkages can be found. Even Knox is forced to admit the importance of history to philosophy during this period. The basis of the method offered is that "philosophical concepts are specified on a scale of forms related to one another as lower to higher in a process of development."[91] The method of philosophy is set off from the methods of natural science and mathematics. What emerges is a dialectical approach similar to the Socratic method and Collingwood's own logic of question and answer. This technique, for Collingwood as for Socrates, rests on a principle most important to his philosophy: "in a philosophical inquiry what we are trying to do is not to discover something of which until now we have been ignorant, but to know better something which in some sense we know already."[92] This principle, firmly established here, surfaces over and over in the later writings on history. Implicit in the principle is the logic of question and answer, absolute presuppositions and the incapsulation of the past in the present. Necessary to the principle and to philosophy as a special kind of inquiry is the idea of the overlapping scale of forms: we need some knowledge to gain knowledge. While science and mathematics put objects into mutually closed species, "philosophical concepts, in contrast, are not coordinate species: reality and goodness, for example, cut across all classifications."[93] This kind of thinking has important consequences for the forms of experience set forth in *Speculum Mentis*, especially for the relationship between philosophy and history. In *An Essay on Philosophical Method,* philosophy is given priority. But there is a definite dialectical relationship—thinking is at once philosophical and historical. There is overlap; both are forms of knowledge. By refusing to distinguish them, as in *Religion and Philosophy,* Collingwood by his own standards committed the "fallacy of identified coincidents." To separate them too rigidly would have been to open himself to the "fallacy of false disjunction."[94] The overlap of classes and scale of forms made more explicit the identity in difference and dialectical interplay between the forms of experience. Art, religion, science, history and philosophy overlap. The superior position of philosophy is shown in that it is implicit in the other forms and "is the act through which the implicit unity of the particular forms is rendered explicit."[95] Truth is gained by reflecting on each form and overcoming its limited view. Each form, although good and true in itself, is bad and false relative to the form above. The error in each form must be overcome. "Each term in the scale . . . sums up the whole scale up to that point."[96]

There is much in this essay that is relevant to the writings on history. However, there is none of the bold historicist sounding statements of the later works. Collingwood emphasized the permanence of philosophical problems such as being and the state. This is in sharp contrast to his position in *An Autobiography* and *An Essay on Metaphysics* where philosophical questions are altered by the winds of historical change.[97] Nonetheless a concern for history comes through here in what is considered the most unhistorical of his works. Even the *Essay on Philosophical Method* may be read as a further attempt at the *rapprochement* between history and philosophy.

After the 1933 book, Collingwood became even more preoccupied with history. For some commentators, as we have seen, this preoccupation constitutes a fall into radical historicism, however it is more correctly judged a continuous yet dialectical outgrowth of his whole philosophy. According to his own account it is during this period that much of what was implicit in his earlier writings is made explicit. The turn to the more explicitly historical and practical can be noted in a revealing letter-essay written in 1934. Philosophy is not an ivory tower exercise but rather an attempt at bringing together theory and practice. His plea here is that philosophical speculation should be brought to bear on political, religious and historical problems. The letter reads like a mid-life *apologia;* it reaches backward to his criticism of the realist school and forward to his criticism of both British politicians and the Nazi-Fascist axis at the dawn of World War II.[98] The letter says much to the problems of epistemology, history, evolution, and politics. Collingwood claims that just as the seventeenth century needed to be convinced that nature is intelligible and that scientific problems are soluble in principle, so twentieth century man needs to be convinced that human progress is possible and moral and political problems are also capable of solution.[99] The understanding of history as the science of human affairs or human nature was gradually becoming his primary interest.

The mid-thirties were the years in which *The Idea of Nature*[100] and *The Idea of History* began to take shape. Collingwood's inaugural lecture as Waynefleet Professor at Oxford was the occasion for his programatic essay, *"The Historical Imagination"* which called for an "inquiry into the nature of historical thinking."[101] History as the science of mind comes to the fore. A clarion call is issued for critical, scientific history as an imaginative constructive process which interpolates "between the statements borrowed from our authorities, other statements implied by them."[102] In this essay, the construction of the historical past is dependent on imagination and less and less on "fixed points supplied from without."[103]

This same line of reasoning about history was continued in the lecture, "Human Nature and Human History" published in 1936. Just as science is the right method for investigating nature, so history is the correct method for studying mind.[104] In order that history not remain chronology but arrive at self-knowledge of mind, the historian must get beyond events to human actions and the thought manifested in the action. Here once again Collingwood has recourse to his important distinction between the "outside" and "inside" of an event.[105] Two important conclusions are drawn which shed light on his approach to history and hermeneutics. First history, in order to be itself, must cast off the shadow of the natural sciences. Statistics, chronology and explanation might form part of history, or contribute to it, but they are different from historical understanding.

Second, past attempts at a science of human nature are unacceptable because they conceive the mind as unchanging. This unhistorical position is unacceptable. Plato's *Republic* can only be a Greek idea. Aristotle's ethics, claims Collingwood, can only be the "morality of the Greek gentlemen".[106] The radical historicism of such statements as these is more palatable when it is related to his hermeneutics.

> If these systems remain valuable to posterity, that is not in spite of their strictly historical character but because of it. To us, the ideas expressed in them are ideas belonging to the past; but it is not a dead past; by understanding it historically we incorporate it into our present thought, and enable ourselves by developing and criticizing it to use that heritage for our own advancement.[107]

The rest of *The Idea of History* was written during 1936–1939. The introduction established the nature, object and method of history. Philosophy is again given priority as the reflective act. The philosopher not only thinks about an object, but also reflects on his thought about the object. Philosophy is "thought of the second degree, thought about thought."[108] Parts one to four of the book constitute a detailed analysis of the history of historiography from Mesopotamia to Croce. Part five, the epilegomena, contains Collingwood's speculations on the philosophical understanding of history and historical method.

The Principles of Art presents some noteworthy discussion which contributes to the infrastructure of his historical-hermeneutical theories. Book two presents a theory in which imagination is the essence of art as a form of experience. This theory has broader implications for understanding the overall structure of experience as a whole. The treatments of imagination, sensation and language provide some of the background detail for the discussion of historical imagination, evidence and re-enactment found in the epilegomena to *The Idea of History*. The relationships described between speaker and hearer, language and thought, and between audience as understander and audience as collaborator,[109] all contribute to a better understanding of his general hermeneutic and bear obvious resemblance to Gadamer's description of the hermeneutical experience as dialogue, conversation, translation and "fusion of horizons."[110]

The accusation of radical historicizing of all thought is principally the result of *An Autobiography* and *An Essay on Metaphysics*. According to the latter, metaphysics is not the study of abstract being. It is the study of the absolute presuppositions which have been held by a person or community. Citing Aristotle in support, Collingwood sets forth a reform of metaphysics which is closely linked to historical study of the changing patterns of human thought.[111] His starting point for the reform is his logic of question and answer. Every question that is raised has a presupposition. Some presuppositions are relative; some are absolute. Absolute presuppositions can neither be questioned nor proven right or wrong. That God exists is for Collingwood such an absolute presupposition. In the absence of it no knowledge is possible. As might have been expected, this proposal for the reform of metaphysics generated much controversy and has borne the brunt of much criticism.[112]

The work which absorbed most of Collingwood's time in the last years of his life was his political treatise, *The New Leviathan*. On the surface, the book appears to have least to say to the questions of history and hermeneutics. He does not deal with the problem of the relation between philosophy and history. However the book is an example of philosophy as thought of the second degree and, as Donagan points out, it is a major component in Collingwood's philosophy of mind.[113] The practical, witty and sometimes caustic bent appears as he discusses politics as the process whereby the state of nature grows into a community. Again he sees the philosopher being called upon to defend civilization, at that time confronted with Hitler. While the book says little directly related to our concern, it is important because it is a political hermeneutic of culture and incorporates into its discussion and applies such questions as whether feelings can be remembered,[114] the role of language as the conveyor of meaning,[115] and the function of the questioning process.[116] Also indicative of the hermeneutical thrust of his philosophy in his treatment of the socialization process. Tradition plays a pivotal role. The passing on, and the appropriation of a tradition is the way civilization happens. "Generally civilization is a mental process which goes on in a community."[117] The transmission of a tradition with its various cultural expressions is most important for Collingwood, especially when the historical circumstances of 1940 are taken into account. Failure to transmit a living tradition is tantamount to capitulating to barbarism. "To civilize is to socialize."[118]

Conclusion

In spite of the complex problems of interpretation, a continuous thread can be seen running throughout Collingwood's philosophical works. This is the hermeneutical thread that informs his historical method and constitutes his contribution to contemporary hermeneutics. Although he would not identify history and hermeneutics, his effort at bringing about a *rapprochement* between history and philosophy amounts to saying that when one does history one must be doing hermeneutics and vice-versa.[119] Hermeneutics as the act by which meaning is recovered is distinguished from history, yet that very recovery is a historical process.

It is the hermeneutical thread in Collingwood that has been seized upon by theology. In the attempt to bridge the gaps between text and event and text and the present, theology has become more conscious of the critical, historical and hermeneutical perspectives. As a result, since Bultmann's use of Collingwood in connection with questions concerning historical understanding and the use of tradition, his name, usually in the company of his better known colleagues, Dilthey and Heidegger, has surfaced more and more in theological literature. Collingwood's influence on this historical-hermeneutical investigation is important, if at times indirect and misunderstood.

Our introduction has served to tease out the various strands in the hermeneutical thread. In the following chapters, the themes which have emerged—the logic of question and answer, absolute presuppositions, historical imagination, the use of evidence and the re-enactment of past thought-will be analyzed and their impact on theological hermeneutics assessed.

NOTES

1. For a discussion of the term "new hermeneutic" see James M. Robinson, "Hermeneutic Since Barth," in *New Frontiers in Theology*, vol. 2: *The New Hermeneutic*, eds. James M. Robinson and John B. Cobb, Jr. (New York: Harper & Row, 1964), p. 77; Paul J. Achtemeier, *An Introduction to the New Hermeneutic* (Philadelphia: Westminster Press, 1969); cf. Richard E. Palmer, *Hermeneutics: Interpretation Theory in Schleiermacher, Dilthey, Heidegger, and Gadamer* (Evanston: Northwestern University Press, 1969).

2. See Ray L. Hart, *Unfinished Man and the Imagination* (New York: Herder & Herder, 1968); Edward Schillebeeckx, *The Understanding of Faith: Interpretation and Criticism*, (New York: Seabury Press, 1974); David Tracy, *The Analogical Imagination: Christian Theology and the Culture of Pluralism* (New York: Crossroads, 1981).

3. Gordon D. Kaufman, *Systematic Theology: A Historicist Perspective* (New York: Charles Scribner's Sons, 1968), p. ix. For a critical assessment of the relation between historical inquiry and Christian faith see Van A. Harvey, *The Historian and the Believer* (New York: Macmillan 1969).

4. Wolfhart Pannenberg, *Basic Questions in Theology*, 2 vols. trans. George H. Kehm (Philadelphia: Fortress Press, 1970), 1:96–97.

5. Rudolf Bultmann, *History and Eschatology: The Presence of Eternity* (New York: Harper Torchbooks, 1957), p. 130.

6. See Hans-Georg Gadamer, *Truth and Method* (New York: Seabury, 1975). German edition: *Wahrheit and Methode* (Tübingen: J.C.B. Mohr, 1960) 2nd ed., 1965.

7. SM, pp. 33–34. "This is the fruit of the Renaissance. If the artist, or the priest, or the philosopher complains, we can only answer 'tu l' as voulu, George Dandin.' He demanded freedom, and he has got it. He wanted a real separation, art for art's sake, truth for truth's sake, religion for religion's sake, each free from all claims on the part of the rest; and now the freedom has come home to roost, in the form of that disruption of life which we analyzed at the beginning. In the middle ages the artist was perhaps not much of an artist, the philosopher was by our standards only mildly philosophical, and the religious man not extremely religious; but they were all men, whole of heart and secure in their grasp of life. Today we can be as artistic, we can be as philosophical, we can be as religious as we please, but we cannot ever be men at all; we are wrecks and fragments of men, and we do not know where to take hold of life and how to begin looking for the happiness which we know we do not possess."

8. SM, pp. 36–37.

9. William M. Johnston, *The Formative Years of R. G. Collingwood* (The Hague: Martinus Nijhoff, 1967), p. 112, n. 26. Collingwood might not have approved of the word "preached," yet there are times when the terms academic preaching does fit his

tone. He jocularly closed EM, p. 343 as follows: "This is my reason for offering to the public what might seem essentially an academic essay, suitable only for readers who are already, like myself, committed to an interest in metaphysics. The fate of European science and European civilizatin is at stake. The gravity of the peril lies especially in the fact that so few recognize any peril to exist. When Rome was in danger, it was the cackling of the sacred geese that saved the Capitol. I am only a professional goose, consecrated with a cap and gown and fed at a college table; but cackle I will."

10. For the influence of Croce see Johnston, *Formative Years,* p. 76; and IH, pp. 190–204. For Dilthey, see IH, 171–76 and H. A. Hodges, *The Philosophy of Wilhelm Dilthey* (London: Rutledge and Kegan Paul, 1952), pp. 315–60.

11. A, p. 77.

12. For an overview of Collingwood as historian and archeologist, with a complete bibliography see, I. A. Richmond, "Appreciation of R. G. Collingwood as an Archaeologist," *Proceedings of the British Academy* 29 (1943): 476–85.

13. IH, pp. 134–41; cf. Lionel Rubinoff, "Introduction" in F. H Bradley, *The Presuppositions of Critical History,* ed. Lionel Rubinoff (Chicago: Quadrangle Books, 1968), pp. 1–74.

14. A, p. 77.

15. SM, p. 241. See Lionel Rubinoff, *Collingwood and the Reform of Metaphysics: A Study of the Philosophy of Mind* (Toronto: University of Toronto Press, 1970), p. 120.

16. IH, p. 209.

17. A, p. 88; IH, p. 282; Rubinoff, *Reform of Metaphysics,* p. 6.

18. IH, p. 10.

19. The importance of family and education is manifested throughout the opening chapters of A. See also Johnston, *Formative Years.*

20. A, pp. 42–43. Where the author refers to a MS written in 1917 "Truth and Contradiction" which he subsequently destroyed.

21. Gadamer, *Truth and Method,* p. 467; Gadamer wrote the introduction to the German translation entitled *Denken* (Stuttgart, 1955); Louis O. Mink, *Mind, History and Dialectic: The Philosophy of R. G. Collingwood* (Bloomington: Indiana University Press, 1969), p. 3, calls *An Autobiography* at best "a reconstruction of the past entirely from the standpoint of his interests and recollections at the time of its writing in 1938"; T. M. Knox, "Editor's Preface" to IH, p. xxi, dismissed it as the result of ill health.

22. A, pp. 1–2.

23. A, p. 2

24. Ibid, p. 12.

25. Johnston, *Formative Years*, pp. 35–36.

26. R. B. McCallum, "Robin George Collingwood," *Proceedings of the British Academy*, 29 (1943): 463–64.

27. A, p. 122.

28. Collingwood, *Religion and Philosophy*. (London: Macmillan, 1916) is out of print; our reference RP and subsequent page numbers will refer to the almost complete text as reprinted in *Faith and Reason: Essays in the Philosophy of Religion by R. G. Collingwood*, ed. Lionel Rubinoff (Chicago: Quadrangle Books, 1968). See James Patrick, *The Magdalen Metaphysicals: Idealism and Orthodoxy at Oxford 1901–1945* (Macon: Mercer U.P., 1985) pp. 77–108.

29. McCallum, "Collingwood", 464. For a list of B. H. Streeter's books see Rubinoff, *Faith and Reason*, pp. 310–11, where he mistakenly refers to B. F. Streeter.

30. William Debbins, ed., *Essays in the Philosophy of History R. G. Collingwood* (New York: McGraw-Hill, 1966), p. xi. While much has been written on Collingwood's illness and its impact on his thought, very little mention is made of his divorce and re-marriage at the end of his life. Only Debbins refers to this. I. A. Richmond, a former student and close friend, alludes in general terms to growing problems related to the illness. Commenting on Collingwood's archeological work in Penrith and disagreeing with his approach, Richmond remarks: "Granted that Collingwood was then physically ill and psychologicaly bedevilled by complicated private and professional entanglements, one has nevertheless the feeling that he had fallen into a pit of his own digging, from which not even the sagacity of his younger days would perhaps have saved him. This was high tragedy, the remorseless fate of those whose brilliance illuminates many fields but not with steady light and conversely, not with steady perception." Richmond, "Collingwood as An Archaeologist," 479.

31. A, p. 50.

32. A, p. 91.

33. A, p. 167.

34. Stephen Toulmin, "Conceptual Change and the Problem of Relativity" in *Critical Essays on the Philosophy of R. G. Collingwood*, ed. Michael Krausz (Oxford: Clarendon Press, 1972), p. 203. Here Toulmin points out that the polemical attacks caused resentful hostility especially after the publication of EM. He is also the only commentator to refer to the "dark rumours that had begun to circulate that he Collingwood had been converted to Marxism, perhaps even to Communism" (p. 219).

35. Knox, "Editor's Preface" to IH, pp. v-xxiv; Alan Donagan, *The Later Philosophy of R. G. Collingwood* (Oxford: Clarendon Press, 1962); Lionel Rubinoff, "Collingwood and the Radical Conversion Hypothesis," *Dialogue: Canadian Philosophical Review* 5 (1966): 71–83; Albert Shalom, *R. G. Collingwood: Philosophe et Historien* (Paris: Presses Universitaires de France, 1967); Rubinoff, *Reform of Metaphysics;* L. Jonathan Cohen, "Has Collingwood been Misrepresented?" *Philosophical Quarterly* 7 (1957): 149–50; G. Buchdahl, "Has Collingwood been Unfortunate in his Critics?", *Australasian Journal of Philosophy* 36 (1958): 327–39.

36. Rubinoff, *Reform of Metaphysics*, p. 26.

37. A, p. 116.

38. A, pp. 42 and 99. See Rubinoff, *Reform of Metaphysics*, p. 397 where he refers to a copy of *Libellus de Generatione* among the papers of de Ruggiero.

39. Knox, "Editor's Preface", IH, p. xii. "In a manuscript written in 1936 Collingwood writes: "St. Augustine looked at Roman history from the point of view of an early Christian; Tillemont, from that of a seventeenth century Frenchman; Gibbon, from that of an eighteenth century Englishman; Mommsen, from that of a nineteenth century German. There is no point in asking which was the right point of view. Each was the only one possible for the man who adopted it."

40. Ibid., pp. x–xi.

41. Ibid, p. xxi.

42. Rubinoff, *Reform of Metaphysics* pp. 21–25; Shalom, E. E. Harris, Nathan Rotenstreich, Leo Strauss and E. W. F. Tomlin are included among those advocating the "radical conversion hypothesis."

43. Ibid., p. 18; Donagan, *Later Philosophy*, p. 12.

44. A, p. 117; An interesting addition to the above quote is made by Rubinoff, *Reform of Metaphysics*, p. 376, n. 17. He quotes John Passmore, *A Hundred Years of Philosophy* (London: Duckworth, 1957), p. 306. n. 1, "It is sometimes suggested by idealist admirers of Collingwood that the brain disease from which he began to suffer in 1933 is reflected in his ultimate heterodoxies. When one contemplates the speculative freedom of these late works, one can only wish that his contemporaries could have been similary affected."

45. Donagan, *Later Philosophy*, p. 12.

46. Donagan, *Later Philosophy*, pp. 14–15; EM, pp. 163–65.

47. Ibid.

48. Mink, *Mind, History and Dialectic*, p. 16.

49. Ibid.

50. Ibid., p. 17.

51. Ibid., p.20.

52. A, p. 77.

53. Rubinoff, *Reform of Metaphysics*, p. 23.

54. Ibid., pp. 87–94; cf. Lionel Rubinoff, "Religion and the Rapprochement between Thought and Action," in *Critical Essays on the Philosophy of R. G. Collingwood.* ed. Michael Krausz, pp. 79–112.

55. Rubinoff, *Reform of Metaphysics*, p. 27.

56. Ibid., p. 24.

57. Ibid., p. 24; cf. Emil L. Fackenheim, *Metaphysics and Historicity* (Milwaukee: Marquette University Press, 1961).

58. Rubinoff, *Reform of Metaphysics*, p. 25.

59. Ibid.

60. Ibid., p. 292.

61. Ibid., p. 292; cf. SM pp. 302–03; see pp. 233–35.

62. Bernard J. F. Lonergan, *Method on Theology* (New York: Herder & Herder, 1972), p. 206.

63. Heinz Kimmerle, "Hermeneutical Theory or Ontological Hermeneutics," *Journal for Theology and the Church*, Vol. 4: *History and Hermeneutic*, ed. Robert W. Funk (New York: Harper Torchbooks, 1967), p. 113.

64. Gadamer, *Truth and Method*, pp. 351–66.

65. Ibid., pp. 333–41.

66. Ibid., pp. 337, 346–47.

67. See James M. Robinson, *A New Quest of the Historical Jesus*, Studies in Biblical Theology, No 25 (London: SCM Press, 1959); Bultmann, *History and Eschatology*, pp. 130–37; Peter Biehl, "Zur, Frage nach dem historischen Jesus," *Theologische Rundschau*, n.s. 24 (1957–1958), 69–76; Niels Tjalve, "Collingwood og theologerne, historie og forstaelse", *Dansk Teologisk Tidsskrift* 35 (1971): 145–85. Tjalve's article published in Danish is the only study found which deals directly with the impact of Collingwood's historical approach on specific theologians. Cf. Paul Merkley, "New Quests for Old: One Historian's Observation on a Bad Bargain, *Canadian Journal of Theology* 16 (1970): 203–18.

68. IH, pp. 9–10.

69. IH, p. 218.

70. Introductions to Collingwood's theory of history are provided by Errol E. Harris, "Collingwood's Theory of History," *Philosophical Quarterly* 6 (1957): 35–49 and G. Buchdahl, "Logic and History: An Assessment of R. G. Collingwood's *Idea of History*," *Australasian Journal of Philosophy* 26 (1948): 94–113.

71. Mink, *Mind, History and Dialectic*, pp. 48–49.

72. RP p. 59.

73. Ibid., pp. 77–78.

74. Ibid., p. 78.

75. RP, p. 78. This is the only place where he deals directly with the question of the historical Jesus. RP in general has not been used as a resource by the theologians who cite Collingwood. Patrick, *Magdalen Metaphysicals,* p. 82, picks up, to some extent the hermeneutical thrust. He states, "In fact the Christian religion was for Collingwood an indispensable intellectual hermeneutic and the *Essay on Metaphysics,* in which Christian dogma appears as the intellectual presupposition of Western Civilization, is the culmination of a consistent development begun in *Religion and Philosophy,* not an anomaly."

76. Ibid., p. 86.

77. Ibid., p. 85.

78. R. G. Collingwood, "Ruskin's Philosophy" in Alan Donagan, ed. *Essays in the Philosophy of Art* (Bloomington: Indiana University Press, 1964), p. 40.

79. Donagan, *Philosophy of Art,* p. 10; Rubinoff, *Reform of Metaphysics,* pp. 223–30

80. Rubinoff, *Reform of Metaphysics,* p. 230.

81. R. G. Collingwood, "Croce's Philosophy of History", in William Debbins, ed. *Essays in Philosophy of History* (Austin: University of Texas Press, 1965), p. 4; cf. Rubinoff, *Reform of Metaphysics,* p. 38.

82. SM, p. 230; cf. Mink, *Mind, History and Dialectic,* pp. 48–49.

83. SM, p. 217.

84. Ibid., pp. 76–80.

85. Ibid., p. 78.

86. R. G. Collingwood, "Nature and Aims of a Philosophy of History," in Debbins, ed., *Philosophy of History,* p. 44.

87. R. G. Collingwood, "Outlines of a Philosophy of Art: in Donagan, ed., *Philosophy of Art,* p. 144; cf. Gadamer, *Truth and Method,* pp. 205–06, 351.

88. R. G. Collingwood, "The Limits of Historical Knowledge" in Debbins, ed., *Philosophy of History,* pp. 90–103.

89. R. G. Collingwood, *"The Philosophy of History,"* in Debbins, ed., *Philosophy of History,* p. 139.

90. From the publication of "The Philosophy of History" in 1930 until EPM, 1933, only book reviews were published.

91. Knox, "Editor's Preface" in IH, p. ix.

92. EPM, p. 11; See Rubinoff, *Reform of Metaphysics,* pp. 55–56.

93. Passmore, *A Hundred Years of Philosophy*, p. 304.

94. EPM, p. 49; cf. Harris, "Collingwood's Theory of History" 49 and Rubinoff, *Reform of Metaphysics*, p. 43.

95. Rubinoff, *Reform of Metaphysics*, p. 13.

96. EPM, p. 85.

97. A, pp. 59–68; EM, pp. 49–57.

98. Collingwood, "The Present Need of a Philosophy," *Philosophy* 9 (1934): 262.

99. Ibid., 264.

100. IN was published posthumously in 1945. A short conclusion "From Nature to History" had been added in 1939.

101. IH, p. 240.

102. Ibid.

103. Ibid., p. 245.

104. Ibid., p. 209.

105. Ibid., p. 213.

106. Ibid., p. 229.

107. Ibid., p. 229.

108. Ibid., p. 1.

109. PA, pp. 247–254; 308–15.

110. Gadamer, *Truth and Method*, pp. 273, 337, 345. See John Hogan, "Gadamer and the Hermeneutical Experience, *Philosophy Today* (1976): 3–12.

111. EM, p. 47.

112. Rubinoff, *Reform of Metaphysics*, pp. 33–34.

113. Donagan, *Later Philosophy*, pp. 16–17.

114. NL, p. 34.

115. Ibid., pp. 40–41.

116. Ibid., p. 74.

117. Ibid., p. 299.

118. Ibid., p. 144.

119. For a criticism of the tendency to lump too many things under the label of hermeneutics, See Lonergan, *Method in Theology,* pp. 154–55.

CHAPTER II

The Logic of Question and Answer

Logic, Theory of Inquiry or Hermeneutics?

It was agreed in the first chapter that Collingwood's attempt at a *rapprochement* between philosophy and history was dependent on an understanding of both disciplines as heremeneutical. Although, as was pointed out, Collingwood does not use the term hermeneutics, his idea of history as an imaginative reconstruction of the past, based on evidence found in the present and accomplished by re-enactment of past thoughts, is a hermeneutical process. The goal of this process is not knowing the past as past but rather knowing oneself. In order to understand this process, it is necessary to examine in some detail his central methodological tool, the logic of question and answer. It is this dialectical form of inquiry which gives direction to the hermeneutical thread. The logic of question and answer is his description of how knowledge is gained and advanced. In spite of the fact that the question and answer process veins all of Collingwood's work, the approach is not made explicit until the publication of *An Autobiography*.[1] The account there is at times overstated and indicates that the author envisioned this form of inquiry as revolutionary in that it abolished both traditional formal logic and modern logic.[2]

While by no means replacing formal logic, Collingwood's dialectic of question and answer has exerted great influence in logic, history, philosophy of science, sociology of knowledge and hermeneutics.[3] This dialogical approach has also exerted influence on the hermeneutical discussion in contemporary theology.[4] Current hermeneutical thought has its starting point in the historical consciousness. It has moved away from a one-pole view of the task of grasping the past as past by way of recovering the original intention which the author meant to express and which the reader was supposed to read out of the text. Two poles must be considered: the text and the interpreter. Both have a bearing upon the act by which the subject matter is recovered. The logic of question answer attempts to get to that subject matter.

Joseph Agassi has acknowledged Collingwood's contribution of the logic of question and answer to the task of the philosophy of science. This contribution is largely still ignored, according to Agassi, because Collingwood failed to relate his theories to traditional formal logic.[5] He seems to have considered his ideas as in complete conflict with other theories. Writing with respect to the philosophy of science, but in terms applicable to hermeneutics, Agassi states concerning Collingwood:

> He explicitly suggested in open conflict with all other logicians, that the meaning of a statement is not a constant proposition but a variable which depends on the question it comes to answer. Even the truth-value of a statement, he was bold enough to assert, can vary from question to question.[6]

The logic of question and answer is a misnomer in that it goes far beyond the investigation of the logical form of propositions. The impact of history on changing questions and answers is included. The form of inquiry is not primarily concerned with truth but rather with the process of how one comes to understand. Its goal is discovery, not proof and, as such, it supplements formal logic but does not replace it. As Mink has noted, it "is not a theory of logic at all, in any ordinary sense of that term, nor is it even a theory of semantics; it is a heremeneutic."[7]

Although the hermeneutical implications of this dialectical inquiry are only beginning to emerge, Gadamer has singled it out as one of his focal metaphors for describing the hermeneutical experience. The following sections of this chapter will analyze Collingwood's unfolding of the logic of question and answer and subsequently Gadamer's understanding of it and application to hermeneutics.

Development of the Logic of Question and Answer

The logic of question and answer was Collingwood's way of expressing his gradually developing determination to cast off the realist model of objective knowledge. With an understanding of experience itself as historical, knowledge is gained by an on-going questioning process. Before being able to articulate such a position, Collingwood himself had to live through the process. His studies in archeology afforded him the appropriate laboratory where the process came to fruition.

He begins his reflection on the logic of question and answer by describing a unique morning conversation he had with himself every day as he crossed Kensington Gardens on his way to work. He looked at the Albert Memorial and was repelled by its ugliness. He would then ask himself what had Scott, the designer, been trying to do?

> What relation was there, I began to ask myself, between what he had done and what he had tried to do? Had he tried to produce a beautiful thing; a thing, I meant, which we should have thought beautiful? If so, he had of course failed. But had he perhaps been trying to produce something different? If so, he might possibly have succeeded. If I found the monument merely loathsome, was that perhaps my fault? Was I looking in it for qualities it did not process, and either ignoring or despising those it did?[8]

It was this questioning process that militated against the realist-intuitionist theories of knowledge, and set off his revolt against the traditional theories of logic. What he had learned in archeology about the need for a well defined question which would call for some well-defined digging, rather than a vague program without any prior understanding of what the archeologist wanted to know, came in quite handy. He claimed that he was discovering in historical research what Bacon and Descartes had found in their philosophical reflection on scientific research. They had claimed that knowledge is acquired only through the asking and answering of questions, that the questions asked must be the right ones, and that they must be asked in the right order. Propositions, statements or judgments do not constitute knowledge in themselves but must be grasped together with the question they claim to answer.[9] The inquirer cannot determine what a person means by merely studying his statements handed down orally or in writing. "In order to find out his meaning you must also know what the question was (a question in his own mind, and presumed by him to be in yours) to which the thing he has said or written was meant as an answer."[10] Question and answer are understood in strict correlation. A detailed and particularized answer responds to a detailed and particularized question, not to some general inquiry. Collingwood next applied the principle of correlativity between question and answer to the idea of contradiction. In contrast to current logic, he claimed that you cannot know what a proposition means unless you know what question it proposed to answer. Contradictions are not, therefore, always so, for "No two propositions, . . . can contradict one another unless they are answers to the same question."[11]

Collingwood sought to replace a logic of propositions with his logic of question and answer. Truth, like meaning, is not something found in any one proposition or in a set of propositions. It belongs to a question and answer complex. The questions and answers must be appropriate to the unpacking of the subject matter. The appropriate question is the one which "arises". The right answer is the one which pushes us along on the questioning and answering process. According to Collingwood, this "right" answer might be false, but it may still be right in that it provides the investigator with a link in the chain of question and answer and promotes the openness that allows for correction and clarification.[12] The truth or falsity of a proposition can be known only after one comes to know the question which it was meant to answer.

Before turning to the application of the question and answer process to history, it will be of help to look further into its structure. While treating art as pure imagination, which neither asserts nor denies, Collingwood argues against a crude empirical approach which claims that assertion and knowledge are identical. Rather the process of knowing is a forward movement, a constant interrogation of what is already known. Understanding, on the other hand is retrospective. Knowing and asserting can be identified only when "the knower looks back over his shoulder at the road he has travelled."[13] In other words question and answer or question and presupposition are related when understood as occurring in processes which are "prospectively open but retrospectively determinate."[14] The questioning process might not always be conscious and clear, yet it is the process in which every real thinker engages.

> People who are acquainted with knowledge at first hand have always known that assertions are only answers to ques-

tions. So Plato described true knowledge as 'dialectic', the interplay of question and answer in the soul's dialogue with itself; so Bacon pointed out . . . that the scientist's real work was to interrogate nature, to put her, if need be to the torture as a reluctant witness; so Kant mildly remarked that the test of an intelligent man was to know what questions to ask; and the same truth has lately dawned on the astonished gaze of the pragmatists.[15]

The same truth has also dawned on theoreticians of hermeneutics. Principles formulated at least by the time of *Speculum Mentis* concerning 1) the primacy of the question, 2) that questioning demands some prior information and 3) that questioning is in essence "a suspension of the activity of asserting,"[16] all have reverberations in the contemporary hermeneutical discussion. The last point mentioned is closely related to Gadamer's openness of the question. Collingwood related this suspension of asserting to the aesthetic imagination. When a question is asked, the non-existent, at least to some degree, is contemplated because raising questions involves envisioning alternatives. Only one of the alternatives can exist.[17] Understanding which is a product of the question and answer dialectic is, as Gadamer also points out, contingent, open and ultimately beyond the inquirer's control.[18] For both philosophers the opening power of the question is focal.

The logic of question and answer is directly related to the historical-hermeneutical problem when it is realized that getting to the question which a piece of art or text was meant to answer is a historical question and demands the application of historical methods. Since writers rarely make explicit their basic convictions, the question to which they are responding is most often left unstated. This makes bridging the gap between reader and text difficult. If the text is separated from the reader by a great span of time or culture, the alienation is incresed. The question has been forgotten or at least does not readily arise, especially if the answer offered in the text is considered the right one. In that case a new question arises from the response and most likely the original question is lost. In order to get to the meaning of a text or piece of art, a method must be found which uncovers the question raised by the original writer. According to Collingwood, this can be accomplished only by reconstructing the question historically.[19] The logic of question and answer backs one into the problem of presuppositions as well as the theory of history as the imaginative re-enactment of past thought. These questions will occupy us in subsequent chapters.

Before moving on to a discussion of the dialectical inquiry and the use made of it by Gadamer, a brief look should be taken at the question and answer interaction in *An Essay on Philosophical Method* and *An Essay on Metaphysics*. These works are often characterized as idealistic and historicist respectively and yet, as we shall see, the same dialectical process of question and answer underlies both. *In An Essay on Philosophical Method,* the terms employed are those of traditional logic. However the flexibility of the logic of question and answer is manifested in the overlap of classes and the scale of forms. What clearly emerges is the need to suppose and the relation of supposing to questioning.[20] The same principle drawn above from *Speculum Mentis* are operative here. The question in the Socratic sense is central. Knowledge is based on information already possessed and questioning demands openness. These principles can be seen to follow from the very hypothesis Collingwood established for his method,

> . . . for if the species of a philosophical genus overlap, the distinction between the known and the unknown, which in a non-philosophical subject matter involves a difference between two mutually exclusive classes of truths, in a philosophical subject matter implies that we may both know and not know the same thing; a paradox which disappears in the light of the notion of a scale of forms of knowledge, where coming to know means coming to know in a different and better way.[21]

This philosophical method clearly influenced Collingwood's approach to history. *An Essay on Philosophical Method*, although defending the systematic *philosophia perennis* with its "single permanent problem," endorses much of his historical-hermeneutical approach. Past philosophies are understood from the present. They exist only in the present. He claims here that the past is "telescoped into the present."[22] Later the term "incapsulation" is used to describe this same phenomena. While the 1933 essay calls for a systematic philosophy, it is clear that the philosophy it sets forth is subject to an ongoing questioning process. It has to remain open, subject to broader synthesis, and flexible in method. In spite of the apparent unhistorical character of the book, the dialectical and historical search for truth which envisions philosophy as an "interim report on the progress of thought down to the time of making it"[23] is evident.

The historicizing implications of the logic of question and answer emerge with *An Essay on Metaphysics*. Metaphysics is presented as an historical discipline which uncovers the absolute presuppositions of a people. In a series of propositions, Collingwood outlines the core of his analysis of presuppositions and prepares the way for his "reform of metaphysics." The logic of question and answer provides the key to this approach. The first proposition, the one pertinent to the present chapter, states, "Every statement that anybody ever makes is made in answer to a question."[24] The emphasis is again placed on the thinking process and, in this work especially, the impact of history on that process. "In proportion as a man is thinking scientifically when he makes a statement, he knows that his statement is the answer to a question and knows what that question is."[25] The questioning process, under the influence of history, goes on, forming a spiral gradually replacing error with truth, but remaining essentially open. The dialectical inquiry of question and answer is what makes compatible the approaches offered in the two essays.

The logic of question and answer is applied most directly by Collingwood in the fashioning of his historical method. It is as it filters through the articulation of this method that the impact of that logic on hermeneutics can be felt at its best. History consists of events that are finished and cannot, in consequence, be perceived. Data and evidence are of no value unless they are interpreted. This is where the logic of question and answer comes into play. The historian begins with a problem or a question. Once the question is clearly articulated in the historian's mind, he can dig through the available evidence in which an answer might possibly be esconced.

> The beginning of historical research is therefore not the collection or contemplation of crude facts as yet uninterpreted, but the asking of a question which sets one off

looking for facts which may help one to answer it. All historical research is focused in this way upon some particular question or problem which defines its subject. And the question must be asked with some reasonable expectation of being able to answer it, and to answer it by genuinely historical thinking; otherwise it leads nowhere, it is at best idle "wondering", not the focus of a piece of historical work. We express this by saying that a question does or does not "arise". To say that a question arises, is to say that it has a logical connection with our previous thoughts, that we have a reason for asking it and are not moved by mere capricious curiosity.[26]

The inquisitive pecking away at historical facts yields nothing. Collingwood learned this early by seeing numerous examples of pointless archeological excavations. History is not erudite antiquarianism but an attempt to answer a particular and limited question. "As no history can be universal, so no history can be final."[27] However, he immediately qualifies this statement while still advocating the ongoing question and answer process. He points out that history can be universal in the sense that it brings us up to date as to the state of knowledge about our question. It illustrates where knowledge stands on the question at the present time. Each generation and each individual raise new questions and gain a different pespective on history. For that reason, the questioning process goes on and history must be re-written by each generation.[28]

The logic of question and answer as it is employed by Collingwood ought most certainly to be understood as hermeneutical. His concentration on what he referred to as obscure subjects, most importantly the history of Roman Britain, forced a hermeneutical approach on him. Knowledge relative to such a subject, for which so little data is available, demands an interpretative and imaginative sifting of a few clues. In such a field the playful and irrational[29] elements of human thought are evident as the historian-interpreter becomes obviously aware of the finitude of the self and all understanding. The well placed question as a starting point provides for half of the act of knowing. Moreover, it is the dialectical building up of questions and answers which open access to the most basic convictions of a person or community. This allows for knowing in its most profound sense, which is, according to Collingwood, knowing "why". This kind of knowing is the goal of the question and answer process. Hans-Georg Gadamer has brought this Socratic dialogue, as interpreted by Collingwood, to the center of the hermeneutical stage.

Gadamer and the Logic of Question and Answer

Gadamer's enthusiasm for Collingwood's logic of question and answer is almost total. If the new hermeneutic can be characterized as a enterprise stemming most specifically from Dilthey, which seeks to understand and interpret the human in contrast to science's attempt to explain nature, Gadamer may be taken as the thinker who has best and most systematically described that enterprise.[30] In this analysis of the historically operative consciousness he returns to the central insight found in Plato's account of Socrates: ". . . contrary to general opinion, it is more difficult to ask questions than to answer them."[31] The value of discourse is that it reveals new knowledge. This can only happen when one of the partners in the discussion wants to know something and thus becomes aware of his not knowing. The object of the discourse is thrown open by the question. However, not just any question will do. In order for a question to accomplish this, it must be pertinent; it must involve both the questioner and the object of the question. A rhetorical question, for example, would not open up a true dialogue. Nor can the question be so wide open as to be "floating." "The openness of the question is not boundless. It is limited by the horizon of the question."[32] It must concern the matter under consideration in the dialogue and the presuppositions of the situation under discussion. The similarity to Collingwood's "right" question, or the question which "arises" becomes apparent when Gadamer raises the problem of the "distorted question." This is the ill-placed question that does not follow the right direction and makes an answer impossible. It is the awkward conversation stopper that does not fit in and contributes nothing to the ongoing discussion of the matter at hand. In order to contribute, the question needs a sense of direction. "Sense is always the direction of a possible question. The sense of what is correct must be in accordance with the direction taken by a question."[33]

Although the question has a definite direction, it is not rigidly limited by this direction. As a constituent of a dialogue, it must remain open to negative and positive judgements. As in any real dialogue, knowledge is both the process and outcome of examining opposites. Admitting ignorance is an essential prerequisite for true knowledge. But of course, as the Socratic *docta ignorantia* sought to show, it is the power of opinion which prevents the admission of ignorance, suppresses the question, and therefore retards the progress toward knowledge. Given the power of opinion, Gadamer asks, "How, then, can the admission of ignorance and questioning emerge?"[34] He responds that questioning emerges in a "sudden" way, that is, in the way a sudden idea *(einfall)* emerges. The idea of this suddenness opens the door to his emphasis on the spontaneity of understanding as well as on its dialogic character.

> But we also know that sudden thoughts do not come entirely unexpectedly. They always presuppose a pointer in the direction of an area of openness from which the idea can come, i.e., they presuppose questions. The real nature of the sudden idea is perhaps less the sudden realisation of the solution to a problem then the sudden realisation of the question that advances into openness and thus makes an answer possible. Every sudden idea has the structure of a question. But the sudden realisation of the question is already a breach in the smooth front of popular opinion. Hence we say that a question too 'comes' to us, that is 'arises' or 'presents itself' more than that we raise it or present it.[35]

The conversation-like character of understanding is shown in the suddenness of the question which opens our thinking and allows for a response. Understanding is much less controlled than might have been thought. As questions arise the interpreter becomes aware of his own limits and finitude. The questioning activity cannot be totally predetermined. It is thrust upon the interpreter by the subject matter at hand. The interpreter finds himself caught in a question in the way in which we "get caught" in a conversation. The dialectical character of thinking is illustrated by Gadamer when he equates the "art of questioning" with the "art of thinking."[36] His similarity to and, to a degree, dependence upon Collingwood may be registered in his description of hermeneutics as a conversation with the text. In contrast to the rigid form that presides over the interpretation of the written statement, the give and take proper to dialogue allows a communication of meaning to emerge. This understanding happens through language which

> . . . represents the restoration of the original communication of meaning. Thus that which is handed down in literary form is brought back out of the alienation in which it finds itself and into the living presence of conversation, whose fundamental procedure is always question and answer.[37]

With the above discussion serving as background to the appropriation of any knowledge, Gadamer returns to the historical-hermeneutical problem. Interpretation becomes a possibility when the historical text presents a question to the interpreter. In order to understand, the interpreter must seek behind what is said. One can gain the sense of the text only by gaining access to the horizon of the question to which the text has responded. The logic of the human sciences is a logic of the question. Gadamer's debt to Collingwood for insight into this form of inquiry is explicity acknowledged.

> Despite Plato we are not very ready for such a logic. Almost the only person I find a link with here is R. G. Collingwood. In a brilliant and cogent critique of the 'realist' Oxford school he developed the idea of a logic of question and answer, but unfortunately never developed it systematically. He clearly saw what was missing in naive hermeneutics founded on the prevailing philosophical critique. In particular the practice that Collingwood found in English universities of discussing 'statements' though perhaps a good training of intelligence, obviously failed to take account of the historicality that is part of all understanding.[38]

Collingwood's dialectic is integral to Gadamer's hermeneutic. Since the question can only be recovered by interpreting the text or the work of art, the appropriateness of the reply turns out to be the "methodological presupposition for the reconstruction of the question . . ." it follows that, "any criticism of this reply from some other quarter is pure mock-fighting."[39]

This axiom brings us back to the hermeneutical circle and Gadamer's "fore-conception of completion",[40] which refers to a presupposition involved in grasping the subject-matter mediated through the text. The German expression used is *Vorgriff der Vollkommenheit*, which means the "pre-grasp of completeness" or the "anticipation of completeness." This is the supposition we all entertain before and as we read a text that the text makes complete sense or that it represents a complete unit of meaning. Only then is it intelligible. As Gadamer indicates, this "anticipation of completeness' is the "nerve" of Collingwood's approach to historical knowledge.

For both philosophers tradition plays an important role. Understanding only happens within a shared tradition. The subject matter of the text is often foreign to us, if only in time. It is strange, and yet there must be a familiarity which makes the task of hermeneutics possible. Gadamer describes the position wedged between strangeness and familiarity which the interpreter occupies as the "Between" between the historically meant object "out there" and the belongingness of that object to a tradition. This "Between" is the "true home" of hermeneutics where a fusion of horizons between text and interpreter takes place.[41]

Precisely how this fusion takes place is problematic for Gadamer just as it was for Collingwood. Both are concerned that it should not be construed as a psychological happening in the sense advocated by Schleiermacher. Both see the event happening as we reconstruct the question that lies behind the utterances of a text or piece of historical evidence. The manner of reconstruction and the basis for that reconstruction is where they differ. Collingwood's emphasis on intentions, motives and thoughts of historical agents is unacceptable to Gadamer. He cites Collingwood's example of the Battle of Trafalgar. The course of the battle is the key which unlocks Nelson's plan. Since that plan was successful, Collingwood assumes that the outcome of the battle reveals what the plan was. By the same token Villeneuve's plan cannot be known since it failed. No evidence remains of it. Gadamer concludes that for Collingwood ". . . understanding the course of the battle and understanding the plan that Nelson carried out in it are one and the same process."[42]

The fusion between past and present takes place according to Collingwood when the interpreter grasps the original thought patterns of the historical agent. This for him constitutes reconstructing the question. It is here that Gadamer's disagreement surfaces. He claims that it would be rare for the course of historical events, such as a battle, to be limited or pre-determined by a plan. While accepting the logic of question and answer he maintains that the use Collingwood makes of it is made ambiguous by an extrapolation on original intention. The shift to language as well as the move away from original intention is emphasized.

> Our understanding of written tradition as such is not of a kind that we can simply presuppose that the meaning that we discover in it agrees with that which its author intended. Just as the events of history do not in general manifest any agreement with the subjective ideas of the person who stands and acts within history, so the sense of the text in general reaches far beyond what its author originally intended. But the task of understanding is concerned in the first place with the meaning of the text itself.[43]

Whether or not Gadamer is doing justice to Collingwood's view of re-enactment of past thought and its relation to original intention will occupy us in the next section. Nevertheless, the Heidelberg philosopher's position clearly indicates the basic move in new hermeneutical theory. Rather than original intention being the *locus* where understanding the past is to be sought, language, that is, the text gains ascendency. The Heideggerian influence can be seen as Gadamer states " . . . language is the universal medium in which understanding itself is realized. The mode of realization of understanding is interpretation."[44] The same view is expressed in his celebrated dictum, "Being that can be understood is language."[45] The text forms the basis on which the interpreter can reconstruct the question. Reconstruction for Gadamer has nothing to do with reconstructing the mental processes of the author. This would appear to conflict with Collingwood's theory of history as re-enacement of past thought in the present. However, as we shall see, Collingwood's rethinking is closely linked to the interpretation of evidence; it runs parallel with Gadamer's interpretation of the text.

Gadamer argues that Collingwood fell into the historicist trap and limited his questioning process to the possibility of reconstructing the author's or historical agent's original intention. The claim in

Truth and Method is that the sense of the text goes beyond original intention of the author or agent. By allowing oneself to be open to the text's question, the interpreter is then able to move with the beyond-direction of the text. The text itself allows the interpreter to gain the question horizon which lies behind and beyond what is written. There is a backward thrust here as the interpreter seeks to know the historical past, but there is also a forward thrust in that no text is ever fully exhausted as to its meaning ". . . every historian and literary critic must reckon with the fundamental non-definitiveness of the horizon in which his understanding moves . . . It is part of the historical finiteness of our being that we are aware that after us others will understand in a different way."[46] This same notion, as we have seen, is found in Collingwood.[47] In spite of his concern for reconstructing original intentions, he too is committed to the radical historicity of the interpreter. Whether these two elements of his approach can be reconciled is questioned by Gadamer. What is behind Collingwood's thinking and re-thinking process? Are historical actions always manifestations of thoughts, questions and intentions? Gadamer is skeptical and sees Collingwood as overly dependent on Hegel.

> But is the construction of intention really an understanding of history? We can see how Collingwood gets involved, against his will, in psychological particularity. He cannot get out of it without a theory of the 'representative of world spirit', i.e. without Hegel.[48]

In spite of the vast area of agreement concerning the dialectical inquiry of question and answer, sharp disagreement exists. In terms of the contemporary hermaneutical discussion, Collingwood is placed in the contextualist camp, where a whole context of factors would determine the framework in which understanding happens. As a textualist, Gadamer would insist on the autonomy of the text itself.[49] More and more this autonomy is linguistic. The overlap between the two positions is great. Collingwood attempts to construct a context but one based squarely upon the text or evidence at hand. And in Gadamer different levels of meaning can be delineated; 1) "the original historical sense," 2) "the effective-historical context" and 3) "the mediation and translation of the text into the situation of the interpreter."[50] In spite of the emphasis on textual autonomy in Gadamer, context still plays a role. Nevertheless, it is clear that language catapults the interpreter beyond intentions consciously entertained. Gadamer's complaint is that Collingwood stopped at conscious intentions. The jump from Nelson's plan to the actual battle is possible for Gadamer only if history is understood in Hegel's sense as party to the unfolding of the world spirit. Of course, Gadamer has touched upon what might be the ultimate justification for Collingwood's whole approach to philosophy and history, especially the re-enactment theory. Collingwood did employ a fairly consistent use of Hegel's system. However, leaving aside the relative merits and demerits of Hegelianism, a response might be made to Gadamer's criticism by means of a more practical historical-hermeneutical analysis of a wider sample of Collingwood's writings.

A Response to Gadamer

Like other critics of re-enactment of past thought, Gadamer seems to be relying on a rigid and limited interpretation of thought, thinking and rethinking. Grasping Collingwood's idea of rethinking as the key to historical understanding is crucial for responding to Gadamer. That grasp is supported by looking at Collingwood the historian and archeologist. His work in these fields amounted to an application of his philosophical theories about history and might be of help in further clarification of his historical-hermeneutical approach. In attempting a response to Gadamer our discussion will be limited to three questions, 1) Does Gadamer's statement of historical reconstruction do justice to Collingwood's complex and dialectical notion of thought? 2) Does that treatment correspond to Collingwood's work as a historian? 3) Is it correct to say, as Gadamer does, that Collingwood limits the meaning of a text to original and conscious intentions of the author or historical agents? The issues raised in these three points will be dealt with further in subsequent chapters. Nonetheless, the paramount role played by Gadamer in hermeneutics calls for a direct response.

While Gadamer accepts as a major contribution the logic of question and answer, he objects, as we have seen, to what he refers to as an extrapolation. That extrapolation has to do with thoughts, purposes or intentions. This approach he attributes to the "seduction of historicism."[51] His problem with Collingwood's re-enactment theory and his charge of historicism are closely tied to his difficulties with Collingwood's notion of thought. In an appendix to his book entitled "Hermeneutic and Historicism," he raised the difficulty entailed in deciding what exactly Collingwood meant by thought. To Collingwood's claim that the historian's task is to penetrate "to the thought of the agents whose acts they are studying," Gadamer responds that,

> It is particularly difficult in German translation to decide exactly what Collingwood means here by 'thought' (Denken). Obviously the concept of Akt in German ('act' in English) has quite a different connotation from what the English author intends.[52]

Some of the obscurity can be dispelled by examining examples of Collingwood's idea of rethinking.

In the hermeneutical process described by Gadamer, a large portion of the task involved is how to gain the horizon of the past. He finds support in the dialectic of question and answer but, outside of his efforts to express the suddenness and openness of understanding through a series of metaphors, he says little about the manner in which the past's horizon is gained. Collingwood's reenactment is precisely that—an attempt to bridge the hermeneutical gap. "The gulf of time between the historian and his object must be bridged . . . from both ends."[53] Allowing the text or evidence to speak and be interpreted is, for Collingwood, the only available entrance to the reconstruction of past thoughts. The questioning process opens up the horizon of the past by letting the historian get at the real subject matter of history, human actions. Human actions, according to Collingwood, have an outside and an inside. It is only when the external action is a response to an conscious experience that the action is human. For this reason the historian must understand the thought of the agent or author. In this way he may grasp the question. In order to understand what a past philosopher taught one must go through the same process he went through. Gadamer, as we have seen, also calls for the interpreter to go behind the text. However, in spite of his metaphors of conversation and fusion, in spite of his insistence on textual and linguistic autonomy, it is still difficult to see how the interpreter goes behind the text. Collingwood's way is re-enactment. The words of the Theodosian Code, for example, even if properly translated, will not deliver to the reader their historical significance. The interpreter must see in the edict what the emperor saw in it.

> He must see the possible alternatives, and the reasons for choosing one rather than another; and thus he must go through the process which the emperor went through in deciding on this particular course. Thus he is reenacting in his own mind the experience of the emperor; and only in so far as he does this has he any historical knowledge of the meaning of the edict.[54]

Getting to the thought behind the text allows the interpreter to grasp, to some degree at least, the basic convictions or presuppositions implied in the text or evidence.

What is, according to Collingwood, the nature of thought, that we can re-enact it? Only conscious thought "can be identical and known to be identical in two different moments, and hence is alone capable of being re-experienced by way of being re-enacted."[55] The ability to re-think one's own past thoughts or another's is the very condition for doing history. Thought here stands for a mental activity the negative peculiarity of which is seen in that it is not an immediate form of experience and therefore is not washed away by the "flow of consciousness." It is distinguished from mere consciousness in its "power of recognizing the activity of the self as a single activity persisting through the diversity of its own acts."[56] Thought involves not mere consciousness but self-consciousness. When consciousness becomes aware of the continuity through the flow of sensations and feelings, thinking occurs. This awareness is more than memory. Mere remembering does not necessarily involve awareness of what one is doing. Historical re-enactment is reflective and is primarily concerned with purposeful, reflective past thought. Because such thoughts survive in texts or evidence, they are able to trigger the process of rethinking and interpretation. Moreover, the continuity of thought, through the historical process, leaves traces in our own thought and therefore opens the possibility of rethinking. Past thoughts are not totally unfamiliar because they remain "incapsulated" in present thinking.

Collingwood sought to avoid the shortcomings of romantic hermeneutics by indicating that it is only thought which survives the flow of consciousness and can therefore be re-experienced. In the *New Leviathan*, he states,

> It follows that *feelings cannot be remembered*. People who think they remember a feeling are deceived, never having been careful to make the distinction, by the fact that a *proposition about a feeling can be remembered*. You cannot remember the terrible thirst you once endured; but you can remember that you were terribly thirsty.[57]

In spite of such strong denials about the re-experiencing of feelings, Collingwood's philosophy of mind, understood dialectically, provides the way for thought to include forms of experience such as feeling and desire. The dialectical structure of thought allows one to include in the subject matter of history ". . . those lower levels of mental functions to which it is usually thought to stand opposed."[58]

Collingwood's re-enactment, then, is by no means naive intuition. It demands careful interpretation of both text and context. It also calls for a sensitive reading of the present in order that it, as a product of the past, might provide the key to that past.

The second point has to do with Collingwood's work as a historian. His principal concern was with historical constitution and not historical explanation.[59] Gadamer's criticism of Collingwood hinges, to some degree, on the view that historical reconstruction is not enough. Interpretation, too, is necessary. Collingwood would respond that the reconstruction and interpretation are inseparable. Constructing history is how one gains the horizon of the past. His theories primarily address themselves to what happened and use the "what" to get at the "why". Rather than an extrapolation from the logic of question and answer, re-enactment of past thought flows from that logic itself and is the very condition for doing history. Gadamer's critique of re-enactment relates to his misgivings about reconstruction.

> A reconstructed question can never stand within its original horizon, for the historical horizon that is outlined in the reconstruction is not a truly comprehensive one. It is,

rather, included within the horizon that embraces us as the questioners who have responded to the word that has been handed down.[60]

Hermeneutics by necessity must always be beyond mere reconstruction. Gadamer's point is valid and would be hard to argue against. However, it might be worthwhile to look briefly at Collingwood the historian and ascertain just what he is doing in his historical practice when he employs his question and answer process coupled with re-enactment of past thought. Does he engage in a reconstruction separate from the interpreter's present?

Leon J. Goldstein examines Collingwood's *Roman Britain* in order to compare its findings with the theories presented in the epilegomena to *The Idea of History*. He is emphatic in demonstrating that re-enactment of past thought is not an attempt at an explanation of history. The object of re-enactment is historical knowledge not historical explanation.[61] Re-enactment allows one to know historically. Rather than being an "immediate, intuitive grasping," as Gadamer implies,

> Rethinking requires a good deal of preparation, and we cannot expect to rethink the thought of any historical actor without knowing a good bit of what he must have known before determining his own course. To re-enact Severus's thought is to determine what he set out to do; it is not to explain why he set out to do it.[62]

His studies of the Roman colonization of Britain indicate Collingwood's use of re-enactment. The lack of available evidence for dealing with that period provides a stiff testing ground for any attempt at gaining the horizon of the past. One of the many examples Goldstein cites may be singled out in order to illustrate how Collingwood constructs history on the basis of the question and answer dialogue and re-enactment of past thought. In *Roman Britain*, there is a description of Antoninus Pius' changes in the British frontier defense system. Just as historians read documents, so Collingwood read the remains of the Antonine wall, a wall which as he shows was of inferior quality compared to its predecessor, the Hadrian wall. As he had previously questioned the Albert Memorial, he now questions this piece of Roman construction. By careful scrutiny of the remains of the "outside" of this event—the wall, he manages to rethink Antoninus' reasons for building such a shoddy and cheap piece of work. What did Antoninus intend to do? Out of this questioning there emerges in Collingwood the re-enactment which comes to expression in his conclusion.

> Both in construction and in organization, then, the Antonine Wall bears the marks of a deliberate effort after cheapness, at the cost of a serious decrease in efficiency. The same thing is to be seen if we consider its strategic position. Both its flanks, especially the left, lie unprotected upon narrow estuaries, easily crossed by the smallest craft in almost any weather. If we recollect the car with which Hadrian . . . fortifies the whole of the northwest Cumberland coast for thirty or forty miles beyond the terminus of the Wall, the complete absence of Roman posts on the Clyde below Old Kilpatrick becomes so striking that we cannot put it down to negligence. These various features of the Antonine Wall when considered together, seem less like a series of oversights than parts of a deliberate policy, based on the assumption that a powerful frontier-work on that line was not needed.[63]

The conclusions drawn here are good illustrations of re-enactment. Interpreting a text or tracing evidence drives the historian beyond it. The horizon of the past is gained by questioning all available evidence and interpreting it by means of cognate knowledge. The rethinking is based on present evidence. And when the evidence is read in relation to its "inside," the purpose and plan or thought, then the subject matter of history, namely, deliberate human actions, emerge. Collingwood's position is that historical rethinking "must take into account everything the historian can think of which may be relevant-rethinking must be rooted in knowledge of historical evidence."[64] Rethinking is not some naive crossing of the time gap, nor is it meant to be an explanation of history; it is, however, an explanation of the available evidence. It happens as a result of carefully reading the traces of the past that are found in the present. It is a starting point which expands rather than limits both the horizons of past and present. Our example from *Roman Britain* indicates that rethinking is a more modest proposal than Gadamer believes; it allows the historian to understand truly human activity-actions informed by thought. Thought can only be known by thinking. Past thought can only be known by re-thinking.

One last point remains in our response to Gadamer. Does Collingwood limit the meaning of a text to the author's original intention? Both men agree that understanding results from a questioning process. Gadamer wants to protect the spontaneity of a process in which ". . . the sense of a text in general reaches far beyond what its author originally intended."[65] Does Collingwood deny this? Our examination of his notion of thought, as well as his historical writing, indicates that he would not limit meaning to original intention. The dialectical nature of thought in his philosophy demands, as we have seen, that the process of question and answer, while being retrospectively determined, is prospectively open. History is never final; it is in constant need of revision. For Collingwood history is the re-enactment of past thought *in the present*. This last phase seems to have evaded Gadamer. The past horizon can only be appropriated by rethinking it from within the present. Past and present are not totally alienated from one another. The past can be known, that is, rethought because it lives on in the present. This is expressed in the "incapsulation" idea which Gadmer does not discuss.

> So long as the past and present are outside one another, knowledge of the past is not of much use in the problems of the present. But suppose the past lives on in the present; suppose, though incapsulated in it, and at first sight hidden beneath the present's contradictory and more prominent features, it is still alive and active; then the historian may very well be related to the nonhistorian as the trained woodsman is to the ignorant traveller. Nothing here but trees and grass, thinks the traveller, and marches on. 'Look', says the woodsman, 'there is a tiger in that grass.' The historian's business is to reveal the less obvious features hidden from a careless eye in the present situation. What history can bring to moral and political life is a trained eye for the situation in which one has to act.[66]

Collingwood was a trained woodsman. He was most certainly aware that the full meaning of the Hadrian or Antonine Wall would never be exhausted. With each imagined or real threat to England in the course of history, new possibilities of meaning for those walls could arise. The past like the future is never really known in itself. Both can only be somehow grasped in the present.[67]

The re-enactment process is the understanding process. It is not a mysterious jump into a mind of the past. It involves a critical re-appropriation of the past horizon similar to the one Gadamer advocates.

> This re-enactment . . . is not a passive surrender to the spell of another's mind; it is a labour of active and therefore critical thinking. The historian not only re-enacts past thought, he re-enacts it in the context of his own knowledge and therefore, in re-enacting it, criticizes it, forms his own judgement of its value, corrects whatever errors he can discern in it. This criticism of the thought whose history he traces is not something secondary to tracing the history of it. It is an indispensible condition of the historical knowledge itself.[68]

Conclusion

In view of Collingwood's position on the dialectical nature of thought, his historical practice and his position on original intention, we would conclude that Gadamer's treatment of Collingwood appears to be less than adequate. We have shown that the logic of question and answer and re-enactment of past thought form the same process. In terms of levels of meaning, the original historical sense is important for Collingwood but it is not isolated from the present. Mediation is possible for him, as for Gadamer, by means of an understanding which operates historically. It is true that Collingwood puts more emphasis on context and original intention. This is undoubtedly due to his historian's instinct which seeks to anchor more securely the questioning process which takes place in the present and opens out to the future. However, the logic of question and answer is a hermeneutic in that it is a process going on in the present which clarifies meaning and not simply meaning-meant.

Since Gadamer was not attempting an in-depth analysis of Collingwood, he should not be faulted. His appreciation for the logic of question and answer is great. Analysis of that logic, in a systematic fashion, is difficult because Collingwood, although employing it throughout his writings, left explicit treatment of it to his last books. Our discussion indicates that Gadamer could have made much greater use of Collingwood in order to clarify the relation between historical reconstruction and historical understanding.[69] On close analysis, both philosophers envision the hermeneutical process as a dialectic of question and answer and a fusion of horizons. Moreover, in spite of the difficulties with the reenactment theory, that theory does represent an attempt to move from strictly metaphorical models of the event of interpretation to a more exacting description of what the historian-interpreter does. In the conversation between Heidelberg and Oxford the last line has not been spoken.

NOTES

1. A, pp. 24–43. Other primary sources are: SM, pp. 76–80; EM, Chaps. IV–VII.

2. A, pp. 44–52.

3. Some examples of the discussion the logic of question and answer has engendered are: A. P. Simonds, "Mannheim's Sociology of Knowledge as a Hermeneutic Method" *Cultural Hermeneutics* 3 (1975): 91–93; Quentin Skinner, "Meaning and Understanding in the History of Ideas," *History and Theory* 8 (1969): 36–39, 50–53; Joseph Agassi, "Questions of Science and Metaphysics," *The Philosophical Forum*, n.s., 5 (1974): 529–56. An overview of Collingwood's theory of history from the question and answer perspective is G. Buchdahl, "Logic and History," 94–113. See also Anthony F. Russell, *Logic, Philosophy and History: A Study in the Philosophy of History Based on the Works of R. G. Collingwood* (Lanham, Md: University Press of America, 1984).

4. Examples of the question and answer logic may be found in many hemeneutical theologians. However, most would appear to be derivative from Gadamer, *Truth and Method*, pp. 333–41.

5. Agassi, "Questions of Science," p. 536.

6. Ibid., p. 542.

7. Mink, *Mind, History and Dialectic*, p. 131.

8. A, pp. 29–30.

9. Ibid., p. 25.

10. Ibid., p. 31.

11. Ibid., p. 33; cf. Donagan, *Later Philosophy*, pp. 59–62.

12. Ibid., pp. 37–38.

13. SM, p. 77.

14. Mink, *Mind, History and Dialectic*, p. 132.

15. SM, pp. 77–78.

16. Ibid., p. 78.

17. Ibid., p. 78.

18. Gadamer, *Truth and Method*, p. 339

19. A, p. 39.

20. EPM, p. 117.

21. Ibid., p. 161

22. Ibid., p. 195.

23. Ibid., p. 198.

24. Ibid., p. 23.

25. Ibid., p. 24.

26. Debbins, ed., *Philosophy of History*, p. 137.

27. Ibid., p. 138.

28. Ibid., p. 138.

29. A, p. 86. For the theme of play see, SM, pp. 102–107; cf. Gadamer, *Truth and Method*, pp. 91–119.

30. See Robinson, "Hermaneutic Since Barth," pp. 19–77; David Linge, "Dilthey and Gadamer: Two Theories of Historical Understanding," *Journal of the American Academy of Religion* 41 (1973): 536–53; Wilhelm Dilthey, *Pattern and Meaning in History*, ed. and intro. H. P. Rickman (New York: Harper Torchbooks, 1962); H. A. Hodges, *Wilhelm Dilthey: An Introduction* (London: Routledge and Keegan Paul, 1944); Theodore Abel, "The Operation Called Verstehen", *American Journal of Sociology* 54 (1948–49): 211–18; Alphonse De Waelhens, "Sur une herméneutique de l'herméneutique", *Revue Philosophique de Louvain* 60 (1962): 583–85.

31. Gadamer, *Truth and Method*, p. 326; Lonergan is also influenced by Collingwood's logic of question and answer. See Hugo A. Meynell, *An Introduction to the Philosophy of Bernard Lonergan* (New York: Barnes & Noble, 1976), p. 142; "Lonergan's theory of knowledge . . . seems to be a version of the 'logic of question and answer' recommended by Collingwood.

32. A., p. 327.

33. Gadamer, *Truth and Method*, p. 327. The German text (p. 346) is even more explicit. In a more accurate translation it reads: "Sense is always sense of direction in a possible question. The sense of what is correct must correspond to the direction which a question has opened up."

34. Ibid., p. 329.

35. Ibid.

36. Ibid., p. 330.

37. Ibid., p. 331.

38. Ibid.

39. Ibid. The orginal German text (p. 352) reads *Spiegelfechterei* which used figuratively as it is here means not "mock-fighting" but "make-believe."

40. Ibid., p. 261. "The significance of this circle, which is fundamental to all understanding, has a further hermeneutic consequence which I may call the 'foreconception of completion'. But this, too, is obviously a formal condition of all understanding. It states that only what really constitutes a unity of meaning is intelligible. So when we read a text we always follow this complete presupposition of completion, and only when it proves inadequate, i.e. the text is not intelligible, do we start to doubt the transmitted text and seek to discover in what way it can be remedied. The rules of such textual criticism can be left aside, for the important thing to note is that their proper application cannot be detached from the understanding of the textual content." In attempting to avoid the connotation of a vicious circle, theological hermeneutics has turned to the term spiral. Cf. E. Schillebeeckx, *God the Future of Man*, tr. N. D. Smith (New York: Sheed & Ward, 1968), pp. 7–8; Hart, *Unfinished Man*, pp. 60–68; Ted Peters, The Nature and Role of Presuppositions: An Inquiry into Contemporary Hermeneutics," *International Philosophical Quarterly* 14 (1974): 211–17.

41. Ibid., pp. 262–63. The English translation reads: "The place between strangeness and familiarity that a transmitted text has for us is that intermediate place between being an historically intended separate object and being part of a tradition. The true home of hermeneutics is in this intermediate area." The German text is particularly difficult to translate. The following is an attempt at remedial translation, German text, (p. 279). "The place between strangeness and familiarity which happens to be the place tradition takes as far as we are concerned, is the Between that is between an objective thing historically meant and out there and the belongingness [of it] to a tradition. It is in this *Between* that hermeneutic finds its true place." Cf. IH, pp. 304–305; Theodore Kisiel, "The Happening of Tradition: The Hermeneutics of Gadamer and Heidegger," *Man and World* 2 (1969): 358–85.

42. Ibid., p. 334; cf. A, p. 70.

43. Ibid., p. 350.

44. Ibid., p. 350.

45. Hans-Georg Gadamer, "On the Scope and Function of Hermeneutical Reflection", *Continuum* 8 (1970): 87.

46. Gadamer, *Truth and Method*, p. 336.

47. See Ch. 1, fn. 39.

48. Gadamer, *Truth and Method*, p. 468.

49. See Skinner, "Meaning and Understanding," 3–53; Christopher E. Arthur, Gadamer and Hirsch: The Canonical Work and the Interpreter's Intention," *Cultural Hermeneutics* 4 (1977): 183–97.

50. Thomas B. Ommen, *The Hermeneutic of Dogma,* American Academy of Religion Dissertation Series No. 11 (Missoula: Scholars Press, 1975), pp. 160–62. Neither Collingwood nor Gadamer should be facilely categorized as "contextualist" or "textualist."

51. Gadamer, *Truth and Method,* p. 336. "It is the seduction of historicism to see in this kind of reduction a scientific virtue and regard understanding as a kind of reconstruction which in effect repeats the process of how the text came into being. Hence it follows the ideal familiar to us from our knowledge of nature, where we understand a process only when we are able to reproduce it artificially." In some way the historicist label is ironic since Gadamer himself has been so labelled. Gadamer's accusation of a natural science approach to history is hard to justify given Collingwood's many attempts at differentiating between historical knowledge and scientific knowledge about nature.

52. Ibid., p. 467. However, Gadamer also admits the mystery involved in the nature of language, pp. 340–46.

53. IH, p. 304.

54. Ibid., p. 283.

55. Mink, *Mind, History and Dialetic,* p. 174.

56. IH, p. 306.

57. NL, p. 134, par. 5.54.

58. Mink, *Mind, History and Dialectic,* p. 166.

59. Leon J. Goldstein, "Collingwood on the Constitution of the Historical Past," in *Critical Essays on the Philosophy of R. G. Collingwood,* ed. Michael Krausz (London: Oxford University Press, 1972), p. 267.

60. Gadamer, *Truth and Method,* p. 337.

61. Goldstein "Constitution of the Historical Past," p. 245. A sizable body of literature has grown up around the controversy of historical explanation in Collingwood. See L. J. Cohen, "Has Collingwood been Misrepresented?," 140–50; Alan Donagan, "Explanation in History," *Mind* 66 (1957): 145–164; W. H. Dray, *Laws and Explanations in History* (London: Oxford University Press, 1957), Ch. IV and V; P. Gardiner, *The Nature of Historical Explanation* (London: Oxford University Press, 1952).

62. Goldstein, "Constitution of the Historical Past," p. 247.

63. Ibid., p. 249.

64. Ibid., p. 253.

65. Gadamer, *Truth and Method,* p. 335.

66. A, p. 100. See D. E. Kennedy, "The Wood and the Trees: The Philosophical Development of R. G. Collingwood," *Australian Journal of Politics and History* 10 (1964): 245–48.

67. See R. G. Collingwood, "Some Perplexities About Time: With an Attempted Solution", *Proceedings of the Aristotelian Society,* n.s. 26 (1926): 135–50.

68. IH, p. 215.

69. See Robert E. Innis, "Hans-Georg Gadamer's *Truth and Method:* A Review Article," *Thomist* 40 (1976): 319.

CHAPTER III

The Doctrine of Absolute Presuppositions

Introduction

While the logic of question and answer enjoys a wide acceptance in many fields, the foundation for that approach, the doctrine of absolute presuppositions, is a center around which a storm of controversy whirls. The remote reason for the controversy relates to what Gadamer refers to as the Enlightenment's "prejudice against prejudice itself, which deprives tradition of its power."[1] Authority was considered the cause of prejudgment and prejudgment the cause of error. As a result, the ideal sought was an unprejudiced human reason which would practice a presuppositionless science. The proximate reason for the controversy revolves around the accusation that Collingwood's later thought, especially as expressed in *An Autobiography* and *An Essay on Metaphysics*, was riddled through and through with relativism. The basis for this relativism is said to be located in his reform of metaphysics whose infrastructure is the doctrine of absolute presuppositions. In terms of understanding Collingwood, the notion of presupposition deserves logical priority; however, it is being taken up after the logic of question and answer because presuppositions are only unveiled as a result of the questioning process. It should also be mentioned that, in contrast to the logic of question and answer, the importance of presuppositions receives no explicit analysis until 1938.[2] The doctrine of absolute presuppositions, with its critique of traditional ontology, has reverberations in logic and epistemology as well as metaphysics.[3] An examination of all that the doctrine entails would bring us far beyond the scope of this study. The present chapter has the more limited objective of analyzing Collingwood's thought about presuppositions, especially those he terms absolute presuppositions, and indicating their relevance to hermeneutics.

Recent hermeneutical discussion has placed considerable emphasis on the importance of presuppositions as inevitable and necessary for any understanding. Presuppositions are the pre-reflective ground of meaning passed on to us by the tradition in which we find ourselves. They are of two types: fundamental or ultimate and contingent presuppositions. The latter are dependent on the former. Contingent presuppositions may be articulated as suppositions or propositions, and become so by drawing out the necessary conditions implicit in the existing propositions. Once the presupposition is articulated, it becomes a supposition. But, as Peters points out,

> ... fundamental or ultimate presuppositions are different. They resist being made into suppositions or propositions. They function to provide the basic framework or pre-understanding which make reflective understanding and articulated propositions possible. They refer us to our fundamental vision of reality and the self-evident truths which are tacitly acknowledged in everything we comprehend and assert. They can be pointed to as ostensively present but cannot themselves be fully drawn up into propositional form. It is this character of standing in the background like a horizon that makes such a presupposition what it is.[4]

The two varieties of presuppositions referred to above correspond to Collingwood's distinction between relative and absolute presuppositions. Absolute presuppositions provide us with our pre-reflective, unconscious "fundamental vision of reality." The term most often employed in hermeneutics is pre-understanding. However, Gadamer uses *"Vorurteil"* which he translates in his lectures as "prejudice." Prejudice is also the choice of the English translators of *Wahrheit und Methode*. Because of the connotation attached to prejudice in ordinary usage, this word may be unfortunate. It is clear, however, that Gadamer uses the word to point to the role of pre-reflective knowledge of the whole, bequeathed to the interpreter by tradition. That knowledge functions as a condition for the understanding and the acquisition of further knowledge. "Prejudice" here does not mean that the outcome of the investigation is determined before hand. A prejudice becomes "ugly" and negative not because it passes judgement but because it does not allow any alteration of judgement when new evidence is presented.[5] It is precisely our fundamental or absolute presuppositions, in Gadamer's terms, our prejudices, which allow us to interpret and understand a text or piece of evidence presented to us. The questioning process brings to the surface presuppositions and roots out illegitimate prejudices. "It is the tyranny of hidden prejudices that make us deaf to the language that speaks to us in tradition."[6]

The notion of presupposition and its effect on understanding is generally acknowledged and plays a large role in theological hermeneutics. In spite of different terminology, the term presupposition describes "a pre-articulated structure of beliefs which directs consciousness to perceive, organize, and meaningfully understand the objects and events it encounters."[7] This same phenomenon forms a core idea in Collingwood and greatly affects his approach to history and hermeneutics. The difference he brings to the discussion is the faith-like character he attaches to "absolute presuppositions."

The Doctrine of Absolute Presuppositions

Collingwood developed his teaching out of his question and answer process. When someone expresses a thought in words, much is left unsaid. What is most often unstated are the presuppositions.[8] Every statement is a response to some question and every question arises from some logically prior statement. If something answers a question, it is a proposition; but if it provokes another question, it is a presupposition. This is what he called a relative presupposition. "By a relative presupposition I mean one which stands relatively to one question as its presupposition and relatively to another as its answer."[9] An absolute presupposition, on the other hand, provokes questions but does not answer them. Absolute presuppositions have been understood in terms of assumptions, basic convictions, a priori concepts, contextual implications and religious faith. And Collingwood, at different times, seems to leave room for such varied interpretations. Summarily, however, he argues that an intelligible statement builds upon presuppositions which eventually may be seen to rest on a foundation of one or more absolute presuppositions. This is a consequence of the nature of understanding itself as historical. All thinking involves an a priori element which, like Gadamer's prejudices, ". . . are an ontological fact, indicative of the facticity of the historically transmitted pre-understanding on the basis of which we can understand anything at all."[10]

The doctrine of absolute presuppositions exploded on the world of English philosophy in 1940. With strands of what many considered to be dogmatism, relativism and historicism, Collingwood claimed that metaphysics is the study of what absolute presuppositions have been held and are being held by a person or community. And that study, he pointed out, is an historical one.

> Metaphysics is the attempt to find out what absolute presuppositions have been made by this or that person or group or persons, on this or that occasion or group of occasions, in the course of this or that piece of thinking. Arising out of this, it will consider (for example) whether absolute presuppositions are made singly or in groups, and if the latter, how the groups are organized; whether different absolute presuppositions are made by different individuals or races or nations or classes; or on occasions when different things are being thought about; or whether the same have been made *semper, ubique, ab omnibus*. And so on.[11]

It is this definition of metaphysics as the study of absolute presuppositions which colors all of Collingwood's later philosophy. Before turning to that philosophy, especially as it is presented in *An Essay on Metaphysics*, we will sketch out the role granted to presuppositions in some of his earlier writings.

A basic faith or trust as a condition for any knowledge received its first formulation in *Religion and Philosophy*. The very existence of reason and science are dependent upon prior forms of consciousness: art and religion. Faith, as a basic attitude which arises out of experience, underlies all thinking. God, the ultimate presupposition of whatever is known, is here conceived of as "the unifying principle of the world, however that principle be regarded."[12] Every philosophy except skepticism has a God in this sense. As soon as a philosophy claims to be systematic and not merely a collection of disconnected ideas it requires a God. Likewise science becomes aware of this absolute presupposition when it is realized that facts do not exist in abstract isolation from one another but get their meaning from a view of the whole.[13] A wholistic view dependent on an underlying principle is not, in Collingwood's opinion, subject to proof. It is not the result of reflection on experience; it is its presupposion.

In spite of his life-long conviction of the need for a religious base for civilization, Collingwood was well aware, as his autobiography attests, of the corruption of consciousness which can befall a people. The restoration of authentic consciousness can only come about through critically examining underlying presuppositions. This is, even at this early stage, the task of philosophy. To be aware of God is religion, to analyze that awareness is the task of philosophy of religion.[14] Doing something and understanding what and how one does it are different things. Philosophy of religion is explored in *Religion and Philosophy* as a metaphysics of experience which merges with a general theory of knowledge and ethics. Basic faith convictions are found by carefully peeling back the various layers that encrust our everyday, secular experiences.

This same search for basic convictions is manifested in the article "The Devil."[15] Collingwood critically examines the use of psychological data in analyzing religious experience. Writing during World War I, he argued against the prevalent currents in psychology and in defense of free will. Throughout his career, free will remained an absolute presupposition for his whole philosophy. The conviction that "no man is compelled to do evil by inexorable action of external forces"[16] is linked up with belief in God and providence and provides the presuppositions for his philosophy of history. Human life is a becoming and self creation. The direction and growth of life is shaped by free will. Life is the process in which real human nature is freely sought.

> But human nature, since man is at bottom spirit, is only exemplified in the absolute spirit of God. Hence man must shape himself in God's image, or he ceases to be even human and becomes diabolical. This self-creation must also be self-knowledge; not the self-knowledge of introspection, the examination of the self that is, but the knowledge of God, the self that is to be. Knowledge of God is the beginning, the center, and end, of human life.[17]

While the themes discussed in *Religion and Philosophy* and "The Devil" will reappear in the later Collingwood and provide the content for his examples of absolute presuppositions, neither work shows much theoretical understanding of how such basic convictions function in human thinking. The most explicit articulation of the role and necessity of presuppositions in the early Collingwood appears in the Ruskin centenary conference paper presented in 1919. Central principles are accepted as "fundamental and incontrovertible" and assumed in all thinking and acting to be true. As we have seen in chapter I, Collingwood refers to these principles as a "ring of solid thought."[18] This ring of principles sounds strikingly like what years later he will refer to as a constellation of absolute presuppositions. The ring ". . . welded together by some force of mutual cohesion" will reappear as "consupponability."[19] These basic convictions are constitutive of a tradition and perhaps can never really be fully and objectively the object of study. As a person's deepest convictions, they often remain unexpressed and even unconscious. They are so much a part of the person that often he is unable to gain any distance from them, not even enough to put them into words. Presuppositions of this fundamental type are received from a historical tradition. The philosopher, operating historically, rummages around in the individual mind or the community's tradition not to do away with fundamental convictions but to allow them to surface in order that a horizon or perspective may be gained. Much of what is later made explicit concerning metaphysics can be found seminally in the Ruskin essay.

The trail of the problem of presuppositions is picked up again in 1927. In "Reason is Faith Cultivating Itself,"[20] a title which says much about Collingwood's doctrine of absolute presuppositions, he unpacks his conviction that reason builds upon a prior belief or trust in the possibility of knowing anything at all. In discussing the relation between faith and reason in the light of Kant's belief in God, freedom and immortality, he informs his readers that such convictions are akin to Descarte's *cogito*. They cannot be proved, since they are too much a part of the person who believes in them; "they are the presuppositions of all proof whatever, not like the Aristotelian axioms, which enter into particular arguments as their premises, but rather as the conditions of there being any arguments at all."[21] The underlying presuppositions are the source from which reason flows. Reason is a systematic development of faith. In a remarkable play on a scholastic axiom, Collingwood writes:

> *Nihil est in intellectu quod non fuerit in sensu* said the schoolmen; if for intellect we read scientific thought, and for sense religious intuition, we may say with substantial truth, that the intellect discovers nothing that faith has not already known.[22]

All knowledge begins with faith, an unprovable conviction that something is there to be known. The conviction inaugurates the questioning process. On the other hand, all action begins with an irresistable and indemonstrable feeling that we are dependent on and supported by a power revealed in our actions. Knowledge and action rest on a foundation of faith. It is in this essay that Collingwood introduces the specifically Christian faith as the basis for the development of Western thought after the Greeks. He returns to this theme in *An Essay on Metaphysics*.

The scattered references to a basic faith or a priori concepts get molded into full-blown theories in *An Autobiography* and especially in *An Essay on Metaphysics*. In the former, the presentation is somewhat sketchy but its impact on metaphysics obvious. Metaphysics does not attempt to go beyond experience. It examines experience in order to ascertain what a people believe about the nature of the world. These beliefs constitute the presuppositions of their physics. Metaphysics also seeks to discover the presuppositions of other peoples and periods in order "to follow the historical process by which one set of presuppositions has turned into another."[23] The metaphysician's task is now clearly an historical one. What presuppositions underlie the physical sciences at a given time is, according to Collingwood, a purely historical question. The metaphysician does not inquire into the truth of such presuppositions because they are not answers to questions. They are not true or false, they simply are. It is these presuppositions which are not the answer to a question but the very ground of questioning itself which he calls absolute.[24]

Absolute presuppositions are described here as a "complex of contemporaneous fact" which arrives on the historical scene as a product of previously held belief complexes. The traditional view of eternal metaphysical problems espoused in *An Essay on Philosophical Method* is rejected. The concepts around which metaphysical problems raged in the history of philosophy are understood as having come upon the scene at "ascertainable times," often in the not very distant past. The realist distinction between the historical question, What did Plato teach? and the philosophical question, Was he right? is reduced by Collingwood to one set of questions and those are historical. Plato's teaching had to be based on the absolute presuppositions of his own time. Only by understanding those presuppositions can the philosopher understand Plato.[25]

An Essay on Metaphysics of 1940 is the place where the doctrine of absolute presuppositions and the reform of metaphysics that such a doctrine supposedly entails received its most complete exposition. At times, the language of the book sounds bombastic and, in relation to traditional ontology, iconoclastic. Metaphysics as the science of pure being or ontology is dismissed as a mistake made first of all by Aristotle.

> But the science of pure being would have a subject matter entirely devoid of peculiarities; a subject matter, therefore, containing nothing to differentiate it from anything else, or from nothing at all . . . You may call this nothing by what name you like—pure being, or God, or anything else—but it remains nothing, and contains no peculiarities for science to examine.[26]

In rejecting Aristotle's first definition of metaphysics, as the study of pure being, Collingwood finds support for his own position in a second definition. Aristotle also considered metaphysics a science which studies the "presuppositions underlying ordinary science." The whole of the 1940 essay is an attempt to explain the meaning of that definition. He begins with the example of seeing a line over one's head and immediately presupposing "clothes-line". The thought "clothes-line" arrives unannounced. "Only by a kind of analysis, when I reflect upon it, do I come to see this was a presupposition I was making, however little I was aware of it at the time.[27] Logicians, in Collingwood's opinion, have tended to neglect the theory of presuppositions. In a series of five propositions, he sets out to fill the gap. Proposition one, "Every statement that anybody ever makes is made in answer to a question,"[28] has already been examined in relation to the logic of question and answer. Proposition two brings us directly to our present concern. "Every question involves a presupposition."[29] Behind the question there is a fundamental belief or an historical fact, which causes a question to arise. Without this presupposition logically and immediately prior to the question, the question would not be asked, or, if asked, it would be nonsensical in this context. Holding a certain presupposition will mean some questions will "arise", others will be held down. What causes a question to arise is the "logical efficacy" of the presupposition. For example when attempting to decipher a damaged inscription, the investigator must first be sure that the mark in question is not accidental. It must be part of the inscription, and therefore be possessed of some meaning. If that presupposition is not present, it must be supposed. That supposition then becomes a presupposition for asking the question "What does it mean?"[30] This prior supposition is the subject of the third proposition, that the logical efficacy depends only on a supposition being made, not upon whether what is supposed is true. In both scientific thinking and practical affairs, it can be of value to argue from suppositions that are known to be questionable or even false. Collingwood cites an example: the family of a woman to whom marriage has been proposed asks the man involved for a written marriage agreement. In this case, the man must realize that the assumption being made is not that he is dishonorable but that one day he might be capable of dishonesty. "He finds no difficulty in distinguishing between their supposing him a rascal and their believing him one, and he does not regard the former as evidence of the latter."[31]

Proposition four introduces the problematic notion of absolute presuppositions, "A proposition is either relative or absolute."[32] Relative presuppositions stand in relation to one question as its presupposition and to another question as its answer. A relative presupposition can be verified. It can be an answer to a question. Absolute presuppositions, however, are not verifiable. They are never answers to questions. Collingwood offers a test for ascertaining whether someone else's presuppositions are relative or absolute. If they are absolute they are at the core of one's whole self-understanding as well as the understanding of one's science or art. The ticklishness of questioning another's absolute presupposition is illustrated by asking a pathologist, "But how do you know that everything that happens has a cause?" The likely response is to "blow right up in your face, because you have put your finger on one of his absolute presuppositions."[33] The idea of cause is taken for granted by the pathologist. Collingwood's fifth and last proposition is, "Absolute presuppositions are not propositions.[34] They are not so, because, as we have seen, they are not answers to questions.

> Hence any question involving the presupposition, such as the question 'Is it true?' 'What evidence is there for it? 'How can it be demonstrated?' 'What right have we to presuppose it if it can't?' is a nonsense question.[35]

Rather than propositions or beliefs which can be argued and proven true or false, absolute presuppositions provide a framework from which reality is experienced. They are not shaped by the self alone but by the character and trend of the community and institutions within which the self is nurtured. Language, culture and history are all ingredient to the way the self is formed and lets in reality. Absolute presuppositions form the horizon or perspective from which, not only beliefs are formed, but also history is known, scientific findings categorized, and other humans understood. The scrutiny of such presuppositions was for Collingwood the task of metaphysics. And because changes occur in a civilization or science, the task is an historical one. The interaction of philosophy and history is necessary because change is the result, ultimately, of presuppositions having gradually been replaced by others. Paradigms based on absolute presuppositions, such as the idea of cause or the existence of God, have formed the very foundation of civilizations that have developed at various times in history. They have also provided for the controlling model of the physical sciences.[36]

It is precisely in history's encounter with absolute presuppositions that various problems emerge. If we are unaware of absolute presuppositions, how can we know them? What is the meaning of the "consupponibility" of absolute presuppositions? If such presuppositions are absolute, how can they be said to change? Finding some response to these problems will shed light on the relation of absolute presuppositions to Collingwood's idea of history and his contribution to hermeneutics. Our first question concerning awareness of fundamental presuppositions is important because of the problems it presents for the understanding of history as re-enactment of past thought in the present. The absence of adequate criteria for identifying absolute presuppositions makes it difficult to ascertain whether an historian has truly re-thought past thinking. This problem is greatly compounded when Collingwood informs his readers that no one is fully aware of his own absolute presuppositions.[37] The lack of awareness would seem to present an insurmountable obstacle to the rethinking process. This problem draws the inquiry into our third question. If people are unaware of absolute presuppositions, they obviously cannot choose between them. Then, how do such presuppositions change?

Before responding to the problems of awareness and change, it is necessary to discuss our second question, the meaning of consupponibility. Consupponibility is the key which unlocks both problems. Collingwood indicates that if metaphysics is, as he claims, an historical science, then absolute presuppositions are "historical facts" and, as such, do not happen and cannot be analyzed singly. They happen in interconnected complexes. Such complexes of historical facts he calls "constellations." The absolute presuppositions in a constellation must be consupponible. That is, while it is not necessary to suppose any individual presupposition, when one is presupposed, then it must be possible to suppose any or all of the others. In spite of its complexity, the constellation still forms a single fact. The various presuppositions making it up converge in one act of thinking.

> They are not like a set of carpenter's tools, of which the carpenter uses one at a time, they are like a suit of clothes, of which every part is worn simultaneously with all the rest. This is to say that, since they are all suppositions, each must be *consupponible* with all the others; that is, it must be logically possible for a person who supposes any one of them to suppose concurrently all the rest.[38]

The complexity and consupposibility of such constellations of absolute presuppositions indicate more clearly the problem involved in our first question about awareness. Neither the historical agent nor the present thinker is usually totally aware of the presuppositions in his thinking. This may be illustrated from a current example: the changing patterns in male-female relationships.[39] As long as certain presuppositions relative to male dominance controlled thinking on the subject, predetermined models of thought and behavior followed. We presently seem to be undergoing a shift in our presuppositions. Controlling images, models and paradigms are being shattered. Thinking about relations between the sexes is being altered, and yet that alteration is happening while most men and women remain unaware that the old paradigms with their constellations of presupposition are being cast aside. This illustrates well Collingwood's emphasis on absolute presuppositions being historical "facts" and yet most often remaining below the level of awareness. The radical changes in an individual or society are much more dependent on historical happenings and involvement in a family, religious or community tradition than is usually realized. Fundamental presuppositions reach down to the feeling level and demand much more than argument to be changed. They also demand an historical-hermentutical perspective in order to be known.

The most likely time for heightened awareness of absolute presuppositions is when they are being called into question. This takes us to our third question and will also shed more light on the problem of awareness. Collingwood only indirectly addressed the problem of how absolute presuppositions change. In a footnote, he points out that such change is not ordinarily a conscious one, yet there is nothing frivolous or superficial about it. "It is the most radical change a man can undergo, and entails the abandonment of all his most firmly established habits and standards for thought and action."[40] Changes in the most basic convictions of an individual or a civilization occur in a particular historical epoch because structures of society, constellations of social or economic facts, for example, are subject to "strains" of various intensity which knock the consupponibility off balance. The strains cause an instability in the received worldview. When the strains become too great, structures change and ways of thinking are altered. In this kind of profound change, there is "a modification of the old with the destructive strain removed; a modification not consciously devised but created by a process of unconscious thought."[41]

We are able, then, to draw some conclusions about awareness and change relative to absolute presuppositions. The modification process has much to do with Collingwood's understanding that the present as a product of its past is the evidential starting point for rethinking the past. The unconscious process by which absolute presuppositions come into being and change need not mean that they lay completely beyond the reach of the historian-metaphysician.

They may be uncovered because they are processed into the present and remain in modified form. Unconscious here does not mean irrational but rather implicit. It is the task of the investigator to make explicit the absolute presuppositions contained in the thought being studied. The presuppositions implied by thoughts and actions are the undergirding of the historical process. Presuppositions which undergo historical change exhibit a gradual progress which, in Collingwood's view, take the dialectical form of the history of errors, progressively being corrected and gradually becoming more consupponible. The historical-hermeneutical task, moving from the present to the past, allows absolute presuppositions to emerge and provides for understanding the process of ongoing modification.[42]

There are obvious difficulties in analyzing one's own absolute presuppositions. They constitute the inner meaning of a culture and are not easily articulated. They represent the limits of the individual's thinking. They are "the summit of a conceptual hierarchy."[43] And, as in Lonergan's horizon analysis, the horizon can only be seen when it is surpassed. When absolute presuppositions are raised to the level of awareness, they are no longer either presuppositions or absolute. For this reason, absolute presuppositions can only be grasped from an historical-hermeneutical perspective. They are also more clearly understood when unearthed in relation to a whole group of people living within a certain historical epoch. This unearthing is a hermeneutical task and sums up much of what is entailed in gaining the horizon of the past. The task, involving a number of allied disciplines from metaphysics to sociology of knowledge, links up the relation between the absolute presuppositions which underlie history and the structure of mind. As Stephen Toulmin states:

> In every field, the beginning of wisdom lies in recognizing how the patterns of conceptual change reflect the presuppositional structures of conceptual systems; and every intellectual discipline develops through a succession of distinct historical phases, characterized by a different set of concepts, questions, and propositions, and forming a self-contained hierarchy of presuppositions.[44]

Coming to grips with a coherent, core meaning or unifying principle of a culture means understanding, to the extent possible, the absolute presuppositions of that culture. On those presuppositions, a whole manner of thinking and acting depends. Interpretation of the past involves the investigator in the dredging up of past presuppositions. It also calls for the dredging to be done while immersed within the waters of one's own presuppositions. Gaining the horizon of the past means allowing the fundamental convictions of a perhaps distant era to break through and converse with our own deepest convictions. That process with all its ramifications for Collingwood's historical-hermeneutic method occupies most of the following chapter. At this point a summary view of one of his examples of absolute presuppositions might help to further clarify.

An Example of the Doctrine

It must be admitted that much of what Collingwood says about absolute presuppositions remains unclear. Even his examples leave themselves open to conflicting interpretations and charges of a total lapse into relativism.[45] However, his use of concrete examples does allow us to move beyond presuppositions which are relative, that is dependent on broader principles, to principles which stand on their own feet. Collingwood offers examples of his theory under three headings; the existence of God, the metaphysics of Kant, and causation. We shall examine only the absolute presupposition, "God exists."[46]

The example "God exists" with all of its implications provides an illuminating illustration for metaphysics as the historical study of absolute presuppositions. Collingwood placed great emphasis on the role of theology in Western culture. Drawing on a strand in Aristotle, he identified theology with metaphysics. Metaphysics in the Greek tradition was concerned with "divine" matters. Collingwood described the Greek philosophers as a "dissenting and sometimes persecuted sect of monotheists in a polytheistic society".[47] Building on a pre-existing tradition of scientific thought, the Ionian thinkers attempted to introduce unity into a polymorphic science. That they failed in this attempt is, in Collingwood's view, the ultimate reason for the collapse of the Roman empire. Irreconcilable contradictions which divided the world into matter and spirit, time and eternity, necessity and contingency blocked the way to the principle Thales and others were approaching:

"The principle that in spite of all the differences between different natural realms and different sciences that study them there is one thing that is Nature, and one science that is natural science."[48]

The failure of that attempt so endangered the Greek worldview that they were left vulnerable to other threats from both within and without. Into this situation stepped Christianity. Christian thinkers were able to offer a solution to the problem of the one and the many by interpreting Greek thought with the help of the Gospel. For centuries, theological reflection on Greek science provided for the absolute presuppositions of science. For these presuppositions, Collingwood credits the patristic writers who corrected Aristotle in his teaching that God did not create the world. His claim is that if the world is simply a fact discovered by the senses as Aristotle said, then it is not "a world of things that happen of themselves and are subject to control by our art or anyone else's."[49] The Fathers, constructing on a foundation provided by both the Greek philosophical tradition and the Hebrew prophets, "corrected" a Greek metaphysical error by proclaiming God creator of the world. They allowed that being the creator of motion in the world is as much a part of the nature of God as being the source of "diversified orderliness" in the world.[50] The *Logos,* as a self-differentiating unity, accounted for God as the source of "diverse realms in nature,"[51] while the Spirit, as the creative activity of God, provided for the source of motion in the world.[52] The doctrine of the *Logos,* in particular was a matrix within which all rational inquiries could be pursued.

In these theological reflections, according to Collingwood, the Fathers, building on the absolute presupposition that "God exists" with its corollaries of creation and providence, accounted for the beginnings of modern science. Behind the idea of a rationally ordered science must be a principal of order. Arguing from a Hegelian perspective, Collingwood pointed out that if mathematics can be applied to nature as is obviously the case, then nature must be rational and have a rational mind behind it. He chides the logical positivists, claiming that if they had more expertise in the history of science, "they would know that the belief in the possibility of applied Mathematics is only one part of the belief in God."[53]

The position taken here, incorporating a curious mixture of

theology and science, places perhaps too much trust in a number of leaps from a faith position to science. For such leaps, Collingwood has been criticized.[54] Nevertheless, the doctrine of absolute presuppositions, exemplified in "God exists," implies no proof or even explanation. It might better be understood as a basic religious trust or faith which provides the starting point for further understanding and action. The beginning of metaphysics is precisely that starting point.

Comparing absolute presuppositions to faith could turn out to be a fruitful exercise in that it will project our understanding of an absolute presupposition like "God exists" beyond a dry, static, ahistorical stance denoted by a "constellation of concepts." The point, represented by such a basic conviction, can be comprehended as a general stance, a habit of mind or an attitutide. That stance, habit or attitude is generally described, in religious terms, as faith. In 1928, Collingwood wrote that, "Faith is the religous habit of mind . . . it is the attitude which we take up toward things as a whole."[55] Analogously faith may be compared to the attitude one takes up toward a limited whole, such as one's country. We know and love a country by living in it. A certain perspective is gained by being part of it. Sacrifices, even death, are sustained for the sake of it. But the analogy ends; a country is not an absolute. Making it so would be idolatrous. However, the starting point in faith or trust shows through the example. Faith is a step on the way to knowledge. It is the most basic step and may be characterized as a kind of preknowledge that the universe is rational. It is an attitude made possible by basic trust and freedom.

> Practical faith consists in the certainty that life is worth living, that the world into which we have been unwillingly thrust is a world that contains scope for action and will give us a fair chance of showing what we are made of; a world in which, if we turn out complete failures, we shall have only ourselves to blame. Practical faith means 'accepting the universe,' or, what is the same thing, knowing that we are free.[56]

It is this understanding of faith, articulated early by Collingwood, which is at stake in his account of absolute presuppositions. Deeper than beliefs which are propositions, faith, like absolute presuppositions, can be neither verified nor falsified. Its origins are vague and its continued existence is often tested by the vicissitudes of personal and communal histories. Anticipating by many years viewpoints expressed by such thinkers as Tillich, Ogden, Erikson and Küng, Collingwood's absolute presuppositions examplified in "God exists" provide the content for the viewpoint of faith as the basis of a lifestyle for an individual or a community.[57]

Perhaps the most striking parallel between absolute presuppositions and religous faith is that the creation, consolidation and perpetuation of such presuppositions is the work of religous institutions. The very guardianship of absolute presuppositions, not only those of religion, but also those of art, science and history, falls ultimately into the hands of the churches. Incidentally since progress is possible only by critically reflecting on the presuppositions which lie at the base of the question and answer dialectic of an age, the role of religious institutions is made ambiguous. On the one hand they must be conservative defenders of basic convictions, and on the other they must attend to the task of critically reflecting on those very convictions. In spite of this ambiguity, the impact of which is felt in every discussion of theological hermeneutics and the development of dogma, the role of the tradition of the community or institution is paramount for understanding, preserving and passing on the absolute presuppositions of faith. This role is brought out by Gordan Kaufman. Acceptance of belief in God is rarely the result of some particular experience or logical proof. It is most often the outcome of a series of linguistic, cultural and familial presuppositions, handed on by a tradition and taken in faith. The decision to move from unbelief to belief usually means moving to a new sociocultural setting where belief has been presupposed and nurtured. The decision most often is not to accept a "new presuppositional framework" but rather to place oneself within a believing community.[58]

Collingwood's doctrine leaves many problems unsolved. The origin, preservation and change of absolute presuppositions remain mysterious. The notion leaves itself open to a variety of interpretations, including a priori concepts, historical facts and faith. But perhaps mysteriousness is inherent in the very nature of something so basic. This section has sought merely to indicate an example, that of the primary religious presupposition, "God exists" and its structure as basic trust or faith. It is for Collingwood *the* fundamental insight which provides the pre-cognitve link between the knower and that which is known. In terms of hermeneutics such an absolute presupposition is received through an historical and linguistic tradition by being a member of a believing community. The community transmits to its members a meaningful frame of reference implied by the existence of God. The shared frame of reference allows understanding to happen. As Peters states, "Presuppositions are inevitable; they are shared; they determine the form of the questions we ask; and they provide the condition for the possibility of acquiring any new understanding."[59] As we shall see in the next section, fundamental or absolute presuppositions provide the power of a tradition which allows one to break into the hermeneutical circle.

Absolute Presuppositions and Contemporary Hermeneutics

The dependence of understanding on presuppositions is generally acknowledged and needs no demonstration. There is widespread agreement in contemporary hermeneutics that, "In order to interpret anything, we must begin by projecting a pre-understanding of what it is we are about to interpret."[60] Although the phrase "absolute presuppositions" is not used by hermeneutic theoreticians, the notion of presuppositions, elevated at times to an ultimate or fundamental level, greatly affects hermeneutics. In this brief section, we will attempt to indicate, in outline form, the use made of fundamental presuppositions by a few of the principle participants in the contemporary hermeneutical discussion, and point out the relation to Collingwood's doctrine.

Emerich Coreth, in discussing the principle that the interpreter ought to be able to understand the author better than he understood himself, claims that it is the distance involved in the hermeneutical experience that allows the interpreter to get not only to what was said, but to what was left unsaid—the presuppositions. The interpreter needs to reflect on that which is in the background. In terms reminiscent of Collingwood, Coreth states:

> If we make explicit the conditionings which determine the unthematized background of the utterances, if moreover we read and understand the particular utterances in their

context, follow single words through their semantic changes, establish the shades of meaning they have in the usage of the author, then we understand that author in a way which is, accordingly, better than the way in which he understood himself.[61]

This illustrates well Collingwood's understanding of the task of the metaphysician-historian. He must bring to the level of awareness the "conditionings" of thought. The question and answer process not only attempts to arrive at the meaning of what was said in a text, but also at the background or presuppositions, which most often remain unsaid. Understanding the past demands grappling with the presuppositions of past thought.

The other pole in any hermeneutical dialogue, the interpreter, is also influenced by the unsaid. Presuppositions on this side of the divide are also given a positive function. Gadamer's "prejudices" serve the same function as Collingwood's absolute presuppositions. This form of pre-understanding is circular. In order to grasp the meaning of a text, the interpreter's own "fore-meaning" is necessary. However, in spite of that "fore-structure of understanding," the interpreter must be open to the meaning of the text. The hermeneutical circle is not a closed, vicious one. The text has its "fore-meaning" and the interpreter his. Only a shared tradition, common to both, permits understanding. For both Collingwood and Gadamer that shared tradition provides the blanket under which the warmth of intelligibility is felt. Gadamer writes:

> In fact history does not belong to us, but we belong to it. Long before we understand ourselves through the process of self-examination, we understand ourselves in a self-evident way in the family, society and state in which we live. The focus of subjectivity is a distorting mirror. The self-awareness of the individual is only a flickering in the closed circuits of historical life. That is why the prejudices of the individual, far more than his judgments, constitute the historical reality of his being.[62]

Gadamer is referring to basic presuppositions, the ordinarily unconscious assumptions that ground our attitudes and behavior. The same idea is expressed by Collingwood.

> The continuity of a cultural tradition is unconscious: those who live in it need not be explicitly aware of its existence. The continuity of tradition is the continuity of the force by which past experiences affect the future; and this force does not depend on the conscious memory of those experiences.[63]

A similar historical perspective, granting full impact to the historicity of understanding implied in absolute presuppositions, is found in Lonergan's notion of horizon. A horizon, like absolute presuppositions, provides the boundaries for our "field of vision" and "range of interest." Horizons are the structured outcome of past achievement, "both the condition and the limitation of further development."[64] The function of presuppositions is well illustrated in one of Lonergan's most celebrated principles. Following suit with Collingwood and Gadamer, he rejects the Enlightenment and Romantic ideal of history without presuppositions. He notes:

> To say that the historian should operate without presuppositions is to assert the principle of the empty head, to urge that the historian should be uneducated, to claim that he should be exempted from the process variously named socialization and acculturation, to strip him of historicity. For the historian's presuppositions are not just his but also the living on in him of developments that human society and culture have slowly accumulated over the centuries.[65]

The function of presuppositions in biblical exegesis was directly addressed by Rudolf Bultmann. In a short essay, "Is Exegesis without Presuppositions Possible?",[66] he assesses both the positive and negative aspects of presuppositions. His argument closely parallels Collingwood's use of presuppositions in historical thinking. Bultmann suppresses dogmatic prejudices or presuppositions which would dictate in advance the results of the inquiry. However, no exegete attacks his texts without his own individuality, habits, weaknesses and biases, *"there cannot be any such thing as presuppositionless exegesis."*[67] Nonetheless, the interpreter should strive to eliminate his presuppositions in order to allow the subject matter of the text to speak. But since exegesis is part of the science of history, the one presupposition which cannot be eliminated is the "historical method of interrogating the text." The determinative aspects of language, for example, which belong to historical method, must be taken into account as well as the cause and effect process underlying the deep sense of historical continuity. The historical method presupposes in principle that it is possible "to exhibit these and their connection and thus to understand the whole historical process as a closed unity."[68]

Bultmann then turns to the more strictly hermeneutical task of overcoming the gap of time by means of translation. Translation for him means historical understanding, and understanding presupposes understanding. A perspective, a way of raising questions, is a necessary prerequisite for the exegete. It is legitimate and will not distort the interpretation as long as the perspective is not considered the only possible one. The fundamental presupposition for understanding history, according to Bultmann, is that the interpreter be related to the subject matter of that history. That relationship he characterizes as "existential," which means that, "for historical understanding, the schema of subject and object that has validity for natural science is invalid."[69] The past cannot be a dead past but must be related, alive to the present. Bultmann's grasp of historical method as a basic presupposition of exegesis is an element of his thought which, as we shall see, is in no small way dependent on Collingwood.

The foregoing survey, in a rudimentary fashion, indicates the way three scholars envision the circular movement involved in the hermeneutical experience. Bultmann, Gadamer and Lonergan manifest, in varying degrees, Heidegger's "hemeneutics of facticity" where the mind's reason can be said to be dependent on history's tradition. *Dasein* is never a completely empty slot and never completely outside the circle of understanding.

> What is decisive is not to get out of the circle but to come into it in the right way. This circle of understanding is not an orbit in which any random kind of knowledge may move; it is the expression of the existential *fore-structure* of Dasein itself.[70]

Collingwood's historical metaphysics, with its absolute presuppositions, also seeks to express the historicity of all human understanding. Certain ultimate presuppositions, while not reducible to sense experience, are simply given by a particular historical situation and in spite of the absoluteness of their claim, they can change. Every human being, by virtue of being human, has already walked half the hermeneutical circle. Absolute presuppositions act as "catalytic agents" which the mind dredges up out of itself, and by means of which it orders experience and converts it into science and civilization. The structure of mind and the structure of history are related. "In other words, the absolute presuppositions which underlie experience have a transcendental grounding in the structure of mind."[71]

Conclusion

The doctrine of absolute presuppositions plays dominant role in Collingwood's approach to history and hermeneutics. Absolute presuppositions and the logic of question and answer form the basis for the historical method. Historical work, according to Collingwood, is carried out by means of a presuppositional or transendental method. The remainder of this study will be concerned with analyzing the fundamental presuppositions of history. History is the imaginative reconstruction of past events. Starting out from existing evidence the historian sets about reconstructing the events presupposed by the evidence. The reconstruction is carried out by means of rethinking past thought which is possible because past thought lives on in the present. Although unable to divest himself of his own presuppositions, the historian cannot fall victim to a wooden reproduction of documents or a robot-like following of "authorities". With his own imaginative picture of the past as the criterion of historical truth, the historian, by means of detailed analysis and imaginative inference, constructs a picture of the past. Presuppositions crowding in from both hermeneutical poles provide the frame for the picture. The very possibility of such a picture however rests on a primary given for historical knowing. This Collingwood refers to as the historical or a priori imagination, the subject matter of the next chapter.

NOTES

1. Gadamer, *Truth and Method,* p. 240; cf. Hans-Georg Gadamer, "The Power of Reason," *Man and World* 3 (1970): 11–12; Peters, "Role of Presuppositions", p. 219.

2. The most important primary sources for the doctrine are: A, pp. 66–67 and EM, pp. 1–77 especially Chapter IV "On Presupposing" and Chapter V "The Science of Absolute Presuppositions."

3. Hartt, Review of *Faith and Reason,* p. 284 states, ". . . hardly any element of Collingwood's philosophy has attracted as much interest or drawn as much fire as his doctrine of absolute presuppositions." Important discussions of this topic are: Vergil Dykstra, "Philosophers and Presuppositions," *Mind* 69 (1960): 63–68; Donald S. Mackay, "On Supposing and Presupposing," *Review of Metaphysics* 1 (1948): 1–20; J. Llewelyn, "Collingwood's Doctrine of Absolute Presuppositions, *Philosophical Quarterly* 11 (1961): 49–60; John B. Post, "A Defense of Collingwood's Theory of Presuppositions," *Inquiry* 8 (1965) 332–54; David Rynin, "Donagan on Collingwood: Absolute, Truth and Metaphysics," *Review of Metaphysics* 18 (1964): 301–33; E. E. Harris, "Collingwood on Eternal Problems," *Philosophical Quarterly* 1 (1951): 228–41; Kenneth Laine Ketner, *An Emendation of R. G. Collingwood's Doctrine of Absolute Presuppositions* (Lubbock: Texas Tech Press, 1973); Michael Krausz, "The Logic of Absolute Presuppositions" in, *Critical Essays on the Philosophy of R. G. Collingwood,* ed. Michael Krausz, (Oxford: Clarendon Press, 1972), pp. 222–40.

4. Peters, "Role of Presuppositions," p. 210; cf. Michael Polanyi, *Personal Knowledge: Toward a Post-Critical Philosophy* (New York: Harper Torchbook, 1958) and Anders Nygren, *Meaning and Method: Prolegomena to a Scientific Philosophy of Religion and a Scientific Theology* (Philadelphia: Fortress Press, 1972).

5. Peters, "Role of Presuppositions", p. 217.

6. Gadamer, *Truth and Method,* p. 239.

7. Peters, "Role of Presuppositions", p. 211.

8. EM, p. 21.

9. Ibid., p. 29.

10. Peters, "Role of Presuppositions", p. 220.

11. EM, p. 47. See Knox, "Editor's Preface" to IH, pp. xii–xvii, where this teaching is considered to be the solidifier of the radical conversion hypothesis. On pp. xvi–xvii, he states, "The absolute presuppositions (i.e. the content of religious faith) are no longer said to be knowledge; as presuppositions they are neither true nor false. And they are no longer universal characteristics of all thought; they are always historically condi-

tioned." He concludes, "It may suffice to remark that while his final historicism has affinities with Dilthey and Croce, his doctrine of absolute presuppositions, with its religious and theological background, has affinities with Kierkegaard and even Karl Barth."

12. RP, p. 56. Collingwood returned to the centrality of God for knowledge and action in his last writings, see R. G. Collingwood, "Fascism and Nazism" *Philosophy* 15 (1940): 168–76.

13. RP, p. 57. Such a position has gained respectability in the sciences and was influenced by Collingwood; cf. Stephen Toulmin, *Human Understanding* (Princeton: Princeton University Press, 1972), vol. 1, pp. 71–80 and Thomas S. Kuhn, *The Structure of Scientific Revolutions* (Chicago: University of Chicago Press, 1962).

14. RP, p. 53.

15. Collingwood, "The Devil" was originally published in 1916 in conjunction with the Streeter group. It has been republished in Rubinoff, ed. *Faith and Reason,* pp. 213–33.

16. Johnston, *Formative Years,* p. 54.

17. Collingwood, "The Devil," in *Faith and Reason,* ed. Rubinoff, p. 232.

18. Collingwood, "Ruskin's Philosophy" in *Philosophy of Art,* ed. Donagan, p. 10.

19. Rubinoff, *Reform of Metaphysics,* p. 224.

20. Collingwood, "Reason is Faith Cultivating Itself," in *Faith and Reason,* ed. Rubinoff, pp. 108–21.

21. Ibid., p. 115.

22. Ibid., p. 120.

23. A, p. 66.

24. Ibid., p. 67.

25. Ibid., 69–72; cf. Fackenheim, *Metaphysics and Historicity,* pp. 17–18.

26. EM, p. 14, 17-20: In spite of language which seemingly attempts to destroy metaphysics, the case has been made that Collingwood was attempting to do the opposite. Rubinoff, *Reform of Metaphysics,* pp. 241—48; Rubinoff argues that EM can be understood as a defense of metaphysics written in response to A. Ayer *Language, Truth and Logic* (London: Gollancz, 1947). It is interesting to note that Ayer's recent work, *Philosophy in the Twentieth Century,* (New York: Vintage Books, 1984), singles out Collingwood's contribution to speculative philosophy, pp. 191–213.

27. EM, p. 22.

28. Ibid., p. 23.

29. Ibid., p. 25; cf. Dykstra, "Philosophers and Presuppositions," pp. 63–64.

30. EM, pp. 26–27; cf. Rubinoff, *Reform of Metaphysics*, pp. 232–33.

31. EM, pp. 28–29.

32. Ibid., p. 29.

33. Ibid., p. 31.

34. Ibid., p. 32.

35. Ibid., p. 33.

36. IN, p. 9.

37. Krausz, "Absolute Presuppositions," p. 226, fn. 1.

38. EM, p. 66.

39. For a provocative discussion on shifting presuppositions in male-female relations see, Eugene C. Bianchi and Rosemary Radford Reuther, *From Machismo to Mutuality, Woman-Man Liberation* (New York: Paulist Press, 1976), pp. 119–31. Perhaps the most striking illustration in theology of critical reflection on fundamental presuppositions can be found in the theology of liberation. Critical reflection, involving a hermeneutic of suspicion, is the basis for doing theology For good summaries see: Juan Luis Segundo, *The Liberation of Theology*, trans. John Drury (Maryknoll: Orbis Press, 1976), pp. 7–38; Alfred T. Hennelly, "Theological Method: The Southern Exposure," *Theological Studies* 38 (1977), 709–35; Haight, *Alternative Vision*, pp. 43–63.

40. EM, p. 48, note to Chapter V.

41. Ibid. Collingwood's understanding of change as the result of modifications in the unconscious thought process has generated much disagreement. Cf. Rubinoff, *Reform of Metaphysics, p. 271;* Knox, "Editor's Preface" to IH, *p. XIV;* Donagan, *Later Philosophy,* pp. 271–75; Toulmin, *Human Understanding,* vol. 1, p. 76, claims that Collingwood "vacillates uneasily between two possible answers, and is unable in good conscience to handle these questions consistently in either of the two ways. Do we make the change from one constellation of absolute presuppositions to another because we have reasons for doing so; or do we do so only because certain causes compel us to? Are questions about the 'modifications' in our intellectual 'structures' to be answered in terms of reasons, considerations, arguments, and justifications—that is in terms of 'rational' categories? Or must they be answered, rather, in terms of forces, causes, compulsions, and explanations—that is, in terms of 'causal' categories?"

42. IH, p. 119; cf. Rubinoff, *Reform of Metaphysics,*pp. 272, 274; Mink, *Mind, History and Dialectic,* p. 156; Post, "Defense of Collingwood," p. 332.

43. Toulmin, "Conceptual Change", p. 206.

44. Ibid.

45. Toulmin, *Human Understanding* "Frege, Collingwood, and the Cult of Systematicity," vol. 1, pp. 52–95 is a clear, concise treatment of Collingwood's "relativism" as compared to Frege's "absolutism." The problem with Collingwood's examples are indicated.

46. Before turning to that examination, however, it should be pointed out that, in general, absolute presuppositions appear to be that which can be taken for granted. Kantian categories or a priori concepts would often appear to be what Collingwood had in mind. Until relatively recently western science has been dependent on various assumptions about cause. The changing use of causation in science manifests the historicity of absolute presuppositions and the fact that their absoluteness is tied to the use made of them. In spite of being absolute, they are subject to change. Collingwood, in an interesting historical insight, traces the absolute presuppositions of science back to the metaphysical speculations of the Church Fathers.

47. EM, p. 201.

48. Ibid., p. 215.

49. Ibid.

50. Ibid., p. 218.

51. Ibid., pp. 219–20. Collingwood refers here to Gibbon's gibe that the *Logos* was taught in 300 B.C. in Alexandria and revealed by John in 97 A.D. He points out that Gibbons lifted the remark from St. Augustine's *Confessions* while "characteristically" failing to acknowledge the source. He also falsified the facts by suppressing the point Augustine was making, that John's doctrine was a new idea in that the Logos was made flesh.

52. EM, p. 221. See, E. W. F. Tomlin, *R. G. Collingwood*, Writers and their Works, no. 42 (London: British Council and National Book League, 1953), p. 34.

53. EM, p. 257. Ultimately, Collingwood's position is traceable to Anselm's argument which, he claims, is the expression of an absolute presupposition. See EM, pp. 189–90; cf. Gilbert Ryle, "Mr. Collingwood and the Ontological Argument," *Mind* 44 (1935), 137–51; "Back to the Ontological Argument," *Mind* 46 (1937), 53–57.

54. Llewelyn, "Collingwood's Doctrine," p. 59. See also Donagan, *Later Philosophy*, p. 304.

55. Collingwood, "Faith and Reason" in *Faith and Reason*, ed. Rubinoff, p. 140.

56. Ibid., p. 141.

57. Hartt, Review of *Faith and Reason* pp. 283, 287–88, refers to the similarities between Collingwood's absoute presuppositions and the notion of faith as basic trust in Tillich and Ogden. A similar approach to faith as basic trust may be found in Hans Küng, *On Being a Christian*, tr. Edward Quinn (New York: Doubleday, 1976), pp. 57–88.

58. Gordon D. Kaufman, *God the Problem* (Cambridge: Harvard University Press,

1972), p. 245. Chapter 10, "The Foundations of Belief", pp. 226–56 is heavily indebted to Collingwood's doctrine of absolute presuppositions.

59. Peters, "Role of Presuppositions," p. 222.

60. Ibid., p. 213.

61. Emerich Coreth, *Grundfragen der Hermeneutik: Ein philisophischer Beitrag* (Freiburg in Br.: Herder, 1969), unpublished trans. by Roger Balducelli, p. 137; cf. A, pp. 39–40.

62. Gadamer, *Truth and Method,*p. 245.

63. Collingwood and J. N. Myers, *Roman Britain and the English Settlements*, 2d. ed. (Oxford: Clarendon Press, 1937), p. 252. quoted in Goldstein, "Constitution of the Historical Past," p. 258.

64. Lonergan, *Method in Theology* pp. 236–37.

65. Ibid., p. 223.

66. Rudolf Bultmann, "Is Exegesis without Presuppositions Possible?" in *Existence and Faith: Shorter Writings of Rudolf Bultmann*, trans. and intro. by Schubert M. Ogden (New York: Meridian Books, 1960), pp. 289–96.

67. Ibid., p. 290.

68. Ibid., p. 292.

69. Ibid., p. 294.

70. Martin Heidegger, *Being and Time,* trans. John Macquarrie and Edward Robinson (New York: Harper and Row, 1962), p. 195, quoted in Peters, "Role of Presuppositions", p. 215; see also Kisiel, "Happening of Tradition", p. 362.

71. Rubinoff, *Reform of Metaphysics,* p. 65; see EM, p. 197; cf. Fackenheim, *Metaphysics and Historicity,* pp. 71–72; see also pp. 39–40, n. 25 where Fackenheim points out the similarity between Collingwood and Heidegger.

CHAPTER IV

The Historical Imagination

Background to the Theory

That there is an historical past, somehow still available in the present, forms an absolute and transhistorical presupposition for all historical knowing. Collingwood's understanding of history as the re-enactment of past thought "incapsulated" in the present gains its dynamism from the constructive capacity of the historical imagination. The historian comes to know *what* happened by means of an imaginative reconstruction of the past.[1] This imaginative reconstruction is possible because the past is neither dead, nor independently existing in itself, but lives on in the present. In contrast to the natural scientist, the historian is not seeking something utterly new but rather a clearer articulation of something about which he is already aware. As we have already seen, Collingwood strove to free history from the methods of natural science. His theory of history is a theory about how present experience is converted into knowledge of the past. This conversion process is the work of the a priori historical imagination. The action of converting is an act of imagination because it is "an attempt to construct what, prior to the construction, is as yet 'non-existent,' but which nevertheless does exist as an implicit part of the historian's present experience."[2] Imagination is the faculty which makes explicit that which is implicit in experience.

The idea of history is innate. Both self-knowledge and our experience of the world are historical. When the mind knows something present, its past is implied and can be regained by interpreting the present. However, the criterion for historical truth is not present evidence but rather the mind's imaginative capacity for reconstruction, the historical imagination.

> That criterion is the idea of history itself: the idea of an imaginary picture of the past. That idea is, in Cartesian

language, innate; in Kantian language, *a priori*. It is not a chance product of psychological causes; it is an idea which every man possesses as part of the furniture of his mind, and discovers himself to possess in so far as he becomes conscious of what it is to have a mind.[3]

Collingwood's theory of historical knowledge is as much or more a philosophy of mind as it is a philosophy of history in the traditional sense. The structures of mind give form to the historian's picture of the past. Historical knowledge should be viewed as an instance of the whole knowing process.[4] The a priori imagination is the activity of mind which constitutes the criterion for history as the autonomous reconstruction of the past. What is the meaning of the historical imagination? How does it relate to the usual function of imagination in the knowing process? What role does it play in the theory of history especially in regard to the problem of historical verification? These problems form the major concerns of this chapter. Before turning to them, however, it will prove helpful to locate the notion of the historical imagination within the context of Collingwood's understanding of history as the science of human nature. Clarification will also be gained by examining the key idea of historical imagination against the wider background of Collingwood's philosophy.

The essay "Human Nature and Human History" begins by stating, "Man, who desires to know everything, desires to know himself."[5] Self-knowledge goes beyond knowledge of body and mind; it attempts to understand the knowing faculties themselves. It seeks to know thought, understanding and reason. How is such knowledge attained? Natural sciences, which study particulars and assign them to general types, do not fulfill the needs of a science of human nature. Past attempts at establishing such a science were led astray by an analogy with the natural sciences. According to Collingwood, "the right way of investigating mind is by the methods of history."[6] The rise of the modern conception of history as critical and constructive makes a true science of human nature possible. In this essay, Collingwood exposes some of his later-to-be expanded presuppositions of scientific history. The chief task of the historian is to get behind external expressions of thoughts. Ultimately, thoughts are that which concern him. Outward expression manifested in events is only important as a vehicle for revealing thought.[7] In a very concrete sense history is self-knowledge of mind. It indicates what mind has known and accomplished in the past. At the same time it is the making present of the past by the redoing of what mind has done in the past. Its object is the activity of thought itself. History is no spectator sport. The historian must re-experience the past by re-thinking it. Past activities to the historian "are objective, or known to him, only because they are also subjective, or activities of his own." By understanding the past of a particular present, the historian better understands himself. "It may thus be said that historical inquiry reveals to the historian the powers of his own mind."[8]

This self-knowing process is only possible because, unlike nature's evolutionary process where the past dies, the historical process keeps the past alive. We "become" human to the extent that we participate in history. In contrast to physical functioning, where, for example, we are not nourished because another has eaten, it can be said that, as far as our mental or spiritual life is concerned, we profit from the experience of others. Knowledge is woven together, and pieces of knowledge affect one another. The past is a kind of bank which houses deposits which continually pay out interest.

> The body of human thought or mental activity is a corporate possession, and almost all the operations which our minds perform are operations which we learned to perform from others who have performed them already. Since mind is what it does, and human nature, if it is a name for anything real, is only a name for human activities, this acquisition of ability to perform determinate operations is the acquisition of a determinate human nature. Thus the historical process is a process in which man creates for himself this or that kind of human nature by re-creating his own thought the past to which he is heir.[9]

Collingwood's conception of history as the science of human nature amounts to admitting that the essence of human nature is historicity. In human actions, human being is self-constituted.[10] Self-conscious historical life distinguishes man from the rest of existence. The specifically rational life only fully arrives on the scene with historical thinking. "It is only by fits and starts, in a flickering and dubious manner, that human beings are rational at all." Collingwood continues:

> Historicity, too, is a matter of degree. The historicity of very primitive societies is not easily distinguishable from the merely instinctive life of societies in which rationality is at vanishing point. When the occasions on which thinking is done, and the kinds of things about which it is done, become more frequent and more essential to the life of society, the historic inheritance of thought, preserved by historical knowledge of what has been thought before, becomes more considerable, and with its development the development of a specifically rational life begins.[11]

Historical knowledge, then, is no luxury or after-thought. It is the life of mind itself. Thought only exists within the historical process. History makes man aware of his rationality and provides the way for creating and appropriating human nature. As the science of human nature, history, according to Collingwood, is the discipline best suited for the interpretation of self and culture.

Having thus claimed such a lofty status for history, he is compelled to ask radical questions about the nature of it. As Kant had questioned natural science, Collingwood now asks, "How is historical knowledge possible?" Mink states that Collingwood was attempting a transcendental deduction of the concept of history. The goal of *The Idea of History* is to show by analysis "the necessary conditions of the possibility of knowing *now* something which happened then."[12] This task includes what has been discussed above: history as the process by which mind comes to know itself. That process presupposes the historical imagination.

The notion of history, as an innate a priori idea, forms an absolute presupposition for historical thinking.[13] By the a priori historical imagination, Collingwood is attempting to spell out that the structure of mind itself, as a product of the past, contains an innate picture of that past or at least the innate capacity to reconstruct that past. Before presenting an analysis of what Collingwood has to say about the historical imagination, some remarks about his general theory of imagination are in order. Pure imagination, the most primitive level of experience, forms the basis for art in *Speculum*

Mentis and was more fully articulated in *The Principles of Art*. It will be of value to relate the general theory of imagination, involving the perceptual imagination and the aesthetic imagination, to the a priori historical imagination. In both cases the functions of imagination might best be described in terms of tying together, supplementing and consolidating. An important function of imagination in the cognitive process is that it consolidates and gives permanence to the data of perception. In his account of perceptual imagination in *Speculum Mentis*, Collingwood indicates that perception itself involves an element of mediation. The source of such mediation is what Collingwood will later call the a priori imagination.

> But even behind the activity of the annalist there is an ultimate form of historical thought which is the most rudimentary of all. This is perception . . . In perception we are immediately aware of our object, which is a concrete and therefore historical fact: perception and history are thus identical. But the immediacy of perception does not exclude mediation, it is not abstract immediacy (sensation) but implicitly contains an element of mediation (thought). When we say that we perceive something, we mean thereby to assert that we are not thinking; but this assertion is an error, and the analysis of perception reveals inevitably the presence of thought.[14]

This perceptual imagination involves thought and this in turn indicates the vital connection between imagination and understanding. Collingwood emphasizes the position that all cognition is a mixture of immediacy and mediation. Pure sensation without imagination and memory would not allow the observer to see anything definite. "Pure sense, apart from thought cannot see the very thing it is looking at: pure thought, apart from sense, finds nothing to think about."[15]

The aesthetic imagination receives its fullest treatment in *The Principles of Art*. Imagination is that which raises preconscious feelings to conscious forms. Not concerned with truth or falsity, it is a "selective attention" which converts sensations and impressions into ideas. Imagination is an activity of mind which is distinct from both sensation and understanding. By connecting and ordering sense data, it serves to link sensation with reason. "Imagination is thus the new form which feeling takes when transformed by the activity of consciousness."[16] Aesthetic imagination is the creative activity of mind which raises a preconscious feeling to the definite form of a work of art.

Both the perceptual and the aesthetic imaginations function in ways that are analogous to the historical imagination. Their mediating and creative role will surface again, especially in the tasks of selection and interpolation in historical thinking. As early as the 1924 essay, "The Nature and Aim of the Philosophy of History," the reconstructive role of imagination in history was presented. The activity of imagining the past is a creative construction building on a past that is present, however vague or hidden. The use of imagination here indicates that imagination and reason overlap. Although the historian's most necessary possession is his imagination, he may in no sense be fanciful. Whereas the artist or novelist imagines for its own sake, the historian must employ an imagination that is disciplined and "subordinated to the pursuit of truth."[17] Although the historical imagination bears resemblance to the perceptual and aesthetic imagination, the contention that historical imagination is subordinate to the pursuit of the truth, indicates that the context in which Collingwood develops his theory of the a priori historical imagination differs from the context in which his general theory of imagination is unfolded.

Louis Mink suggests that the essay "The Historical Imagination" can best be understood as a commentary on F. H. Bradley's *The Presuppositions of Critical History*. Collingwood's esteem for Bradley as the father of critical history is evident. "Scissors and paste" history is finally overcome by Bradley's criticism of sources. He however failed to make the next critical step and pass over to what Collingwood calls "scientific" history. By this term is meant an interpretation of the past which is based on historical thinking itself as autonomous, with its own principles and method. "The Historical Imagination" attempts to set forth the criteria for this new historical consciousness.[18] In earlier sections of *The Idea of History,* Collingwood gives some indication of his indebtedness, most directly to Kant, Fichte and Hegel. Following Kant, Fichte had discovered the a priori elements in history. The historian is not God and cannot view history except from within it. The conditions of historical knowledge are based on the fact that the knower is in the present and looks at the past from the present perspective. But the historian's axiom must also be that the historical event is located in the past. This is not something that is empirically discovered; it is an a priori correlation of historical knowledge. Both conditions are absolute presuppositions of history. Fichte was claiming that events in time are a "schematized representation" of logical or conceptual relations. Collingwood states that since Plato, philosophers have agreed that there exists some relation between time and eternity, the historical and the logical. There is a necessary time sequence between events which is similar in character to the necessary sequence in which one point leads to another in a non-temporal logical sequence. In other words, the historian's picture of the past must have a certain conformity to the structures of the historian's mind.

> If this is denied, and if it is maintained that temporal sequence and logical implication have nothing to do with each other, historical knowledge becomes impossible, for it follows that we can never say about any event 'this *must* have happened'; the past can never appear as the conclusion of a logical inference. If the temporal series is a mere aggregate of disconnected events, we can never argue back from the present to the past. But historical thinking consists precisely of arguing back in this way; and it is therefore based on the assumption (or, as Kant and Fichte would have said, on the *a priori* principle) that there is an internal or necessary connection between the events of a time-series such that one event leads necessarily to another and we can argue back from the second to the first.[19]

This passage illustrates well the historical imagination as the necessary projection of a past for a particular present. History then picks up on that projection and analyzes the process by which the present came into being. This picture of history with its own logical structure and dynamic relations corresponds to Collingwood's dynamic logic of history which can be teased from a dialectical interpretation of mind and history.

It was Hegel who was to take the ideas outlined in the previous paragraphs and bring them to fruition. He is Collingwood's principal philosophical ancestor and his influence is pervasive. Here, we can only briefly mention Hegel's influence on the notion of the a priori historical imagination. For Hegel, as for Collingwood, all history is the history of thought. It manifests the self-development of reason. History presents us with "logical transitions set out on a time-scale". Historical developments, according to Hegel, are never accidental. Such developments "are necessary; and our knowledge of an historical process is not merely empirical, it is *a priori*, we *see* the necessity of it."[20] Following his remarks on Hegel, Collingwood adds that necessary connections are not seen in mere events, since events contain no necessary connections; they are evident in human actions because actions have "insides", thoughts, which are bound to other thoughts by logical connections.[21]

The instrument by which the mind constructs an imaginary picture of the past based on the present is the historical imagination. Collingwood characterizes it as a priori because he uses it in a sense corresponding to Kant's categories.[22] It is creative, autonomous and necessary but also based on evidence found in the present. After this background discussion we are ready to directly examine the key document for the theory of the a priori historical imagination.

The Historical Imagination

As the topic of his inaugural address as Waynefleet Professor of metaphysical philosophy at Oxford, Collingwood chose *The Historical Imagination*,[23] and explicitly proclaimed what he had long held, i.e., that the nature of historical thinking was both a legitimate and necessary aspect of philosophy. He claimed that history had by that time worked out a method of its own. It no longer fell under the shadow of its elder sister, natural science, since its method and results were no less certain than hers. As a particular form of knowledge, history can no longer be subsumed under perception and scientific thinking, as so many English philosophers up to that time had done. His thinking on the relation of history to perception shows signs of development. History is like perception in that it is individual. However, it gains its independence from perception and at the same time becomes problematic when it is realized that

> Its objects are events which have finished happening, and conditions no longer in existence. Only when they are no

longer perceptible do they become objects for historical thought. Hence all theories of knowledge that conceive it as a transaction or relation between a subject and an object both actually existing, and confronting or compresent to one another, theories that take acquaintance as the essence of knowledge, make history impossible.[24]

Because historical events are no longer perceptible, history differs from natural science. However, history resembles science in that it, too, is inferential and reasoned. The theoretical difference between history and science is emphasized in that science studies the world of abstract universals, while history is concerned with concrete individual things located in space and time. The object of history is not changeless and abstract. Collingwood here is reiterating his long held stance in opposition to the realist school, that history's object is the concrete universal. This is the main idea of historical consciousness. History is a form of knowledge which combines, yet goes beyond, knowledge by acquaintance and knowledge by description. This approach may be traced back at least as far as *Speculum Mentis* "... concrete universality is individuality, the individual being simply the unity of the universal and particular."[25] This notion is developed in *The Historical Imagination* by way of distinguishing between history and nature or the concrete and the abstract. Collingwood claims that current philosophy attempts to give an account of history as a combination of perception of the "here and now" with the abstract grasp of the "everywhere and always." But, just as history cannot be identified with either, so it is not a combination of both. Neither partly acquaintance with transient events nor partly reasoned knowledge of abstractions, history presents a third possibility for knowledge. "It is wholly a reasoned knowledge of what is transient and concrete."[26]

To account for this third way Collingwood first deals with the common-sense theory of history. By this he means history whose essentials are memory and authority. "History is then believing some one else when he says that he remembers something. The believer is the historian; the person believed is called his authority."[27] He immediately repudiates such a view by pointing out exacty how the historian tampers with the statements handed on by his authorities. The practicing historian is well aware that in regards to what he finds in his authorities he selects, he interpolates, he criticizes. It is precisely in these three tasks that the autonomy of historical thought comes to the fore. The responsibility of the historian is seen first in selection. No historian merely copies his authorities. He puts in his own biases and, very importantly, leaves out much that he cannot use. It is he who is responsible for selection, not his authority. Interpolation is an even clearer illustration of the historian's autonomy. By interpolation is meant historical reconstruction. At the least, interpolation is the key to that construction process. Authorities pass on points in the historical process; they leave out intermediate phases. The historian then necessarily interpolates the missing phases. The importance of the imaginary picture of the past, the product of historical imagination, becomes manifest. The picture of the subject, drawn in part from authorities, is seen to depend increasingly on the historian's own inferences from evidence.

> In this part of his work he is never depending on his authorities in the sense of repeating what they tell him; he is relying on his own powers and constituting himself his own authority; while his so-called authorities are now not authorities at all but only evidence.[28]

The historian's autonomy, according to Collingwood, may be pushed even further. This is most clearly demonstrated in historical criticism. By cross-examining his authorities, the historian can move beyond the text and extract from his witness even that which has been withheld in the original statements. Read critically, the dispatches of a commander which report a victory might reveal a concealed truth, or a less than critical evaluation of a preceeding historian.[29] Selection, interpolation and criticism, the functions of the historical imagination automatically project the historian beyond the autonomy of the text. The historian's power to reject something of what has been passed on, and to replace it with something else, illustrates Collingwood's criticism of "scissors and paste" history. The historian, he maintains, possesses his own criterion of historical truth.

Memory and authority have little or no weight in this approach to history. Basing history on statements passed on by authorities provides the infrastructure for the very "scissors and paste" history which Collingwood rejects. Nor can history depend on memory. The use of memory alone betrays a breakdown in the critical method which rejects the use of authorities, including one's own memory. Memory, one's own and that of others, must be subjected to adequate critical control. It is suspect, since "memory is not history, because history is a certain kind of organized or inferential knowledge, and memory is not organized, not inferential, at all."[30] When the historian simply accepts his own memory as history without scrutinizing what is remembered, as any other piece of historical evidence, he has rejected sound historical method. When he uncritically accepts what is remembered by another witness, he is doing the same. Moreover the historian may rediscover something which has been completely forgotten. Through critical examination of statements in his written sources and the use of unwritten evidence he may even discover something that "until he discovered it, no one ever knew to have happened at all."[31]

With the repudiation of authority and memory, what is left as a criterion of historical truth? Are there any criteria for knowing the past? Before offering his response to this question, Collingwood mentions Bradley as a milestone along the way to historical knowing. Bradley's answer to the question was what he called "our experience of the world."[32] It is this experience that lets us know that some things happen while others do not. Our present becomes the criterion for establishing what happened in the past. Collingwood has much respect for Bradley's position and claimed that his probings have brought about the "Copernican revolution in the theory of historical knowledge." What Bradley failed to realize in his critical history, however, is the other and more positive way of going beyond the given authorities. This involves conceiving of history as a constructive enterprise. Here Collingwood returns to interpolation as the constructive task of the historian. He describes "constructive history" as interpolating between the statements taken from authorities other statements implied in their remarks. "Thus our authorities tell us that on one day Caesar was in Rome and on a later day in Gaul, they tell us nothing about his journey from one place to the other, but we interpolate this with a perfectly good conscience."[33] Since the role of imagination is so central to historical construction, it would appear that the distinction between history and merely fanciful thinking is erased. Collingwood disassociates himself from this view. The historian's interpolation differs from that of the historical novelist in that its content must be called for by logical inference from the available evidence. If the construction is in agreement with what the evidence demands, it is not only legitimate but necessary. What is inferred in this way is imagined and, Collingwood adds, in order to make sense of the past, necessarily imagined.[34] This constructive activity is the function of the a priori historical imagination, and may be seen as related to that of the perceptual and aesthetic imaginations. It supplements and consolidates, bridges gaps and lends "the historical narrative or description its continuity." It differs from the peceptual and aesthetic imaginations in that its object, the past, is not perceivable and yet can become, through the historical imagination, an object of thought.[35]

In a manner not totally dissimilar to the function of the aesthetic and perceptual imaginations, the a priori historical imagination is the instrument whereby the historian can construct an imaginary picture of the past. The past appears as a "web of imaginative construction stretched between certain fixed points provided by the statements of his authorities." Collingwood is speaking of imaginative reconstruction where the imaginary picture is constantly checked by evidence, "and runs little risk of losing touch with the reality which it represents."[36] This theory appears to be a partial repudiation of the common-sense theory of history, in that it demands critical reflection in the present. However, its dependence on "fixed points" exposes it to the accusation that it, too, is merely "scissors and paste" history, circumscribed namely by statements handed on by authorities. However, Collingwood adds another radical qualification to his theory of history. Certainly it was creative on his part to assert such a strong role for the imagination in the study of the past. That strong a dosage of imagination is usually reserved for the study of the future. However tying the imaginative constructive role to solid fixed points left ample space for the roles of authority and "hard facts". The position may still be comfortable with the traditional aproaches to history.

At this point, however, Collingwood interjects one of his strongest sounding principles and appears to deliver the death blow to any notion of historical data as such. "I am now driven to confess that there are for historical thought no fixed points thus given: in other words, that in history, just as there are properly speaking no authorities, so there are properly speaking no data."[37] The statement is strong and, admittedly, in need of explanation. Historians think of themselves as working from data. "Facts" play a large role in Collingwood's own work as a historian. What he is attempting to proclaim is a principle which has gained wide acceptance in contemporary historiography: facts, like feathers, are hard to pin down. Data is not historical past fact but something existing in the present and in need of interpretation. Some facts might be accepted by historians as fixed or settled in meaning but remain so only until they are revisited and scrutinized once more. The weaving of the fabric of the imaginary past cannot be understood as contingent on certain points passed on and fixed. The historian is responsible for the fabric's nodal points as well as for the connecting material. Selection, criticism and appropriation of so-called facts are also part of his task.

This approach has been severely criticized, The criticism often has been based on the position that Collingwood is discounting all evidence and testimony and basing history on a fanciful, imaginative formulation of the past. To cite one example, Coady correctly states that Collingwood's main argument is that all history is inferential and systematic, with imaginative reconstruction or re-enactment of the past as the criterion of historical fact. But he goes on to add:

> "There is nothing other than historical thought itself, by appeal to which its conclusions may be verified . . . Consequently, reliance upon testimony (or for that matter upon pots and tombs) cannot be treated as providing the historian with data."[38]

This kind of criticism can only be fully responded to in terms of Collingwood's understanding of historical evidence and history as re-enactment of past thoughts. Both topics are dealt with in the following chapters. For the present, it may be pointed out that even a superficial perusal of his historical works sufficiently indicates the importance of data for the historical researcher. The point in this discussion of data is that fixed points cannot be based only on the testimony of an authority but can be legitimately accepted only as the result of inferential thinking grounded solidly on evidence found in the present.[39] It is data in this sense which unearths the thought behind it, and allows the past to be understood. Data as raw fact, understood as being somewhere out there, is of no help to the historian. It becomes evidence when it manifests thought which integrates the past into the present. Collingwood does not deny the importance of data with a certain element of fixity in it. He merely means to indicate that both the data and its fixity get meaning through interpretation. Coady's mention of "pots and tombstones" is a particularly unfortunate example since such archeological remains provide most of the grist for Collingwood's historical mill.

Both the use of evidence and its place in imaginative reconstruction of the past can be illustrated by taking another look at Collingwood, the practicing historian. Ironically, it is precisely a tombstone which provides the example. Goldstein relates that the last chapter of *Roman Britain* depicts the gradual disappearance of the Romanization of Britain. The island became Celto-Roman and lost its Roman culture. In recounting this process, Collingwood states:

> This backwash of Celticism over the romanized regions . . . is traceable by archeological evidence. At Silchester a tombstone was found . . . written in the Irish, as distinct from the British, form of Celtic. An Irishman who died in Silchester and left friends able to make him an epitaph in his own language must have been a member of an Irish colony in the town . . . the Silchester inscription shows a state of things in which parties of Scots are settling down peacefully in the lowland zone, and retaining their own language and customs.[40]

This is an illustration of the working of the historical imagination. No texts tell Collingwood of an Irish colony. However by searching out all the evidence available about the time and place, he can get behind the tombstone to its wider implications for history. According to Goldstein, the whole question and answer complex which history is, involves conjecture. The Irish colony, although it cannot be logically inferred, is "postulated," on the evidence of the tombstone. The historical event of an Irish colony, imaginatively reconstituted, is what best explains the available evidence. Contrary to Coady's interpretation, data and evidence play a large role in Collingwood's historical method. However, rather than raw data being the criterion for the truth or falsity of an historical event, it is the historical event which imaginatively reconstituted, explains the data.[41]

With both the facts of history and the narrative thrown back on the constructive powers of the historian, Collingwood must return to answering questions about what constitutes the criterion for historical truth. The justification of sources used, whether tombstone or text, no matter how well accepted by authorities, is always open to question. The instrument for criticism, as we have seen, is the a priori historical imagination. Any piece of evidence must be critically appropriated as fitting in with a picture which makes sense. That picture is neither a fanciful nor intuitive grasp of the past. It is, however, an imaginary picture. The historical past is the coherent and continuous picture which results necessarily from the imagination being brought face to face with historical evidence.[42]

Before looking at the historical imagination as the criterion for historical truth, it may be well to turn briefly to the relation of this theory to hermeneutics. With the a priori imagination, Collingwood further exposes the structure of understanding as historical. The a priori historical imagination is the motor that drives the historically effective consciousness. Imagination is that capacity within us to sense the possibilities and alternatives present in the givenness of the past, the immediacy of the present and the openness of the future. It involves intellect and will, as well as feeling and appetite. The imagination, operating historically, is a further specification of imagination, i.e. imagination with the capacity to flesh out the givenness of the past. It is our capacity to project, one might even say, to necessarily or automatically construct a context out of a text or an artifact which confronts us as a question. That imaginative reconstruction is not done however in a mechanical fashion according to "rules" of interpretation, it is rather built up while interpreting the text or evidence and any allied data.

What is important for theological hermeneutics is how the past is integrated into the present. For Collingwood, of course, the re-enactment theory is the key. However, re-enactment is fundamentally possible only because of the a priori capacity to know the past and grasp it as coherent and continuous with our present understanding and future hopes. Imaginative participation, the excitement caused by evidence, an aliveness of the understanding subject, all are ingredients in the contemporary theological hermeneutics discussion. That discussion is grounded in experience and imagination as the gateway to understanding. Echoing Collingwood's position that the condition for the past being known is that events "vibrate in the historian's mind," Bultmann remarks,

> . . . genuine historical knowledge demands a very personal aliveness of the understanding subject, the very rich unfolding of his individuality. Only the historian who is excited by his participation in history (and that means - who is open for the historical phenomena through his sense of responsibility for the future), only he will be able to understand history. In this sense the most subjective interpretation of history is at the same time the most objective. Only the historian who is excited by his own historical existence will be able to hear the claim of history.[43]

Perhaps the most concrete endorsements of the historical imagination in theological hermeneutics may be found in Lonergan. In his effort to relate historical reconstruction and historical understanding to hermeneutics, he employs Collingwood's ideas about the historical imagination. The past for Lonergan is not known when a "string of credible testimonies" has been re-edited. The historical past is truly understood only when the present thinker is able to grasp imaginatively "what was going forward," which most likely was unknown or only vaguely known to past historical agents.[44] Grasping "what was going forward" is the result of the historian's efforts at selection, criticism and construction. For the analysis of these tasks, Lonergan is clearly in Collingwood's debt. He refers to the essays on imagination and evidence as "brilliant and convincing."[45]

The Criterion for Historical Truth

In the closing sections of *The Historical Imagination* Collingwood seeks to clarify what he means by the a priori imagination as the criterion for historical truth. His explanation is designed to avoid both skepticism and a crude authoritarian realism. Returning to his comparison between the historian and the novelist, he points out that both wish to construct a picture which includes narration of events, descriptions of situations, revelations of motives and character analysis. Both want to produce a coherent whole where character and situation come together. Charaters act and the plot unfolds according to internal necessity. In both, the judge of this necessity is the imagination. "Both the novel and the history are self-explanatory, self-justifying, the product of an autonomous self-authorizing activity; and in both cases this activity is the *a priori* imagination."[46] The difference between the two constructions is that the historian's picture is meant to be true. He does want to understand what really happened. The novelist, on the other hand, needs only concern himself with the internal coherence of his picture. Accordingly, Collingwood points out three rules of method which differentiate the historian from the novelist and set up limits for the historical imagination. First, the historian's picture of the past must be localized in space and time. Secondly, "all history must be consistent with itself." Everything in the historical world must stand in some relation to everything else, even if the relationship be "only topographical and chronological." Thirdly, and most importantly, "the historian's picture stands in a peculiar relation to something called evidence."[47]

The imaginative reconstruction process aims at reconstructing the past of a particular present. It cannot be divorced from that present. The approach espoused here is to use the entire past through which the present came to be. The historian reconstructs the past of the present in which he lives. However, from a pratical perspective, this reconstrution is never fully achieved. For this reason, "in history, as in all serious matters, no achievement is final."[50] Because questions change, the principles by which evidence is interpreted change. Therefore, each generation must rewrite history. Collingwood is quick to point out, however, that he is not advocating historical skepticism but only illustrating "a second dimension of historical thought, the history of history."[51] This entails the realization that the historian is part of the process he is studying, and enjoys no God's-eye view. He can only study that process from his place within it.

Rather than advocating or fostering historical skepticism, Collingwood is illustrating that the criterion for historical truth is not raw facts passed on by authorities, or the various methods or rules of interpretation. The correspondence theory of truth sheds no light on the problem of historical truth, since there is no longer an object out there by appeal to which conclusions can be justified. The picture of the past is, in essence, a logical reconstruction grounded on evidence found in the present and "verified" by the principle of coherence. Each historian's efforts contribute "to an increasingly more coherent picture of the past."[52] In the final analysis, the criterion is the idea of history itself, "the idea of an imaginary picture of the past." It is an idea which arises from the spontaneity of the mind itself. No fact of experience corresponds exactly to it. It is an idea never totally within grasp. And so the historian's work is never complete. The historical imagination constantly pushes him on to further interpretation. The picture of the past will never be exactly what it ought to be. Nevertheless, it is governed in its course by an idea which is clear, rational and universal. "It is the idea of the historical imagination as a self-dependent, self-determining and self-justifying form of thought."[53]

Conclusion

Collingwood's theory of the a priori historical imagination as the criterion for historical truth allows for an understanding which is very compatible with the new hermeneutic. The historical imagination is his articulation of the hermeneutical principle that all experience and understanding is given form by ideas and language that structure our consciousness and are themselves part of a continuous historical process. Likewise, a text or artifact automatically confronts the mind, not as an orphan, but rather as the offspring of a context and a past. Two points stand out: our knowledge of the past is dependent on mind and dependent on the present. Mind-dependence should not be understood in a subjectivist sense, namely as dependence on the peculiarities of individuals, but rather as a dependence based on the shared meanings passed on by a tradition.[54] With regard to the second form of dependence, the very presence of the present demands a reflected presence, which entails a picture of the past. The past of a particular present emerges as a question. The picture of the past, when fleshed out, permits certain knowledge but nevertheless, knowledge which remains open to revision and reinterpretation based on the availability of evidence. The discipline of history is itself an ongoing and continuous picture of the past. The past is knowable only because it lives on in the imagination. Collingwood differs from most philosophers of history in that he was not concerned with explaining history; he was, however, concerned with explaining evidence. The picture of the past is a true one if it adequately explains present evidence. That explanation is more than an abstract objective analysis; it is also a concrete, imaginative construction.

Participation in history as the self-knowledge of one's own mind allows historical truth to emerge. The discipline of history is a continuous dialogue where the picture of the past is confirmed by present evidence and present evidence is confirmed by the picture of the past.[55] The criterion for coherency and continuity is the mind's imaginary picture of the past but that picture "stands in a peculiar relation to something called evidence." The closest the historian comes to what "really" happened is not some proved event but rather an inferred or, at times, conjectured event that best explains his evidence.

NOTES

1. Debbins, "Editor's Introduction" in *Philosophy of History*, pp. xvi–xxii.

2. Rubinoff, *Reform of Metaphysics*, p. 280; cf. EPM, p. 11.

3. IH, p. 248; cf. Rubinoff, *Reform of Metaphysics*, p. 287.

4. Lonergan, *Method in Theology*, p. 175 says the same and cites Collingwood for support.

5. IH, p. 205. For a good background discussion see Appendix I, "Positivism, Historicism, and The Idea of a Science of Human Nature," in Rubinoff, *Reform of Metaphysics*, pp. 338–63.

6. IH, p. 209.

7. Ibid., p. 217.

8. Ibid., p. 218

9. IH, p. 226; cf. Gregory Bateson, *Steps to an Ecology of Mind* (San Francisco: Chandler, 1972), p. 21.

10. Rubinoff, *Reform of Metaphysics*, pp. 347–63. The author traces this kind of thinking from Droysen, through Dilthey to Collingwood; cf. Fackenheim, *Metaphysics and Historicity*, pp. 26–28.

11. IH, p. 227.

12. Mink, *Mind, History and Dialectic*, p. 161.

13. Rubinoff, *Reform of Metaphysics*, pp. 274–86 places the past as an innate idea among Collingwood's absolute presuppositions of history. See also Mink, *Mind, History and Dialectic*, p. 176, 183–86. Donagan, *Later Philosophy*, pp. 210–11, takes a different position. "An *a priori* idea of an imaginary picture of the past must not be confounded with an absolute presupposition about it. Although absolute presuppositions are *a priori* in the sense that they are not empirical, they are not *a priori* in the Kantian sense; for no absolute presupposition is part of the furniture of every mind."

It is important to note that Collingwood was an astute enough historian to realize that historical consciousness, which allows self knowledge of mind, did not arrive full blown in the middle and late nineteenth century. Traces of this innate or absolutely presupposed idea go back to antiquity. However, he would probably hold that truly historical thinking would not have been possible before the patristic writers, especially Augustine. As we have seen in Chapter III, the Fathers reworked the Greek concept of nature and posited by faith the doctrine of a free creation. It is only by a free process that history can come about. Without freedom there is no story. Nature remains a *fatum*. There is no history, only fact or fate. For this reason, Collingwood attaches so much importance to the Church Fathers as forming the absolute presuppositions of western thought. The late arrival of historical consciousness of course could be traced to many sources but the key for him would be found in the notion of God the creator. See IH, pp. 20–25, 46–49; EM, 185–227.

14. SM, p. 204; cf. Rubinoff, *Reform of Metaphysics*, pp. 275–76. Art as pure imagination is discussed in SM, pp. 58–63.

15. Collingwood, "Sensation and Thought," *Proceedings of the Aristotelian Society* 24 (1923–24): 65; cf. Rubinoff, *Reform of Metaphysics*, p. 276.

16. PA, p.215. Collingwood's theory of art with its discussion of imagination, expression, language and symbol would demand a separate study. See PA, especially Books II and III. cf. Donagan, *Later Philosophy*, pp. 94–133.

17. Collingwood, "The Nature and Aims of a Philosophy of History" in *Essays in Philosophy of History*, ed. William Debbins (Austin: University of Texas Press, 1965), p. 48; cf. Rubinoff, *Reform of Metaphysics*, pp. 142–43.

18. Mink, *Mind, History and Dialectic*, pp. 183–86. See Chapter I, fn 13; cf. Harvey, *Historian and the Believer* pp. 70–77, 88–91, 113–114.

19. IH, p. 110; cf. Rubinoff, *Reform of Metaphysics*, p. 283.

20. IH, p. 117; cf. Buchdahl, "Logic and History", pp. 104–05.

21. IH, p. 118. Chapters V and VI below will discuss the "inside" and "outside" distinction and history as a re-thinking process.

22. Collingwood considered the historical imagination as innate and a priori. However, locking that idea too closely to Kantian categories might tend to rob it of its practical implications for the historian. Goldstein, "Constitution of the Historical Past," writes: "The historical imagination is simply Collingwood's way of referring to the techniques and autonomy of history in the reconstruction of the historical past. It is surely not a category in any sense" (p. 263, n. 1).

23. Collingwood, *The Historical Imagination: An Inaugural Lecture*, (Oxford: Clarendon Press, 1935). This lecture was republished as part of the epilegomena to IH, pp.231–49.

24. IH, p. 233; cf. Lionel Rubinoff, "History and Perception: Reflections on Collingwood's Theory of History", *Philosophical Forum*, n.s. 2 (1970): 91–102.

25. SM, pp. 220–21; cf. Rubinoff, *Reform of Metaphysics*, pp. 154–60; Mink, *Mind, History and Dialectic*, pp. 48–53.

26. IH, p. 234.

27. Ibid., pp. 234–35. For a critique of the treatment of testimony see C. A. J. Coady, "Collingwood and Historical Testimony", *Philosophy* 50 (1975): 409–24.

28. IH, p.237; cf. Shalom, *Philosophe et historien,* especially the section, "La connaissance historique: le passé et la pensée," pp. 190–204.

29. IH, p. 237.

30. Ibid., p. 252, quoted in Leon J. Goldstein, *Historical Knowing,* (Austin: University of Texas Press, 1976), 146.

31. IH, p. 238; Collingwood's thinking here shows the influence of his training in archeological research which was then gaining importance in historical studies. His views on memory in history should also be considered in light of such modern techniques of carbon-dating and structural linguistic studies. For a critical assessment, see Coady, "Historical Testimony", p. 413; cf. Brevard S. Childs, *Memory and Tradition in Israel,* Studies in Biblical Theology, (Naperville, Ill.: Alec R. Allenson, 1962), pp. 86–87, 89.

32. IH, p. 239.

33. Ibid., p. 240.

34. Ibid., p. 241; cf. Debbins, "Editor's Introduction" in *Philosophy of History,* pp. xvii–xix; Rubinoff, *Reform of Metaphysics,* p. 241.

35. IH, pp. 241–42.

36. Ibid., p. 242; cf. Debbins, "Editor's Introduction" in *Philosophy of History,* p. xix.

37. IH., p. 243. Coady, "Historical Testimony", claims that the historian cannot do without testimony and data, which he thinks Collingwood is completely disallowing. Collingwood's response, no doubt, would have to do with his understanding of the subject-matter of history as thought, the "inside" of an event. Historical fact, for Collingwood, is interpreted data. There is no uninterpreted data. In that sense, there is no fixed data. Neither data nor testimony can be accepted on face value. Cf. Harris, "Theory of History," 39–40; Carl L. Becker, "What are Historical Facts?" in *The Philosophy of History in Our Time,* ed. Hans Meyerhoff, (Garden City: Doubleday, Anchor Books, 1959), pp.120–37.

38. Coady, "Historical Testimony, p. 414; in part Coady is quoting IH, p. 243.

39. Debbins, "Editor's Introduction" in *Philosophy of History,* p. xix.

40. Quoted in Goldstein, "Constitution of the Historical Past" p. 262. See Collingwood, *Roman Britain* p. 282. In this quote "Scots" indicates inhabitants of Ireland.

41. Goldstein, "Constitution of the Historical Past" pp. 264–65.

42. IH, p. 245.

43. Bultmann, *History and Eschatology,* p. 122.

44. Lonergan, *Method in Theology,* p. 186.

45. Ibid., p. 188, fn. 9. For a summary of Lonergan's position on historical evidence and reconstruction see *Method in Theology*, pp. 205–06. His position is very dependent on Collingwood.

46. IH, p. 246.

47. Ibid.

48. Ibid., p. 247.

49. Ibid.

50. Ibid., pp. 246–47.

51. Ibid., p. 247.

52. Debbins, "Editor's Introduction" in *Philosophy of History*, p.xxi. See also Goldstein, "Constitution of the Historical Past" pp. 263–66.

53. IH, p. 249. The problem of verification or explanation is not a central concern of this study. In hermeneutics the problem is raised by Hirsch and Betti. See Emilio Betti, *Teoria Generale della Interpretazione*, 2 Vols. (Milano: Guiffre, 1955); Eric D. Hirsch, Jr., *Validity in Interpretation*, (New Haven: Yale University Press, 1967), see especially, Appendix II, "Gadamer's Theory of Interpretation," pp. 245–64. Lonergan's treatment of "Judging the Correctness of One's Interpretation" is close to Collingwood's theory. The criterion of correctness has to do with whether one's insights are invulnerable of "whether or not they hit the bull's eye." The interlocking of questions and answers form a unity. An "enclosure" is the goal. "For it is the emergence of that enclosure that enables one to recognize the task as completed and to pronounce one's interpretation as probable, highly probable, in some respects certain." See Lonergan, *Method in Theology* pp. 162–64. This unity or enclosure would appear close to Collingwood's imaginary picture. Although Lonergan would probably not allow such a judgement role to imagination, the role of imagination in the reconstructing process is central for both philosophers.

54. See the helpful distinction of two senses of mind-dependence, "the idosyncratic and the non-idiosyncratic," suggested by Leon J. Goldstein, "Collingwood's Theory of Historical Knowing," *History and Theory* 9 (1970): 22–23.

55. For the possibility of evidence disconfirming the historian's picture see, Mink, *Mind, History and Dialectic*, p. 184.

CHAPTER V

Historical Evidence

Introduction

As indicated in the preceding chapter, the picture of the past is constructed by the historian when he enters what Collingwood calls a "peculiar relation" to evidence. Past events are reconstructed through the sifting and weighing of evidence found in the present. The reconstructed event explains the present evidence. Present and past are dialectically related; one is unintelligible without the other. History is constituted by present questions, provoked by various forms of evidence, which point to a past. Indeed, the main body of *The Idea of History* can be read as an attempt to explain how past historians used evidence. The earliest historiography indicated complete dependence on "reports of facts given by eyewitnesses of those facts".[1] Before critical thinking about historical sources, the historian was, to a great extent, limited to memory and testimony. Concerning the Greek historical method Collingwood writes:

> Their method tied them on a tether whose length was the length of living memory: the only source they could criticize was an eye-witness with whom they could converse face to face. It is true that they relate events from a remoter past, but as soon as Greek historical writing tries to go beyond its tether, it becomes a far weaker and more precarious thing.[2]

With the awakening of historical consciousness, historical study matured to the degree that it learned the difference between the hard facts of physical science and historical evidence. The use the archeologist makes of strata is different from the use made by the geologist. The geologist locates the strata according to periods and correlates them with strata of the same type. The archeologist, on the other hand, does not simply accept the strata as stone, clay and metal; he interprets them as fragments of buildings, potsherds and coins which reveal purpose. Such findings only become historical evidence when there comes upon the scene someone who understands what they were used for.

> Before the nineteenth century, a natural scientist might have replied that the same was true of his own studies: was not every task in natural science a contribution to the decipherment of the purposes of that mighty being whom some called Nature and others God? The nineteenth century scientist would answer quite firmly that it was not. And the nineteenth century scientist is right as to the facts.[3]

Purpose is not a working category for the scientist. Yet, according to Collingwood, it is for the historian. History consists of "narrations of purpose" and traces of the past become historical evidence only when their purpose has been deciphered. The new historical consciousness was bound up with this changing concept of historical evidence. Evidence has to be interpreted, and meanings and purposes somehow re-experienced. A document, for example, must be analyzed as to the purpose for which it was written. Only when the historian understands in some detail why the document was produced and for whom can he be said to understand it. Only then is he aware of a past conscious act, which, for Collingwood, is the core of history. A true historical source is that which is evidence of a past conscious act. It opens up the possibility of re-thinking past thoughts. The same applies to unwritten sources. History, as a discipline, consists of narratives of

> ... purposive activity and the evidence for them consisted of relics they had left behind (books or potsherds, the principle was the same) which became evidence precisely to the extent to which the historian conceived them in terms of purpose, that is, understood what they were for . . .[4]

An 'iron implement' found amidst a Roman ruin is of no value to a historian as long as it remains of 'uncertain use'. However, once its use is ascertained, much can be inferred. If the implement turns out to be a flour-mill for example, questions can be raised as to how widespread the production of wheat was and how it was grown and used.[5]

As this new understanding of historiography was emerging in the nineteenth century, hermeneutics, descended from Schleiermacher, was also coming into its own. For Dilthey, to understand historically means to relive *(nacherleben)* or to reproduce *(nachbilden)*. Understanding is re-experiencing through objective expressions of man, experiences which reflect meaning and reveal the relationship of parts to a whole.[6] The vehicle for reliving the historical past is provided to the interpreter by the text upon which he trains his eyes. The written text affords access into the creative mind behind it. In spite of his criticism of Dilthey's unhistorical emphasis on psychology, Collingwood is definitely influenced by his hermeneutical approach. As the previous chapters have indicated, history is a hermeneutical undertaking. Historical thinking is largely a process of interpreting evidence which, in turn, is a vehicle for re-experiencing or rethinking the past. Collingwood's use of evidence is a central issue in his historical method which, correctly understood, evidences the hermeneutical thrust in his approach.

Whether or not a text or artifact becomes historical evidence is dependent upon the use the historian makes of it. The historian uses traces of the past in order to reconstruct the past. The interpreter is concerned with the thing in itself. Both are interpreters, but their goals are different. A field such as Roman Britain, so highly dependent on archeological remains, virtually demands the reconstruction of the historical past. Textual autonomy is highly unsuited to a period and place for which texts are so few and fragmentary.

While the goal of hermeneutics differs from the goal of history, for Collingwood the interpretive-understanding task of the hermeneutical thinker and the constructive task of the historian do, by and large, coincide. Both are interpretive ventures, and what is being interpreted is the present. His approach to evidence, be it text or potsherd, does not differ greatly from Gadamer's approach to a text. For Collingwood however, the process of interpretation draws the interpreter-historian into the reconstruction of the past. Text opens out to, and even demands, context; evidence inevitably points to event.

The goal of history is the reconstruction of the past. Evidence is the starting point. Traces of the past, interpreted and linked with other traces, lead through inference to a past event with its own past and future. History is, "a science whose business is to study events inferentially, arguing to them from something else which is accessible to our observation, and which the historian calls 'evidence' for the events in which he is interested."[7]

Although historical understanding and meaning go far beyond original intention, history is knowledge of past conscious acts. Interpreting evidence allows the historian-interpreter to move from evidence to past thoughts. The process, as we shall see, is a hermeneutical one. The element of language, while not as crucial as it is for Gadamer, is important since what is understood and interpreted is human expression left behind in different kinds of evidence.

This chapter will concentrate on Collingwood's understanding and use of evidence and inference. It will also serve to introduce his view that history is essentially concerned with the "insides" of historical events—thoughts. His distinction between the "inside" and "outside" of an event provides a key to his historical methodology. This distinction, or at least the vocabulary describing it, had been put to much use in theological hermeneutics.

Evidence: The Starting Point of History

The past as such is not the object of history. Although Collingwood by no means wishes to deny a "real past," he claims that the concern of scientific history is not the past. The goal of the discipline of history is the reconstruction of the past in the present. As Goldstein has pointed out, reconstruction, in Collingwood's use of the term, corresponds well with the phenomenologist's use of the term constitution. Husserl's notion of constitution does not lead to subjectivism, since he is not seeking to prove that we encounter objectivity; he rather wants to explain how it is intelligible. Although he emphasizes the role of intentionality in the constitution of meanings and objects, he does not leave out the usual empirical indicators of external reality. He wants to explain how subjectivity "constitutes" objectivity.[8] This process of constitution is parallel to Collingwood's understanding of historical knowledge. We have, he claims, no direct access to the past except by reconstructing it by means of historical research. He is adamant in his opposition to realist thinkers who hold out for immediate knowledge of the past, and insist upon using the "real past" as a measuring rod for testing the truth or falsity of the historically reconstructed past. As pointed out in the preceding chapter, history is autonomous. The measuring rod is the historical imagination.

As we have seen, "scissors and paste" history, with its twin supports of testimony and memory, is not acceptable. Scientific history demands grounds that justify knowledge. Testimony and memory, in order to contribute to organized, inferential knowledge which history is, need to be supported by evidence.

> If I say 'I remember writing a letter to So-and-so last week', that is a statement of memory, but it is not an historical statement. But if I can add 'and my memory is not deceiving me; because here is his reply', then I am basing a statement about the past on evidence; I am talking history.[9]

If historical knowledge is to be knowledge at all, it cannot be the simple acceptance of what has been preserved and handed on. Any claim to knowledge must be justified by appeal to grounds. The long battles against realism and skepticism come to a resolution in the theory of historical knowledge.[10] The object of historical study is never gained by immediate apprehension or direct acquaintance. Nonetheless, historical knowledge is possible. Historical events can be known by interpreting historical evidence found in the present, and by inferring or hypothesizing an event which best explains the evidence. As we have already indicated, that position seems to have been formulated by Collingwood in the course of his own work as a historian. The movement from concern with a "real past" to the critical interpretation of evidence can be documented as early as 1928.

> For historical thinking means nothing else than interpreting all the available evidence with the maximum degree of critical skill. It does not mean discovering what really happened, if 'what really happened' is anything other than 'what the evidence indicates.' If there once happened an event concerning which no shred of evidence now survivs, that event is not part of any historian's universe; it is no

historian's business to discover it; it is no gap in any historian's knowledge that he does not know it.[11]

Historical knowledge provides the clearest illustration of the proposition that knowing makes a difference to what is known. In historical knowing, it is the knowing that constitutes the known. "What really happened . . . [is] not only unknown but unknowable, not only unknowable but non-existent."[12] The only past that can be known is the past that lives on in the present.

The use of evidence is that which differentiates history as a scale of forms, admittedly with overlap, moving from "scissors and paste" or "common sense" history through critical history to scientific history. Scientific history is non-intuitive and inferential. It begins, as we have seen, with the imaginative reconstruction of the past which accounts for the available evidence. The construction is subjected to internal criticism. Consistency is constantly checked. New evidence is continually taken into account. Evidence and inference are the means to the reconstructed past. However, unlike natural scientists, historians do not employ laws which might be supported or weakened by evidence or event; "and, unlike a scientific observation report, a piece of historical evidence is not a datum, for it has value only when interpreted, and any interpretation may be challenged."[13]

Before moving on to the interpretation of evidence, some remarks are in order about Collingwood's understanding of historical inference. In common with any other science, the historian must justify his claim to knowledge. He must be able to exhibit the grounds upon which his knowledge is based. This is what is meant by describing history as inferential. There is no easy road to knowing the past. It must be scientifically reconstructed from available evidence. Collingwood discusses the two kinds of inference, deductive and inductive, but does not tie his method completely to either procedure. Historical inference is an application of the logic of question and answer. By means of the questioning process, scientific history provides warrants and grounds which may be judged true or false. Although history remains open to new evidence and to the reinterpretation of present evidence, it demands and is able to deliver certainty. Collingwood seems even to opt for a certainty which characterizes inference in the physical sciences, where, if the premises are affirmed, the conclusion is inevitable. He refuses to accept an inductive agreement which allows only "permissive" conclusions. "An inductive argument with a negative conclusion is compulsive, that is to say it absolutely forbids the thinker from affirming what he wishes to affirm; with a positive conclusion, it is never more than permissive."[14] Historical criticism, that is criticism of passed-on documents, produces only a "permissive" conclusion. It does not produce the kind of history Collingwood seeks. Although not necessarily in a deductive sense, history allows for a positive and conclusive result. "Nothing matters to [the historian] except that his decision, when he reaches it, shall be right: which means, for him, that it shall follow inevitably from the evidence."[15] Scientific history, in Collingwood's sense of the term, involves a broad use of inference whereby statements or artifacts are interrogated until the events behind them are revealed. In the same way that a detective reconstructs a crime from the available clues, the historian reconstructs events by systematically relating pieces of evidence.

Our references above to the Antonine wall and the tombstone at Silchester illustrate well Collingwood's use of evidence for the reconstruction of the past. Other illustrations from his historical studies could be added.[16] But in terms of relating his use of evidence for reconstruction to the hermeneutical concern for interpreting a text, it will prove more enlightening to examine the example offered in *The Idea of History*, under the heading "who killed John Doe?" This may well be Collingwood's most celebrated example.[17] In this Sherlock Holmes-like plot he describes the homicide detective's task as analogous to the task of the historian. The tale serves to single out his use of evidence as an important, if unnoticed, contribution to hermeneutics. John Doe is found dead of a stab wound in the back. Detective-Inspector Jenkins of Scotland Yard is called in to assist the local constable in the investigation. His approach to the identification of the murderer exemplifies the logic of question and answer and the imaginative reconstruction of an event. The detective's thinking does not depend on testimony as fact. This is not to imply that testimony cannot be of immense importance, only that to be of value it must be properly understood. Of course, as in most crimes, testimony was forthcoming. An elderly spinster asserts that she killed Doe because he had made a dastardly attempt on her virtue. The village poacher testifies that he had seen the Squire's gamekeeper climbing in the dead man's window. Both depositions are disposed of quickly by the police. However a full confession, given in a state of agitation by the rector's daughter, is the cause of puzzlement on the part of the investigators. Her statement only serves to point up that testimony is a piece of evidence which must be interpreted and used in conjunction with other evidence. Richard Roe, the young lady's boyfriend and a medical student, was staying at the rectory the night of the murder. He surely would have known the swiftest route for the blade. His shoes were wet the morning after the crime, which forced him to admit that he had gone out in the middle of the night; "he refused to say where or why." But was there a motive? Was he protecting someone? The testimonies of the daughter and Richard provide excellent examples of the distinction between intentional and unintentional data, "between what a witness intends to tell us and what he unintentionally reveals in the process of telling us."[18]

As it turns out, the detective reasons his way to the identity of the murderer by interpreting testimony and other available clues. The daughter is protecting Richard. Since Richard has no motive, whom might he be protecting? The ashes and metal buttons in the dustbin are deciphered as the remains of letters and gloves. Also paint smears matching that of the freshly painted iron gate between Doe's garden and the rectory turn up on a clerical jacket only that day awarded to a needy parishioner. John Doe had in fact been stabbed by the rector whom he had been blackmailing over a youthful infidelity on the part of the rector's deceased wife.

Collingwood's treatment of testimony, as evidence to be interpreted, rather than fact, proves most insightful, not only for the reconstruction of the past, but for the interpretation of a text.

> Confronted with a ready-made statement about the subject he is studying, the scientific historian never asks himself: 'Is this statement true or false?' in other words 'Shall I incorporate it in my history of that subject or not?' The question he asks himself is: 'What does this statement mean?' And this is not equivalent to the question 'What did the person who made it mean by it?', although that is doubtless a question that the historian must ask, and must be able to answer. It is equivalent, rather, to the question 'What light

is thrown on the subject in which I am interested by the fact that this person made this statement, meaning by it what he did mean. This might be expressed by saying that the scientific historian does not treat statements as statements but as evidence: not as true or false accounts of the facts of which they profess to be accounts, but as other facts which, if he knows the right questions to ask about them, may throw light on those facts.[19]

The above quote embodies a critical junction for Collingwood's understanding of history as the reconstruction of the past based on evidence found in the present. Both statements and material clues are evidence to be interpreted. If, for example, the rector's daughter's testimony is looked upon as fact, no progress is made in the investigation. Numerous false confessions bear this point out. Very often, the importance of a testimony is not *what* is said, but *that* it is said. Collingwood's insights into historical understanding and the role of evidence in that understanding shed light on the hermeneutical question of interpretation of texts. Just as no progress is made in the reconstruction of the past if testimony is accepted as fact with its own meaning-meant, likewise no progress is made in the interpretation of a text unless the meaning of the text is tied to and interprted out of a complex of questions constituted in the present. The text or testimony cannot be limited to the intention of the writer or speaker but must be interpreted in light of other information which the interpreter has about the subject-matter under discussion. Both the hermeneutical transaction of understanding and the historical transaction of reconstruction are interpretive events of the present.

As might be expected, Collingwood does not mean to overtax his analogy and claim that criminal detection is identical with scientific history. "The student of historical method will hardly find it worth his while, therefore, to go into rules of evidence, as these are recognized in courts of law."[20] The administration of justice demands of a jury not only that they arrive at a verdict but that they do so now. The historian is under no such constraint. He always remains open to new evidence; he can ask questions about the evidence but when he does, he should do so in the manner of a master sleuth, by cross-examining his sources. By sources, Collingwood means evidence and evidence only delivers meaning when it is measured by a question.

Collingwood's approach does not put primary emphasis on the truth or falsity of evidence.[21] He is more concerned with the hermeneutical question of what the evidence means. And yet, truth is the historian's goal. In the detection of crime, probability suffices; history demands certainty. With proper employment of the historical method, the careful investigator is able to infer truth about the past. Historical truth is inferentially grasped in the ongoing questioning and assessing of historical evidence. This process of drawing inferences is actually for Collingwood the rethinking of past thoughts. The past is truly known, not by comparison with some now nonexistent "real past," but only when it is rethought in the present. By means of the historical imagination, the historian is able to interpret evidence and thereby rethink the motives and intentions of past agents.

> Such rethinking is done by asking questions of past documents and artifacts and by drawing inferences. This procedure adds an objective ingredient, and Collingwood believes that public verifiability is possible, that everyone who rethinks a historical intention will draw the same inferences.[22]

The historian imaginatively reconstructs the past by rethinking it. That rethinking process is made possible by two interrelated components of historical understanding. First, the past leaves physical, observable traces in the present-evidence. And evidence, as we have seen, can be interpreted and inferences drawn. A past event lives on physically. Secondly, the past leaves traces in a more subtle way. Past thought continues on in the process of human thought. Its impact can still be experienced because past thought is "incapsulated" in present thinking. A past event lives on mentally. The past event is part of a continuing process. From the world of perceptible things the historian is able to reconstruct in his own mind the very process in which his own present came to be. This rethinking process will be introduced in the next section and developed more fully in chapter VI.

From Evidence to Thought: The Outside and Inside of Historical Events

At this point, we must ask what is the nature of an historical event. Why is it able to be rethought while being reconstructed out of present evidence? Packed within this question is another, what is the subject-matter of history? The response to both questions constitutes what Collingwood means by calling history the self-knowledge of mind. In a very real sense, history is the study of how an individual and community come to be what they are. The response to these questions also points up the hermeneutical dimension of his historical method: the historical event or fact is the result of interpretation of evidence. The reconstructive move behind the fact, or better still through the fact, constitutes a hermeneutic of event which happens in the present and evokes present meanings.

Beginning with the second question, the subject-matter of history is for Collingwood human action. The historian studies *res gestae*, things done by humans. History is not directly concerned with acts of nature or rote mechanical actions. It seeks out purposeful action. But how does human action as the subject-matter of history fit in with the event constructed out of evidence? If history properly so called is the history of human affairs, its subject matter is complex and, to say the least, difficult to get at. Human affairs encompass both the natural and the physical, as well as the mental and the spiritual. Both the geologist's interpretation of fossils and the archeologist's interpretation of human artifacts can be recruited for historical service. A special problem arises, however, for the historian: it concerns the nature of historical event as the expression of human thought. To deal with this problem, Collingwood offers a key methodological insight. He distinguishes between the outside and inside of an event.[23]

The outside of the event is "everything belonging to it which can be described in terms of bodies and their movements", for example Caesar's crossing of the Rubicon or his assassination on the Senate floor. The inside of the event is described in terms of thought, motives or intentions. The historian must of course be concerned with both aspects. His initial task is the examination of outward and visible expressions, but he has not understood an historical event until he has grasped it as an human action which is a unity with an inner and outer aspect. The historian is only interested in the crossing of the Rubicon and Caesar's bloody demise in terms of their relation "to a constitutional conflict . . ." His work may begin by discovering the outside of an event, but it can never end there; he must always remember that the event was an action, and that his main task is to think himself into this action, to discern the thought of its agent."[24]

Collingwood has often been accused of limiting history to thought. This is considered to be the logical result of his idealism. Yet his historical works are heavy with dates, "facts" and evidence. All of which constitute the outside of the historical event. Although the thought of the historical agent is the key to history, the reading of evidence is the only path to that thought. Outside and inside are interdependent. They can be distinguished but not separated.

A note can be inserted here about Collingwood's method in relation to the so-called covering law theory and historical explanation. As we have mentioned, the historian must discern the thought within an historical event. The scientist, in contrast, regards nature as a phenomenon for observation. He observes events apart from any outside-inside distinction and searches for the "causes or laws of events." The scientist "discovers" an event by perceiving it, assigning it to a class, and relating that class to other classes. The historican "discovers" an event only when he has penetrated to the thought expressed in it.

> To discover that thought is already to understand it. After the historian has ascertained the facts, there is no further process of inquiring into their causes. When he knows what happened, he already knows why it happened.[25]

The notion of cause, however, is not foreign to history, but it is used in a special way. Collingwood is definitely committed to free will and the uniqueness of historical events. The question "Why did Brutus stab Caesar?" means for him, "What did Brutus think, which made him decide to stab Caesar?" In history, the cause of an event is the thought of the person "by whose agency the event came about: and this is not something other than the event, it is the inside of the event itself."[26]

Because Collingwood's emphasis on thought has been interpreted as if thought were equivalent to the author's or historical agent's original intention, his contribution to hermeneutics tends to be underestimated. However, his understanding of the historical event as a reconstruction resulting from the interpretation of present evidence runs parallel with the hermeneutical event of understanding, resulting from the interpretation of a present text. His approach to history and specifically his understanding of historical knowledge as the interpretation of evidence, written or unwritten, is extemely pertinent to contemporary hermeneutics. While Gadamer admits that the historian cannot divest himself entirely of the prejudices of his own time, and therefore must view the past from that perspective, he still leaves the impression that this constitutes a limit or even a "failure."[27] Collingwood's historical method probes more deeply the historically effective consciousness and claims that moving beyond one's own horizon not only cannot be done but should not be done because it is a theoretically false method for history. History is a hermeneutical enterprise in that historical knowing is precisely the knowing of the past through the prism of the present. The key to the inside-outside distinction and the re-enactment theory is the interpretation of evidence. Both the historical event and the hermeneutical event are interpretations of statements or evidence. The historian has the added task of reconstruction but reconstruction cannot be divorced from interpretation of evidence. The reconstructed past is always the past of a particular present.

By making history as a discipline dependent on the present, Collingwood moves history toward a qualitative and hermeneutical view of evidence. Instead of a quantitative approach which, by the sheer weight of statistics and facts, claims to establish a "real past" with a corresponding meaning-meant, Collingwood opts for a qualitative approach, which meticulously interprets what is available, and by bringing together the outside and inside aspects, reconstructs the unity of the event and evokes meaning in the present. The reconstruction takes place through the hermeneutical experience, where an ongoing dialogue is carried on between the thought expressed in the evidence and the thought of the historian. The presuppositions in both poles are permitted to surface. Neither the evidence and the thought it expresses nor the questioning of the historian is denied its own historicity. As the John Doe detective story indicates, neither testimony nor text may be accepted as statements. Both must be treated as evidence. The historian and the hermeneut, to be true to their respective callings, must emulate the probing detective and reflectively define their own present situation and from that horizon interrogate and interpret the available evidence. Understanding happens for Gadamer when the right questions are asked of the text. For Collingwood, the same kind of interrogation, not only of texts but of all kinds of evidence, provides the basis for reconstruction. The reconstructed historical event, like the hermeneutical event, evokes meaning in the present.

Conclusion

A number of conclusions can be drawn out of our discussion of historical evidence. All of them further indicate the contribution, or at least the potential contribution, of Collingwood's ideas to theological hermeneutics.

First, the central position afforded to the intepretation of present evidence indicates the interdependence of hermeneutical and historical understanding. Like hermeneutics, historiography is not a quantitative science. The application of quantifying methods is of limited value. Historical evidence or "fact" gains its importance by "meaning" of interpretation.[28] Interpreting evidence means for Collingwood imaginatively rethinking the thought expressed in the evidence. This process, which is preeminently hermeneutical, delivers not a reproduced "real past" but a past inferentially reconstructed on a present horizon out of present evidence. Knowing the past as past means precisely to grasp the past "in the context of later happenings."[29] The interpretation of evidence in light of present knowledge is a constitutive factor in all true historical knowing.

Second, the distinction between the outside and inside of a historical event with the corresponding interpretive movement from outer occurrence to inner thought has had wide application in theology. It has provided theologians with a formidable tool for clarifying the distinction between *Historie* and *Geschichte* for the English speaking world. The central events in the life of Jesus are apprehended under an outer and inner aspect. A distinction between "fact" and "meaning", although far more dichotomous than Collingwood would have allowed, is often applied in his name to the crucifixion and resurrection. As one critic puts it, getting on the "inside" of the life of Jesus has been accepted by some theologians as "the *kerygmatic* key in the lock of the Gospels."[30] Reserving further discussion for chapter VII, at this point, we will cite only one example.[31] Macquarrie discusses the need for the historian to participate in the object of his reflection. He illustrates this with Bultmann's treatment of the crucifixion. His illustration clearly shows the imprint of Collingwood.

> Considered objectively, from the outside, how could a past event, such as the crucifixion of Jesus, be regarded as also an atonement which is still efficacious today? . . . if we seek to understand this event from the inside—by thinking ourselves into it, by participation, or however we care to express it—then its character as an atonement becomes clear. For is it not the case that the Christian who gets inside this event—by being "crucified with Christ", by "taking up his cross and following Christ"—experiences the event as the attaining of wholeness, as an atonement? This account of the matter seems at least to make sense.[32]

Third, an unexpected dividend can also be gained from our analysis of Collingwood's approach, especially his creative use of evidence. An important and problematic question for the theologian and biblical scholar is how the mythic consciousness functions and how to relate myth and history.[33] Collingwood's method discloses that a similarity exists between the ways in which the historical and mythic imaginations function. In both cases, the imagination is concerned with the task of ordering reality and uncovering the absolute presuppositions of order. Thus, both history and myth emerge from reflective-restrospective thinking, as they seek to construct an explanation for a present state of affairs. As we have seen in detail, the historian reconstructs the past presupposed by the present. The past he constructs provides the most intelligible interpretation of how a particular present came about. Relying on present evidence, he reconstructs the past of *this* person or *this* community. The interpretation of evidence in the present is also the point of departure in the construction of myth.

This has been clearly perceived by Gordon Kaufman. He states that the origin of myth does not represent such a radical shift from strict historical method to pure speculation, as might at first be believed. The myth-maker employs the same "presuppositional" or "transcendental" method as the historian. The reconstruction of the imaginative picture which is presupposed by present evidence is also what controls the construction of myth. Likewise, for both history and myth, the measure of truth is the "convincingness" of this one picture, as an explanation for available evidence. According to Kaufman, although myth moves beyond the particularities with which history is concerned, the historian's approach to reconstruction and "verification" may be applied, for example, to such mythic narratives as the Genesis account of the fall and its consequences (Gn. 3). Of course, here we are concerned not with events presupposed by historical documents but with occurrences presupposed by all historical documents and facts, namely, with the human condition itself. All the same, the mythic imagination seeks to posit those events the happening of which accounts for the way the human condition appears in the present. The historian does the same, with regard, not to the human condition, as such, but to particular pieces of evidence which the past has left behind, and the present makes available. To this extent a parallel exists between the ways the mythic and the historical imaginations work.[34]

Finally, Collingwood's understanding of the function of text as evidence may have a bearing on the question of whether biblical theology ought to be a historical discipline. An affirmative answer to this question marks the beginning of biblical theology, and is still advocated by Krister Stendahl.[35] According to Stendahl, biblical theology has a constructive, descriptive task which is historical. This task must be kept separate from the hermeneutical task of systematic theology. A sharp distinction between meaning-meant and present meaning is maintained. "The distinction between the descriptive function as the core of all biblical theology on the one hand, and the hermeneutics and up-to-date translation on the other must be upheld if there is to be any chance for the original to act creatively on the minds of theologians and believers of our time."[36] Such a dichotomy is undermined by the method we have presented. Obviously the hermeneutical, systematic theologian interprets texts in and for the present. If Collingwood's historical method has any validity at all, the scientific historian and descriptive biblical theologian do the same. Both understanding and reconstruction depend on meanings in the present. Of course, the tasks have different emphasis, but, as we have seen, they are interdependent and parallel. To repeat, the key for understanding the interdependence between the historical or descriptive and the hermeneutical is the use of evidence. For scientific history, in Collingwood's sense, the biblical texts are not ready-made statements with a frozen meaning-meant. They are pieces of evidence, which, when questioned and interpreted, release a reconstructed past within a context of present meaning.

Dividing the question of meaning into two tenses, past and present, as Stendahl does, gives the impression of reducing a descriptive biblical theology to a kind of "scissors-and-paste" theology. If descriptive biblical theology allows of no interpretation, then it involves simply the piecing together of ready-made statements. It is concerned only with the "outside" of events. This would appear to be less than theology, and, for Collingwood, certainly much less than history. Scientific history contains no ready-made statements. The same may be said for scientific theology. The descriptive theologian and historian, respectively, describe and reconstruct, but out of present questions put to present evidence. Past meanings can only be grasped in dialogue with present meanings.

The need to relate the historical task and the hermeneutical task, the outside and inside of an event, the descriptive and systematic in theology, would find numerous adherents. Opposition to Collingwood's approach comes about when the interpretation of evidence is directly related to knowledge of past thought. For him, the core of history, past thought, is only known when it is rethought in the present.

NOTES

1. IH, p. 24.

2. Ibid., p. 26; cf. Goldstein, "Theory of Historical Knowing," pp. 24–25.

3. A, pp. 108–09.

4. Ibid., p. 109.

5. Donagan, *Later Philosophy*, p. 180; cf. A. pp. 109, 127–28.

6. Palmer, *Hermeneutics*, pp. 116–17; Hodges, *Dilthey: Introduction*, pp. 121–24.

7. IH, pp. 251–52. An area such as Roman Britain calls for a historian who has what it takes to create context. Collingwood filled this need superbly. Bateson, *Steps to an Ecology of Mind*, p. xiv, refers to him as "the first man to recognize—and to analyze in crystalline prose—the nature of context."

8. Goldstein, *Historical Knowing*, pp. xx–xxi; for his understanding of Husserl's notion of constitution, Goldstein's source is Robert Sokolowski, *The Formation of Husserl's Concept of Constitution* (The Hague: Martinus Nijhoff, 1964).

9. IH, pp. 252–53.

10. For the development of Collingwood's thought about realism and skepticism in relation to history, see Goldstein, "Theory of Historical Knowing," pp. 10–11.

11. Collingwood, "Limits of Historical Knowledge" in *Essays in Philosophy of History*, ed. William Debbins (Austin: University of Texas Press, 1965), p. 99; cf. Goldstein, "Theory of Historical Knowing", 15.

12. Collingwood, "Limits of Historical Knowledge," in *Philosophy of History*, Debbins, ed., p. 99.

13. Alan Donagan, "The Verification of Historical Theses," *Philosophical Quarterly* 6 (1956): 196; cf. IH, pp. 244–45, 261–62.

14. IH, p. 261; for a negative assessment, see, L. B. Cebik, "Collingwood: Action, Re-enactment, and Evidence," *Philosophical Forum*, n.s. 2 (1970): 70.

15. IH, p. 268.

16. See Collingwood, *Roman Britain*, pp. 133–39 and A, pp. 120–46; cf. Goldstein, "Theory of Historical Knowing", 28–34.

17. IH, pp. 266–68; cf. Coady, "Historical Testimony," 415–20.

18. Harvey, *Historian and Believer*, pp. 276–77.

19. IH, p. 275; cf. Joseph B. Tyson, *A Study of Early Christianity* (New York: McMillan, 1973), p. 8.

20. IH, p. 268.

21. To deal extensively with the truth question here would bring us beyond the scope of this study. This however does not mean that the question of judgement and truth can be left out of the hermeneutical discussion. Cf. IH, pp. 252–63 and Lonergan, *Method in Theology*, pp. 162–67. Lonergan discusses "Judging the Correctness of One's Interpretation" as one of the basic operations of interpretation.

22. Tyson, *Early Christianity*, p. 9.

23. IH, pp. 213–14; cf. Rubinoff, *Reform of Metaphysics*, pp. 297–98; Donagan, *Later Philosophy*, pp. 192–93; Mink, *Mind, History and Dialectic*, pp. 189–90; Debbins, "Editor's Introduction" in *Philosophy of History*, pp. xvi–xvii.

24. IH, p. 213; cf. Harris, "Theory of History," 40. The inside-outside distinction has occasioned much critical comment. Collingwood's terminology is metaphorical. As we shall see in the next chapter, getting to the "inside" of an event does not bespeak a magical, intuitionist approach as some commentators have held. Cf. Gardiner, *Nature of Historical Explanation*, pp. 46–51. Buchdahl, "Logic and History," 94–113; W. H. Walsh, *Introduction to Philosophy of History*, 3rd rev. ed. (London: Hutchinson's University Press, 1967), pp. 48–58. For a response see Goldstein, "Theory of Historical Knowing," 34–35, fn. 53, he replies to those who attribute an intuitionist position to Collingwood's inside-outside distinction, "All he intended by the expression is that human action consists of behavior informed by thought, and it is difficult for me to see how any fair-minded reader could fail to see that."

25. IH, p. 214. See above chapter II, fn. 61 for references to historical explanation. Harvey, *Historian and the Believer*, p. 45, sums up the discussion: "What are the grounds upon which some judgements about a course of past events are more entitled to credence than others? The answer to this question serves to divide philosophers of history into roughly two groups: (1) those who have maintained that entitlement to credence is directly proportionate to the degree to which historical explanations approximate scientific explanations; and (2) those who have argued that historical explanations are of a unique sort and require no reference whatever to the hallmark of scientific explanations, the subsumption of a statement under a law." Harvey (p. 65, n. 17) puts Popper and Hempel in the first category and Collingwood and Dray in the second. Dray's, *Laws and Explanation in History* is an extended critique of the "covering law model." Cf. Wolfhart Pannenberg, *Theology and the Philosophy of Science*, trans. Francis McDonagh (Philadelphia: Westminster Press, 1976), p. 147; Donagan, *Later Philosophy*, pp. 200–09. Collingwood himself is very critical of historians who attempt to make historical inquiry a science, in the sense of finding laws and patterns under which historical events may be categorized. In IH, pp. 263–66, he refers to this as "pigeonholing." This is a method where the historian collects facts and attempts to organize the resultant history into laws and patterns. Collingwood says "extrapolating such patterns into the remote past, about which there was very little information, and to the future,

about which there was none, gave the 'scientific' historian just that sense of power which scissors-and-paste history denied him." He concludes that such "schemes" are the "offspring of caprice."

26. IH, pp. 214–15.

27. Gadamer, *Truth and Method*, pp. 465–66.

28. Richard R. Niebuhr, *Resurrection and Historical Reason: A Study of Theological Method* (New York: Charles Scribner's Sons, 1957), p. 25. Niebuhr is referring here to C. H. Dodd.

29. Georges Florovsky, "The Predicament of the Christian Historian," in *God, History and Historians: Modern Christian Views of History* ed. C. T. McIntire (New York: Oxford University Press, 1977), p. 420.

30. Merkley, "New Quests for Old", 207.

31. In chapter VII, the use made of Collingwood by Bultmann, the New Questers and Pannenberg will be analyzed. Numerous other examples of the application of the outside-inside distinction to biblical theology can be cited. Cf. C. H. Dodd, *The Founder of Christianity* (New York: Macmillan, 1970), pp. 1–16; Richard R. Niebuhr, *Resurrection and Historical Reason*, pp. 92–102, 137–38; H. Richard Niebuhr, *The Meaning of Revelation* (New York: Macmillan, 1962), pp.81–90; Harvey, *Historian and the Believer*, pp. 234–42; Carl Michalson, *The Hinge of History: An Existential Approach to the Christian Faith* (New York: Charles Scribner's Sons, 1959) pp. 26–27.

32. John Macquarrie, *The Scope of Demythologizing: Bultmann and his Critics* (London: SCM Press, 1960), p. 84.

33. The works of Eliade and Ricoeur are most important for this area. Two general discussions of the problem are W. Taylor Stevenson, *History as Myth: The Import for Contemporary Theology* (New York: Seabury Press, 1969) and Lee W. Gibbs and W. Taylor Stevenson, *Myth and Crisis of Historical Consciousness* (Missoula: Scholars Press, 1975).

34. Kaufman, *Systematic Theology*, p. 366, fn. 1. Kaufman's Yale dissertation dealt in part with Collingwood, see Gordon D. Kaufman, *Relativism, Knowledge and Faith* (Chicago: University of Chicago Press, 1960).

35. The beginning of biblical theology as a self-conscious theological discipline is usually traced back to Johannes Phillipus Gabler and his programmatic "oratio" *De iusto discrimine theologiae biblicae et dogmaticae regundisque recte utriusque finibus* (Altdorf, 1787). Cf. Werner Georg Kummel, *The New Testament: The History of the Investigation of its Problems*, trans. S. MacLean Gilmour and Howard Clark Kee (Nashville: Abingdon Press, 1972), pp. 98–100. See *The Interpreter's Dictionary of the Bible*, 1962 ed. George A. Buttrick et. al (Nashville: Abingdon, 1962), pp. 418–437, s.v. "Biblical Theology: Contemporary", by K. Stendahl; K. Stendahl, "Method in the Study of Biblical Theology" in *The Bible in Modern Scholarship*, ed. J. Philip Hyatt (Nashville: Abingdon Press, 1965), pp. 196–209. See also Avery Dulles' response to Stendahl in this same volume, pp. 210–216. For further development, see Stendahl, "Bible as Classic and the Bible as Holy Scripture", 3–10.

36. Stendahl, "Biblical Theology," p. 423.

CHAPTER VI

The Re-Enactment of Past Thought

Introduction

The elements which go into Collingwood's historical method such as the question and answer dialectic, presuppositions and the imaginative reconstruction inferentially built up by interpreting evidence are widely accepted principles; indeed some have even become truisms of modern historiography. While critics abound, for the most part historians no longer seek some frozen, existing out-there, uninterpreted "real past." To a great extent they understand their task as Collingwood describes it: the imaginative reconstruction of the past based on evidence found in the present. It is only when he moves beyond this theory of historical knowledge and describes with precision what, in his opinion, the historian does when practicing this theory that he runs head on into a major confrontation with both philosophers of history and hermeneutical theoreticians. Since the historian can neither confront the past directly nor rely on just any testimony about the past, Collingwood asks, "How, or on what conditions, can the historian know the past?" His outside-inside distinction and his views on the subject matter of history provide insight into his response: only thought somehow survives the flow of time. The answer to the above question constitutes his most controversial statement, ". . . the historian must re-enact the past in his own mind."[1] Seemingly lost in the clouds of idealism, this statement is perplexing and open to misunderstanding.

W. H. Walsh's description of Collingwood's historical thinking as "the standard idealist account" has given direction to most of the misconceptions that have cropped up around the re-enactment theory.[2] According to Walsh, Collingwood's theory amounts to saying that history involves a direct and immediate form of knowledge. The thoughts of the past are grasped in a "unique way" which is non-discursive and non-inferential. Historical knowledge is reduced to a kind of "intuition". This misconception has dominated the intepretation of Collingwood's approach to history until relatively recently. The rethinking process has been misunderstood as a self-certifying and almost magical transference to a "real" past. Walsh's "intuition" has been supported by other commentators who use such terms as "telepathic communication with past thoughts"[3] and "empathic understanding."[4] Buchdahl refers to the "miraculous power whereby we can, as it were, slide into the thought of the past."[5] The received interpretations understand re-enactment as an intuitionist theory of historical verification. However, as both Donagan and Goldstein have demonstrated, Collingwood is not claiming some mysterious cognitive power whereby the historian discovers past thoughts. He maintains rather that by the interpretation of evidence the historian is able to rethink past thoughts by imaginatively discerning them in the available evidence.[6] Neither a theory of historical explanation nor a psychological or romantic interpretation is supported by a more rigorous analysis of Collingwood's own thought, nor by a hermeneutical intepretation of the same.

The analysis will show that re-enactment of past thought is not tied to some immediate identification with the past. Past thought can be re-enacted only because it survives in the present. It is incapsulated in present thought. The re-thinking theory is born of a very existential concern for understanding in the present. A hermeneutical interpretation will demonstrate in turn that the misconceptions mentioned earlier fail to do justice to Collingwood's thought. Re-thinking may then be understood as further articulating in clearer language the dialogic and conversational manner of the hermeneutical experience. A hermeneutical grasp of the rethinking process will serve to link the three elements in the hermeneutical experience: understanding, interpretation and application.[7] All are implied in Collingwood's rethinking process. What Gadamer refers to as the "fusion of horizons" is expressed by the re-enactment process and the incapsulation theory. Re-enactment of past thought corresponds to what happens when a reader is confronted by a text. The meaning of the text is not limited to the text but is constructed by being rethought in the historical process of transmission and interpretation.

History as the Rethinking of Past Thought

In spite of the fact that past events are not immediately knowable, the discipline of history is being practiced. This is possible because the historian ultimately is concerned with thought. Historical thinking begins by examining and interpreting the relics of the past. However the goal of that examination and interpretation is to understand past thought in the present. From the words in a historical text, the historian wants to find out ". . . what the person who wrote those words meant by them. This means discovering the thought . . . which he expressed by them. To discover what this thought was, the historian must think it again for himself."[8]

Here Collingwood adds parenthetically that he is referring to thought in the "widest sense of the word." His notion of the nature of thought demands further analysis. Thought or thinking is that which is able to continue in existence in a way which cannot be said for physical, social or psychological events. Since past thought survives or is able to be revived, it can be rethought. While some commentators have tried to make the re-enactment theory part of a methodological solution, others have categorized it as an absolute presupposition for doing history. Collingwood seems simply to claim two points: that re-enactment is the central condition for knowing the past and that it is a description of what in fact historians do.

Collingwood's own language at times has lead to the accusation that he limits history to thought. He does put much emphasis, perhaps too much, on the rationality of human behavior. However, his claim, as his historical works indicate, is that human action is behavior informed by thought, but not limited to thought. Moreover, while sensations, feelings, and physical states and occurrences influence behavior, they are carried away by the flow of consciousness. An idea or plan can be reconstructed from evidence, whereas anger, sympathy and fear are not retrievable in themselves.

In a long discussion introducing the re-enactment theory Collingwood goes so far as to state that the historical actor's thought and the historian's thought can be one and the same. To use one of his own examples, the historian can re-think the same, identical thought of Euclid.

> If he thought 'the angles are equal' and I now think 'the angles are equal,' granted that the time interval is no cause

> for denying that the two acts are one and the same, is the difference between Euclid and myself ground for denying it? There is no tenable theory of personal identity that would justify such a doctrine. Euclid and I are not (as it were) two different typewriters which, just because they are not the same typewriter can never perform the same act but only acts of the same kind. A mind is not a machine with various functions, but a complex of activities; and to argue that an act of Euclid's cannot be the same as an act of my own because it forms part of a different complex of activities is merely to beg the question. Granted that the same act can happen twice in different contexts within the complex of my own activities, why should it not happen twice in two different complexes?[9]

To the objector who claims that no two human beings can ever think identical thoughts, Collingwood responds that such a position could only lead to historical scepticism and ultimately to solipsism.[10]

Thought is an activity in which the succession of states of consciousness can be stopped thus allowing the general structure of consciousness to be apprehended. That structure is seen as a framework in which the past lives on together with the present and can be compared with it. Thought alone stands outside the flow of consciousness. For Collingwood, not only the object of thought is outside the flow, but the act of thinking also. It is possible that one act of thought may continue on through a lapse of time, be in abeyance and later revive.[11]

It is apparent that Collingwood's own language, to some extent at least, is responsible for the misinterpretations which surround the re-enactment theory. In order to counteract the misconceptions it will again be necessary to study Collingwood's historical work. Rethinking is not a transhistorical leap into the past which provides an explanation for history. The reenactment theory should be understood as a hermeneutical contribution to historical knowing. Not a case of identifying psychologically with a past figure, rethinking is what happens as a result of careful interpretation of evidence.

> We shall never know how the flowers smelt in the garden of Epicurus, or how Nietzsche felt the wind in his hair as he

walked on the mountains; we cannot relive the triumph of Archimedes or the bitterness of Marius; but the evidence of what these men thought is in our hands; and in recreating these thoughts in our own minds by interpretation of that evidence we can know, so far as there is any knowledge, that the thoughts we create were theirs.[12]

Rethinking past thought however does not limit history to abstract theoretical reasoning. It involves the process of question and answer which, building on evidence, calls forth the past from the present. The "act of thought" is not some isolated "thing" that can suddenly be grasped by an observer. Rather past thought is woven together, admitting and even illustrating the complexities and circumstances that influenced past motives, intentions and plans. Although the historian can re-enact past thought, he cannot apprehend the individual act of thought as it really happened. What is apprehended of the individual is something that has been shared. "It is the act of thought itself, in its survival and revival at different times and in different persons: once in the historian's own life, once in the life of the person whose history he is narrating."[13] Collingwood, then, is not claiming that the historian experiences the actual act of thinking of the historical agent. He does claim, however, and claims it as absolutely essential to historical understanding, that the historian can reconstruct the thought behind an historical event because that thought has been shared with others and is still manifest in forms of expression. Rethinking is possible because past thought has been mediated through evidence. Obviously, this rethinking takes place in a different context and perhaps different language. Examining the process in which Collingwood was able to fashion purpose and motive out of archeological and written evidence dispels any hint of an intuitive gimmickry and reveals re-enactment as a sound interpretive and inferential theory of historical knowing. The present presuppositions of the historian are not ignored; they are necessary to the re-enactment. As we have seen in our dialogue with Gadamer, "rethinking" does not necessarily fall into the trap of a narrow conception of "original intention." The time gap between thought in the past and its rethinking in the present must be bridged from both sides.[14] To be historically effective the historian should share a common tradition with the object of his study. His mind must offer "a home" for the revival of past thought. His thought needs to be "pre-adapted" to become the host of a past thought. The inquirer's present interest must give him the openness required to enter into dialogue with the unfamiliar. Rethinking as a hermeneutical experience, involving a "fusion of horizons", is indicated when Collingwood relates an experience that is familiar to most scholars concerned with historical studies.

> A man who at one time of life finds certain historical studies unprofitable, because he cannot enter for himself into the thought of those about whom he is thinking, will find at another time that he has become able to do so, perhaps as a result of deliberate self-training. But at any given stage in his life the historian as he stands is certain to have, for whatever reason, a readier sympathy with some ways of thinking than with others. Partly this is because certain ways of thinking are altogether, or relatively, strange to him: partly it is because they are all too familiar, and he feels the need of getting away from them in the interests of his own mental and moral welfare.[15]

The past cannot be rethought in its immediacy. It is rather by questioning the evidence from one's present horizon, supported by a tradition which extends back to the past horizon, that the investigator can reconstruct the thought inferred by the evidence. As the above passage indicates, both in spite of and because of its alienation due to pastness, the thought or purpose can be grasped because it is still a shared instance of thinking with which the present inquirer can identify.

Two illustrations from *Roman Britain* may be inserted here to put to rest the contention that rethinking is an immediate, intuitionist approach to history, bolstered only by a shaky idealism. The first concerns the interpreting of unwritten sources. Collingwood refers to an earthwork constructed to the south of Hadrian's wall, the so-called Vallum. He sees in it a second obstacle running parallel to Hadrian's Wall "and provided with a corresponding series of controlled openings for traffic, differing from it in its deliberately unmilitary design."[16] The function of this second barrier long remained a problem for historians. Drawing on the full range of his knowledge of the Roman Empire, Collingwood offered a solution. Claiming no more than that his account "fits the facts,"[17] he attempts to rethink Hadrian's thoughts, that is those thoughts that determined the construction of such a frontier wall.

A Roman frontier has two principal functions, one military, the other economic. These are separate functions, for the sentries reported to the commandant and the customs officers to the procurator. The relation between the two operations was a delicate one, for they involved distinct jurisdictions. Before Hadrian's Wall, frontier works had been separate from garrison forts. In the absence of proof, Collingwood conjectures that openings in the wall were controlled by customs officials, while sentries guarded their own gateways. Hadrian's Wall presents an innovation in that the customs checkpoints and the military barriers formed one wall.

> From a military point of view this new method of planning the forts in relation to the barrier was no doubt an improvement. If traffic crossing the line of the barrier was compelled to pass through a fort, the military control over such traffic was tightened. But the question must now have arisen, how to provide for the customs officers? Hadrian, a stickler for military discipline, may very well have thought it unwise to give the procurator's man an official position at fort gateways where the authority of the commandant should be undisputed. The simplest solution on paper; though a cumbrous and expensive one, would be to have a second barrier behind the Wall; to make this barrier look as un-military as possible, consistent with efficiency; and to provide it with a crossing opposite each fort, where the customs officers could do their work. The Wall as a whole would be controlled by the governor, the Vallum by the procurator; the distinction between the two reflecting and symbolizing the separation between the military and financial services.[18]

This passage is an instance of historical rethinking as Collingwood understands it. We notice there how dumb archeological remains handled carefully and deciphered in relation to Roman military, economic and administrative policy come alive and make statements as to purposes, motives and intentions. By scrutinizing the evidence, Collingwood is able to rethink the thoughts of which the evidence is the expression. Goldstein is right to observe: "The essential considerations which presumably passed through Hadrian's mind as he came to the decision to have the Vallum built have passed through Collingwood's as well."[19]

A second example more directly concerned with written sources gives further support to the contention that rethinking is essentially a hemeneutical endeavor. The motives behind Caesar's invasion of Britain had long evaded the historian's grasp. Caesar himself never discloses in has writings what he intended to bring about by invading the island. And yet, unless his intent is known, "the mere narrative of his campaigns must remain unintelligible." Thus, Collingwood sets about to reconstruct Caesar's intent. In his account of the campaigns in Gaul, Caesar offers a clue to that intent as he complains that "in almost all his Gallic campaigns, contingents from Britain had been fighting on the side of his enemies."[20] The problem of keeping the peace in Gaul was uppermost in Caesar's mind. Rebellion on the part of the fiercely independent tribes was a constant threat. That threat was, to a great extent, the motive for the British expedition.

> As the event of his expedition showed, Caesar was on the horns of a dilemma. So long as Gaul was restless, Britain, a refuge and reservoir of disaffection within a few hours' sail, was an added danger: for the sake of Gaulish security, therefore, Britain must be made harmless. But so long as the restlessness of Gaul was acute a campaign across the Channel was hazardous: it was an incitement to revolt in Gaul while the Roman armies were overseas. Either way there was a risk.[21]

Here is a perfect example of the logic of question and answer being applied as well as the interpolative function of the historical imagination. Caesar's text, as well as collateral information, are put to the question in order to extract from them that which they leave unsaid. Alternatives must be sought out, and the motives and intentions which best explain the evidence reconstructed. By means of a tightly argued case, Collingwood makes it obvious that the British invasion was not simply a large-scale raid, a punitive war to warn the Britons against interference in Gaul. Caesar meant much more. Again the rethinking process by means of interpretation of all the known evidence is carried out. The intention of annexing the whole of Britain is reconstructed.

> [Caesar] knew the size of Britain with a fair degree of accuracy; he knew that its inhabitants were less civilized and less highly organized both in politics and in war than the Gauls; he meant in the following year to invade the country with five legions and to keep them there for the winter; and when all these facts are considered at once, it can hardly be doubted that his plan was to conquer the whole island.[22]

Neither example contains a hint of an intuitive entering into the existential experience of a past situation by means of reproducing feelings or emotions. There is no dependence on a psychological transference; rethinking is done on the basis of interpretation of evidence. Our illustrations show how the rethinking process can cut through layers of historical evidence, written and unwritten. Thought, history's object, is that which "can be detached from the original context of action and be reproduced in the later context of historical inquiry, hence [it] . . . is universal not existential."[23]

Both examples manifest that the re-enactment of past thoughts is directly related to the questioning process in the present. Rethinking allows the historian to share the perspective of both Hadrian and Caesar but it is only the distance of time which grants entry to that sharing. In order to revive Caesar's thoughts, the historian has to take into account the context of that thought, and thereby grasp it in its "widest sense." It may be that Collingwood's approach affords the possibility of transcending the two orthodoxies in the history of ideas, and more closely relate text and context and thereby bring more cross-fertilization to history and hermeneutics.[24]

Rethinking does not limit the meanings of an event to the straitjacket of original intention. Like Gadamer's hermeneutical experience, it is a description of how one knows the past. In response to Gadamer's misgivings about re-enactment of past thought, Collingwood would claim that the text itself does not necessarily expose the question horizon of the past; rethinking does. Indeed, as we shall see in the next section, the processive nature of human thought disallows a really restricted notion of original intention. Nonetheless, past thought, as part of an ongoing process, contributes in no small way to present meanings. While rethinking is neither a methodological tool nor an explanation of history, it contributes to both. It is more correctly understood as a transcendental reduction of historical understanding. Rethinking the past is the condition for understanding the past. The actual doing of history is methodologically accomplished when that condition is met by means of the imaginative and inferential process of interpreting evidence.

Event, Process and Incapsulation

The rethinking or re-enactment of past thought is Collingwood's description of historical understanding. In our response to Gadamer in chapter II, it was indicated that rethinking takes us beyond a metaphorical description such as "fusion of horizons" but is essentially concerned with the same experience. The retrieval of the past as part of a shared tradition is a common concern of both Collingwood and contemporary hermeneutics. Rethinking happens by interpreting expressions of past thought. The "outside" of an event leads one to an "inside." Both together constitute a human action. However, until more is understood of Collingwood's conception of thought as an on-going continuous process, it remains somewhat obscure how precisely interpretation allows one to see "through" an event. The reenactment process is made clearer by the "incapsulation" theory presented in *An Autobiography*.[25]

The past an historian wishes to know is one which, in some way, makes a claim on the present. As the examples from *Roman Britain* show, that claim might only be apparent to the trained historical observer. However, for the Christian reader of the New Testament, for example, a past which makes a claim on the present is essential to his very existence as a believer. We are historical beings. Our thoughts and experiences form a continuous process in which our present is formed, to a great extent, by our past. Our very ways of perceiving are affected by our own past experiences and those of our communities. Present actions and manners of thinking are the products of social habit dependent on tradition. Present, past and future are inextricably interwoven. Without a shared tradition, Caesar's campaigns, as much as the gospels, would remain unintelligible. The present needs its past in order to be understood, and the past cannot be made intelligible without the present on-going process of human questioning. Tradition for Collingwood is like the dynamic functioning of a corporate mind. It is the process whereby the past is personally, although not necessarily consciously, brought into the present and opens up the future. As we have already seen "The continuity of tradition is the continuity of the force by which past experiences affect the future; and this force does not depend on the conscious memory of those experiences."[26]

The "outside" of rethinking is accounted for by the interpretation of evidence. The function of tradition which Collingwood describes in his "incapsulation" theory presents the "inside." It should be emphasized that terminology here is strictly metaphorical. Rethinking and interpretation are one process. However, interpretation penetrates to past thoughts because,

> historical knowledge is that special case of memory where the object of present thought is past thought, the gap between present and past being bridged not only by the power of present thought to think of the past, but also by the power of past thought to reawaken itself in the present.[27]

The possibility of reawakening the past is dependent on a prior condition that the past is somehow present—even though dormant. This is what Collingwood means by the incapsulation of past thought in the present. The theory provides the foundation for history as the ongoing process of human thought, and for history as a discipline, as the plugging into that process. It is only within a process perspective that the past may be found thriving and exerting an influence on the present. The past that is of interest is a living past. Collingwood formulated his first principle of history thusly,

> . . . that the past which an historian studies is not a dead past, but a past which in some sense is still living in the present . . . I expressed this by saying that history is concerned not with "events" but with "processes"; that "processes" are things which do not begin and end but turn

into one another; and that if a process P_1 turns into a process P_2, there is no dividing line at which P_1 stops and P_2 begins; P_1 never stops, it goes on in the changed form P_2, and P_2 never begins, it has previously been going on in the earlier form P_1. There are in history no beginnings and no endings. History books begin and end, but the events they describe do not.[28]

The importance of this notion of process cannot be over-estimated. Indeed history as the re-enactment of past thought would be unintelligible without it. Material evidence provides the vehicle for rethinking, but for that rethinking actually to occur more than material evidence is necessary. Documents and potsherds are stimulants for the historical imagination but, according to Collingwood, rethinking of past thought would not occur unless past ways of thinking still existed and could be traced in present thought. In other words, past thoughts survive. However, the survival need not be continuous. "Such things may have died and been raised from the dead, like the ancient languages of Mesopotamia and Egypt."[29]

The reconstruction of the "inside" of the historical event is possible because past thought lives on in the present. The past is not ushered on stage as a problem-solver. It has been present, though unnoticed, all along. The practical importance of being able to recognize the presence of the past may be seen in the reluctance with which social change is met in a society. Only on reflection, after the fact of change, is the continuity between past and present revealed. Progress and change are rarely seen as good precisely because the past has not been studied and understood.[30] The function of history is to inform us about the present. It does so however, by means of its ostensible subject-matter, the past, which is incapsulated in the present.

How does this incapsulation of the past in the present relate to the rethinking and interpreting process? If, for example, a thought of Nelson's is still somehow present in my thought, would not my identity be placed in jeopardy? Although Collingwood's language does open him to this objection, he proposes a way out of the dilemma. The thought I re-enact is the same as the thought of the historical agent. Yet, in some way, the thoughts are different. The difference, as we have seen, is one of context. For Nelson, his thoughts were present ones. For the historian, it is a past thought living in the present, and, as Collingwood puts it, "incapsulated, not free." What is the meaning of an incapsulated thought? It is a thought, which does not form part of the question and answer complex in the present. It is not an everyday, "real" question. On a superficial or obvious level, one does not usually ask why Caesar invaded Britain or why Nelson made a particular statement. But even a superficial level of questioning may prompt the inquirer to switch into a deeper dimension. By more reflective questions, the historian stops merely thinking about his subject and is able to think with him. An intimate conversation with a historical text invites identification. "I plunge beneath the surface of my mind, and there live a life in which I not merely think about Nelson but am Nelson, and thus in thinking about Nelson think about myself." This identification is not some mystical taking leave of the present. It is immediately clarified and qualified by the incapsulation theory. The identification with a past historical agent Collingwood refers to as a "secondary life." However, this "secondary life" as a way to explain how one understands the past does not include abandoning the present. "But this secondary life is prevented from overflowing into my primary life by being what I call incapsulated, that is, existing in a context of primary or surface knowledge which keeps it in its place and prevents it from thus overflowing."[31] Another "proposition" of historical knowledge is thus formulated: "Historical knowledge is the re-enactment of a past thought incapsulated in a context of present thoughts which by contradicting it, confine it to a plane different from theirs."[32]

This proposition sums up Collingwood's response to a focal problem for the philosophy of history and hermeneutics. On the one hand unless the past can somehow be identified with the present, it can never be known. On the other hand, unless the past is differentiated from the present, knowledge of it is not distinguishable from knowledge of the present. In that case, historical knowledge is negated. The "sameness" and "difference" of the historical past is insured by the incapsulation theory. Rubinoff elucidates Collingwood's solution to this problem against the Hegelian background of *Speculum Mentis*. The present is conceived of as a synthesis of past and future. This implies a doctrine of time in which the past is both immanent in and transcendent to the present. The past, because it is incapsulated in the present is existentially real. At the same time, it is ideal because it can be reconstructed and made an object of thought. The past is called into being by historical thinking which disentangles the past from the present where it actually exists and transforms it into the thought it was. "What prevents the past, so conceived, from becoming a mere mode of present experience is its quality of 'transcendence,' while what prevents it from being a mere object of 'acquaintance' is its quality of 'immanence' ".[33]

Re-enactment of past experience or thought entails two tasks which overlap and are carried out simultaneously: the interpretation of evidence and the reawakening of past thought incapsulated within present thought. Thus understood, re-enactment or rethinking provides a sound description of the historical-hermeneutical process. Incapsulated past thought is brought to a conscious level through the interpretation of evidence. Rather than an abandonment of the present, rethinking, which is an imaginative and inferential process, cannot happen unless the historian-interpreter is reflectively present to his own present. Without that, the past implied in that present will never surface. Only reflection on present meanings can provoke questions about past meanings and allow the "continuity of force" to affect the future. Rethinking and incapsulation provide a hermeneutical grasp of a historical tradition and help to account for Collingwood's view that history is a self-knowing and self-making process.

Re-enactment and Theological Hermeneutics

The theory of re-enactment has its principal theological advocate in Rudolf Bultmann. He states, "The historian cannot *perceive* the thoughts as a scientist perceives natural facts, but must *understand* them by re-enacting the process of thought."[34] While Bultmann and some of his followers make use of the theory, re-enactment of past thought in general does not seem to have endeared itself to contemporary theoreticians of hermeneutics. Lonergan's position would seem to sum up much of the reaction, including Gadamer's. While endorsing most of what Collingwood has to say about historical knowledge, Lonergan claims that the position on history as re-enactment "is complicated by idealism."[35] In biblical hermeneutics in particular, post-form-critical scholars are reluctant to accept an approach involving rethinking. The claim made there is that because of the nature of the New Testament texts for example, they simply cannot be said to "disclose thoughts of Jesus, let alone permit us to luxury of re-thinking them or re-enacting them."[36] However, the examples cited throughout this study illustrate well the complex process of interpretation and rethinking which, by penetrating various layers of texts or remains, permits and even calls for the inferring of an event. Collingwood would readily admit that the redactive nature of the gospels makes rethinking an arduous and delicate task. He would hasten to add, however, that the remains of the Vallum do not exactly furnish us with a verbatim transcript of Hadrian's plans.

Without denying that Collingwood's idealistic philosophy and language, as well as the exploratory and tenative nature of many of his writings, contribute greatly to misconceptions, we maintain that much of the disagreement with the re-enactment theory comes from identifying it with either a leap into past psychological states or a theory of historical explanation. Both interpretations, as our examples indicate, are oversimplifications. By way of illustration, Van Harvey appears to fall into both traps. He rightly calls attention to the distinction between how we come to know something and how we come to certify the validity of that knowing. In terms of history, for Collingwood, the former relates to rethinking; the latter relates to the mutual confirmation which takes place between the imaginatively rethought picture and the available evidence. However, as we have seen, the two procedures go on together. Historical imagination is the criterion for truth, but it can never be divorced from evidence. Harvey uses Collingwood's example of the reconstruction of a crime. "The imaginative reconstruction of the crime is only a hypothesis, and whether it is right or wrong can be justified by its accounting for what is certainly known."[37] With the exception perhaps of the word "hypothesis", for which he would have preferred perhaps "inference" or "conjecture" (from evidence), Collingwood would be in complete agreement. However, Harvey, returning to the need to distinguish between how historical knowledge is gained and the justification of that knowledge, makes an obvious, if misguided, reference to Collingwood.

> This distinction is important, because some historians who insist that history is the re-enactment of past thought or

experience sometimes talk as if the historian had some special intuitive powers by virtue of which he could "get inside" other minds in a self-authenticating fashion. They argue that the historian does not infer what the agent is thinking or feeling but grasps it immediately and directly. Moreover, these historians sometimes insist that the historian does not have merely a thought or experience similar to the subject he is investigating, but an identical one. He does not only rethink the thought of a past agent but has the identical thought.[38]

This assessment of Collingwood fails to take into account that a question is being asked in the present, that the context of the question is past, and that the answer emerges from an interpretation of evidence. Harvey's opinion, apparently heavily dependent on Patrick Gardiner, is that the view expressed in the paragraph above "leads to insuperable problems." He maintains the problems stem not from the imaginative rethinking, but from the fact that the rethinking solution "confuses a highly useful and perhaps indescribable method for arriving at a hypothesis about the 'inside' of an event with the ways in which one would go about confirming that hypothesis."[39] The verification of an hypothesis, Harvy insists, would require that the event posited in the hypothesis be corroborated by other events, facts and data. Again, Collingwood would be in agreement. For him, rethinking the "what" of the historical event points to the "why", but corroboration is totally dependent on evidence. Our examples from *Roman Britain* indicate that Collingwood too would have "insuperable problems" with the view attributed to him in the passage quote above. Rethinking is not an immediate, self-authenticating getting inside of an event which would make justification through evidence superfluous. Harvey too falls victim to the received interpretation.

Implicit in the rejection of the re-enactment theory by hermeneutical thinkers such as Gadamer and Harvey is that Collingwood leaves out the function of the present, and therefore does not get to understanding as such. In view of the incapsulation theory this criticism is beside the mark. This theory manifests well the historicity of all understanding and the dialogue between present and past. All rethinking involves a dialogue between the self and the past. The past only becomes manifest in the present by passing through the screen of critical reflection. The historian re-enacts past thought but only in the context of his own knowledge. In re-enacting it, he criticizes it and passes judgement on its value. In rethinking the past, he "corrects whatever errors he can discern in it." Collingwood continues, "All thinking is critical thinking; the thought which re-enacts past thoughts, therefore criticizes them in re-enacting them."[40]

In agreement with most of the contemporary hermeneutical thinkers, Collingwood was most certainly concerned with the critical appropriation of meaning in the present. Historical texts or remains are signs indicating past human actions whose meanings can be gleaned. However, those meanings only become available when there is sufficient shared experience between the historian-interpreter and the past he is attempting to understand. As in Gadamer's metaphor of conversation, there must be some degree of intellectual sympathy. Collingwood, like Gadamer, identifies understanding nd interpretation. Understanding in the German sense of *Verstehen*, as a personal involvement and sympathy which gets to the inside of a human action, is what Collingwood means by historical understanding.[41] To understand the past means to share meanings with the past. Re-enactment of past thought is for Collingwood the only route to that sharing.

While not necessarily directly dependent on Collingwood, Coreth is one scholar who apparently accepts re-enactment as integral to the hermeneutical experience.

> ... there will be no understanding unless I co-enact and re-enact the alien thinking in terms of its own grounds and context. I must strive to understand it in its own terms and it its entirety. ... It does not concern the meaning that was meant. Co-enactment does not mean, to be sure, that I agree with all the assertions, and that they become my own convictions. But I have indeed understood an author only if I perceptively understand that, given his viewpoint and his reasons, one can think and speak as he does, and that it is possible for someone to arrive out of honest conviction to such judgements and to such a global view of things.[42]

The Collingwoodian overtones in this passage are obvious. Similarity of expression and meaning are also apparent when Coreth describes tradition as the hermeneutical arch which makes understanding the past possible. The arch corresponds to the incapsulation theory. Coreth's interpretation of tradition as an hermeneutical arch serves to support Collingwood's claim that, "Incapsulation is not an 'occult entity',"[43] but a description of how tradition functions. According to Coreth, the arch

> spans from the event that happened once in the past over the historical effects of it and of its interpretation and all the way to the understanding we have of that event today. It puts the past in touch with the present, and confers significance on the past in terms of the future.[44]

Conclusion

In conclusion it may be said that while Collingwood's philosophy of history maintains close ties to Hegel's unfolding of absolute mind, his mature thought about history and his practice of history, including the re-enactment and incapsulation theories, betray an all pervasive concern for the hermeneutical question of meaning and understanding. Understanding history by the rethinking of the past is not a methodological solution nor an explanation theory but rather a description of how the mind works historically and what in fact an historian-interpreter does. It is interesting that Collingwood's response to his critics is not unlike that of Gadamer to his. Collingwood's claim in regard re-enactment is: like it or not, that is what historians do. To do less than rethink the past is to accept something less than understanding.[45] Gadamer employs a similar rubric in his response to Betti. "Fundamentally I am not *proposing a method,* but I am describing *what is the case.* That it is as I describe it cannot, I think, be seriously questioned . . ."[46] In spite of critical differences, Collingwood and Gadamer agree on many points. For both philosophers the "reality of history is essentially and vitally dialogical" and historical thinking "must always operate in critical awareness of its own historicality."[47] The key for Collingwood is the rethinking process. But that process, as we have seen, is closely interwoven with the hermeneutical understanding of tradition and the interpretation of evidence. Rethinking by means of interpretation of evidence provides the means for moving beyond the text or archeological remain to a hermeneutic of event.

Collingwood's approach to history, interpreted from the perspective of contemporary hermeneutics, reveals the components in that approach as major contributions to the whole hermeneutical discussion. Our next and last chapter will survey the use made of his contribution by specific theologians.

NOTES

1. IH, p. 282. Primary sources for the re-enactment theory include: IH, pp. 282–302; 302–15; A, pp. 95–106, 110–19; and RP, pp. 77–79; 262-64. The theory has spawned a large literature. See for example, Goldstein,"Theory of Historical Knowing", pp. 27–34; Mink, *Mind, History and Dialectic*, pp. 159–70; Donagan, *Later Philosophy*, pp. 192–96; Debbins, "Editor's Introduction" in *Philosophy of History*, pp. xxii–xxix; Rubinoff, *Reform of Metaphysics*, pp. 39–43; Rubinoff, "Religion and the Rapprochement, pp. 95–96; Buchdahl, "Logic and History", pp. 95–98; Cebik, "Action, Re-enactment, and Evidence," pp. 68–90.

2. Walsh, *Philosophy of History*, pp. 43; 48–58; 70–71; cf. Donagan, "Verification of Historical Theses", 193–95; Goldstein, "Theory of Historical Knowing," p. 32, fn. 48.

3. Gardiner, *Nature of Historical Explanation*, p. 39. Gardiner later altered his position. Cf. Patrick Gardiner, *The Philosophy of History* (London: Oxford University Press, 1974), p. 5; Idem, "Historical Understanding and the Empiricist Tradition," in *British Analytical Philosophy*, ed. Bernard Williams and Alan Montefiore (New York: Humanities Press, 1966), pp. 267–84.

4. F. D. Newman, *Explanation by Description* (The Hague: Mouton, 1968), p. 51. The test actually reads *emphatic* but *empathic* is meant.

5. Buchdahl, "Logic and History" 112; cf. Donagan, "Verification of Historical Theses," 195; Goldstein, "Theory of Historical Knowing", 34–35, fn. 53.

6. Donagan, "Verification of Historical Theses", 205.

7. Gadamer, *Truth and Method*, p. 274.

8. IH, pp. 282–83.

9. Ibid., pp. 287–88.

10. Ibid., pp. 288–89; cf. Debbin's "Editor's Introduction" in *Philosophy of History*, pp. xxiv–xxv.

11. IH, p. 287.

12. Ibid, p. 296.

13. Ibid., p. 303; cf Goldstein, "Theory of Historical Knowing," 31.

14. IH, p. 304. See above Chap. II, "A Response to Gadamer."

15. Ibid., pp. 304–05.

16. Collingwood, *Roman Britain*, p. 133; cf. Goldstein, "Theory of Historical Knowing," 29.

17. Collingwood, *Roman Britain*, p. 134; cf. Goldstein, "Theory of Historical Knowing," 29.

18. Collingwood, *Roman Britain*, p. 134; cf. Goldstein, "Theory of Historical Knowing," 30.

19. Goldstein, "Theory of Historical Knowing," 31–32.

20. Collingwood, *Roman Britain*, p. 32.

21. Collingwood, *Roman Britain*, pp. 32–33; cf. Donagan, "Verification of Historical Theses," p. 197.

22. Collingwood, *Roman Britain*, p. 34; cf. A, pp. 111–12. Theological examples of rethinking can be cited. Re-thinking or re-enacting past thoughts in a new context and different language would seem very much to be the task the theologian faces concerning for example, the meaning of the eucharistic celebration. A classic historical example of the need for rethinking is one which Collingwood himself refers to, the development of doctrine in the early church and the ensuing christological and trinitarian heresies. To understand those debates with any degree of accuracy, one must enter into them. Although Lonergan has misgivings about Collingwood's re-enactment, he offers an example of his own understanding of re-enactment which seems quite compatible with our interpretation of Collingwood. In *Method in Theology*, p. 165, Lonergan states: "Thomas Aquinas effected a remarkable development in the theology of grace. He did so not at a single stroke but in a series of writings over a period of a dozen years or more. Now, while there is no doubt that Aquinas was quite conscious of what he was doing on each of the occasions on which he returned to the topic, still on none of the earlier occasions was he aware of what he would be doing on the later occasion, and there is just no evidence that after the last occasion he went back over all his writings on the matter, observed each of the long and complicated series of steps in which the development was effected, grasped their interrelations, saw just what moved him forward and, perhaps, what held him back in each of the steps. But such a reconstruction of the whole process is precisely what the interpreter does. His nest of questions and answers is precisely a grasp of this array of interconnections and interdependences constitutive of a single development".

23. Goldstein, "Theory of Historical Knowing", p. 32. Goldstein goes on to show that, although Collingwood's primary concern was for historical knowing, he does become involved in historical explanation. "For history, the object to be discovered is not the mere event, but the thought expressed in it. To discover that thought is already to understand it. After the historian has ascertained the facts, there is no further process of inquiring into their causes. When he knows what happened, he already knows why it happened" (IH, p. 214). On page 34, Goldstein says, "When Collingwood knows what the Vallum really is, he knows why it was built. When he knows what Caesar's strategy was, he knows the record of the ideal observer . . . not as behavior, but as the movement of troops. In sum, what is involved in the passage quoted from Collingwood is simply the claim that the object of the historian's research is human action, not behavior understood physicalistically." He concludes, "what Collingwood is trying to say is that the historian studies action—an 'outside' informed by an 'inside'—not behavior. Any-

thing exhausted by its immediacy cannot be reproduced in the mind of the historian." Explanation as paradigmatic in the natural sciences and understanding as applicable to the human sciences is a discussion with a long history. Dilthey is central to that discussion. For a contemporary treatment Paul Ricoeur is most important, see for example, Ricoeur, *Interpretation Theory: Discourse and the Surplus of Meaning* (Fort Worth: Texas Christian University Press, 1976), pp. 71–88.

24. Cf. Skinner, "Meaning and Understanding," 3–53 and Simonds, "Mannheim's Sociology of Knowledge," 81–104.

25. A, pp. 89–119.

26. Collingwood and Meyers, p. 252 as quoted in Goldstein, "Constitution of the Historical Past", p. 258.

27. IH, p. 294; Rubinoff, *Reform of Metaphysics*, p. 281 commenting on the relation between perceiving evidence and rethinking states: "At the epistemological level this ontological distinction between an event and an action gives rise to the distinction between perceiving and what Collingwood calls 'rethinking': a distinction, incidentally, which must be understood according to the terms not of propositional but of dialectical logic, so that what Collingwood calls rethinking, rather than being radically distinct and separate from the act of perceiving, is on the contrary, the becoming explicit of what is already implicit in perception. Perception and rethinking, in other words, do not mutually exclude one another, they overlap".

28. A, pp. 97–98.

29. Ibid., p. 97.

30. IH, p. 326; cf. Herbert McCabe *What is Ethics All About?* (Washington, D.C.: Corpus Books, 1969), where he makes this same point with respect to the Irish rebellion of 1916. "We may, indeed, rightly assert after the event that the minority of active revolutionaries did in fact speak for the deepest desires of the apparently indifferent majority, but most people could not be aware of this at the time" (pp. 116–17).

31. A, p. 113. While thought constitutes the universal medium for understanding for Collingwood, this does not greatly separate him from Gadamer's emphasis on language as the universal medium. Collingwood too realizes the closeness between thought and language. See PA, p. 251.

32. A., p. 114.

33. Rubinoff, *Reform of Metaphysics*, pp. 144–45; cf. Collingwood, "Some Perplexities About Time," 135–50.

34. Bultmann, *History and Eschatology*, p. 131; for a summary statement see p. 135; cf. Robinson, *New Quest*, pp. 66–72; Jasper Hopkins, "Bultmann on Collingwood's Philosophy of History," *Harvard Theological Review* 58 (1965): 227–333.

35. Lonergan, *Method in Theology*, p. 175, fn. 1.

36. Iain Nicol, "History and Transcendence," in *God, Secularization and History, Essays*

in Memory of Ronald Gregor Smith, ed. Eugene Thomas Long (Columbia: University of South Carolina Press, 1974), pp. 77–78; cf. Joseph A. Fitzmyer, "Belief in Jesus Today", *Commonweal* 101 (Nov. 1974): 140–41.

37. Harvey, *Historian and the Believer*, p. 92.

38. Ibid.

39. In *Historian and the Believer*, Harvey's reference (p. 101, fn. 49) is to Gardiner, *Nature of Historical Explanation*, pp. 120–33.

40. IH, pp. 215–16; cf. Rubinoff, *Reform of Metaphysics*, p. 262.

41. Cf. Theodore Abel, "The Operation Called Verstehen," *American Journal of Sociology* 54 (1948–49): 211–18; S. Beer, "Causal Explanation and Imaginative Re-enactment," *History and Theory* 3 (1969): 6–29.

42. Coreth, *Grundfragen der Hermeneutik*, pp. 132–33.

43. A, p. 141.

44. Coreth, *Grundfragen der Hermeneutik*, p. 147.

45. IH, p. 263 and A, pp. 111–12.

46. Gadamer, *Truth and Method*, p. 465.

47. Nicol, "History and Transcendence," p. 85.

CHAPTER VII

Some Theological Applications of Collingwood: Bultmann and Pannenberg

Introduction

The gradual awareness of the historicity of understanding has shaped the current hermeneutical discussion in theology. Historical consciousness and hermeneutical consciousness form one another. At least since the publication of Barth's commentary on Romans, the actual work of understanding the Christian message in a particular historical setting has become the principle focus of theologians. For Bultmann and his followers, "hermeneutics is the real work of Theology."[1] That focus, exemplified but not reduced to a movement from history to hermeneutics, has its best theoretician in Gadamer. It emphasizes the task of overcoming the distance between the biblical message and the present age. The hermeneutical task, however, has not been able to sever its ties to the more properly historical task, emphasized by some of Bultmann's followers of somehow penetrating the text to the events they describe. This second movement from hermeneutics to history has its principal advocate in Wolfhart Pannenberg.[2]

Both movements accept the shift from a hermeneutical-historical method strictly speaking to a concern for "the life-situation of the interpreter and the intrinsic power of the matter to be interpreted to affect his understanding of himself."[3] The background for this shift is most often traced to Dilthey, Heidegger and Collingwood. Dilthey and Heidegger have been the subjects of much theological reflection. On the other hand, although Collingwood's position has been described as the "*Magna Carta* of the historian, and more particularly of the historian of the origins of Christianity,"[4] his approach has been pressed into the service of theology without the benefit of detailed examination.[5] This is not to contend that his influence on theological hermeneutics has not been important. On the contrary, it is the burden of the present study to indicate the breadth of that influence. The present chapter is designed to examine some of the details and dimensions of that influence on theological hermeneutics. Such an examination turns out to have the added effect of contributing to the necessary linkage between the hermeneutical process and scientific historical methodology. Collingwood's contention that an event is historical when it responds to a question asked in the present has close affinity with the new hermeneutic. His equally pressing concern for historical evidence which permits the historian to reconstruct the thought behind an event strikes a cord reminiscent of the more traditional historical quests in theology.

Collingwood's contribution to theological hermeneutics is too large to be contained within the scope of this chapter.[6] We have already indicated something of his impact on Gadamer and Lonergan. At this point, we shall turn to the application of his principles by two specifically biblical theologians. Our approach here will be one of illustration. It is not meant to be comprehensive. The use and, at times, abuse of Collingwood in the development of hermeneutics will be illustrated by surveying the application of some of his ideas by Rudolf Bultmann and Wolfhart Pannenberg. Our goal is to indicate how the elements of Collingwood's historical approach, especially the linkage of historical reconstruction and hermeneutical understanding in the theory of re-enactment, has been understood by theologians.

In the interest of clarifying and strengthening our contention about the importance of Collingwood's contribution, our comments will focus, whenever possible, on directly documented use of his writings. Critical response will be offered where appropriate.

Rudolf Bultmann

Bultmann's dependence on Heidegger is well known and needs no elaboration here. Far less known is his appropriation of Collingwood's understanding of history. The remark that Collingwood's approach to history, especially the distinction between the "outside" and "inside" of events,is the *Magna Carta* of the historian of Christian origins is not too great an exaggeration in the case of Bultmann.

Of course, Bultmann's approach to history and hermeneutics predates any influence of Collingwood. Nonetheless, *Jesus and the Word* introduces a viewpoint and a method which raise questions similar to those raised by Collingwood. Because we are historical beings, Bultmann contends, we cannot be neutral observers. The events of the past are able to move us "and only when we are ready to listen to the *demand* which history makes on us do we understand at all what history is about."[7] An approach to history which seeks, in a one-sided fashion, to achieve objectivity misses the real significance of history. This work, published in 1926, exhibits an historical thrust but fastidiously avoids any trace of psychological or biographical interpretation. Bultmann also recoils from taking a position beyond history. In a Collingwoodian fashion, he seeks the event in time, not the personality of Jesus. His attention is entirely limited to what Jesus proposed, "and hence to what in his purpose as a part of history makes a present demand on us."[8] The goal of historical research is not the personalities of great historical figures. Interest in personality "does not touch that which such men had at heart; for *their* interest was not in their personality but in their work."[9] And that work, for Bultmann, is the cause for which the historical agent has given his life. Accordingly the object of New Testament research is variously described by Bultmann as the teaching, work, cause or purpose of Jesus. His whole career, down to his last writings, was spent in articulating how that goal may be reached.

Having long practiced the arts of history and hermeneutics, Bultmann years later turned to theoretically explaining his practice. Although that explanation may be found throughout his later books and articles, the most important statements would seem to be the 1941 lecture, "New Testament and Mythology,"[10] the 1950 essay "The Problem of Hermeneutics",[11] and the 1955 Gifford lectures entitled *History and Eschatology*.[12] The first lecture on the task of demythologizing appeared before the publication of *The Idea of History*. The second essay, an exposition of general hermeneutical principles, while containing no reference to Collingwood, embodies the questions and problematic Collingwood had long faced. Bultmann supplements traditional hermeneutical rules with Schleiermacher and Dilthey's psychological method, but finds their view too "one-sided." Certainly an interpretation is oriented to the subject matter spoken of in the text, but the interpretation is also governed by a "prior understanding of the subject."[13] The logic of question and answer and the theory of re-enactment implicitly function in this essay as tools for understanding the Bible. The questions raised about the psychological method of interpretation mirror at once Bultmann's acceptance of the need to re-enact the past and at the same time his misgivings about Schleiermacher's and Dilthey's understanding of that re-enactment.

Like Collingwood who claims that the question the archeologist seeks to answer must be clearly articulated before the digging begins, Bultmann claims that all understanding of the text should be directed by the "objective" of the inquiry. Thus a "pre-understanding" or presupposition provides the opening for the question guiding the interpreter. In the case of the New Testament, understanding is possible because both the interpreter and the authors share a *"life-relationship to the matter under investigation.*[14] Preunderstanding allows the interpreter to question the text and be questioned by it. The New Testament provides the perfect model for the study of history. Ultimately history is studied in order to learn the possibilities of human existence. The hermeneutic, in the sense of a disciplined interpretation of the Bible, is Heidegger's existential analysis of *Dasein.* "Existentialist philosophy, while it gives no answer to the question of my personal existence, makes personal existence my own personal responsibility, and by doing so it helps to make me open to the Bible."[15] New Testament study becomes a study in self-understanding.

Although by no means as a-historical as he has been accused, Bultmann's concern is not for historical fact but for the understanding of meaning. That meaning, however, remains tied to history; in order to be uncovered it calls for a very personal involvement of the understanding subject in history. It is from this existential view of history that the New Testament is studied. Faith and history are related but in a tenuous fashion. Faith has its grounding in an historical event, but history provides no guarantee. The demythologizing hermeneutic is designed to lay bare the bones of faith. It attempts a "task parallel to that performed by Paul and Luther in their doctrine of justification by faith alone without works of law." De-mythologizing applies the doctrine of justification by faith to the realms of history and epistemology. "He who abandons every form of security shall find true security. Man before God has always empty hands."[16] While Bultmann's hermeneutics receives it focal insights from Heidegger, a fully articulated understanding of history and the philosophy of history is absent until *History and Eschatology.* It is here that Bultmann lavishes high praise on Collingwood and therefore brings him into the thick of theological debate.[17]

Although faith cannot be made dependent on historical research, God's word is encountered in historical events. Bultmann's view of history as an encounter between present existence and past event as manifested in texts demands philosophical and historiographical confirmation. For that confirmation, he looks to Collingwood's *The Idea of History*. After discussing the views of Dilthey, Croce and Jaspers, he turns with approval to Collingwood's view of history as self-knowledge of mind and re-enactment of past thought. He uses the Oxford philosopher to bolster his own distinction between scientific fact and historical event. By stringing together almost six pages of quotes from *The Idea of History*, he testifies to Collingwood's impact on his thought.[18] The object of history is the "actions of human beings that have been done in the past" and "all history properly so-called is the history of human affairs." Bultmann endorses both the distinction between the "outside" and "inside" of an event and the re-enactment theory. Although the distinction between *Historie* and *Geschichte* has a considerable history,[19] Bultmann's own development of it owes much to Collingwood. The historian begins his work by discovering the outside of the event. But he cannot stop there. A wooden record of what Jesus said and did would not necessarily make great impact on modern man. It is only when such words and deeds are grasped as revealing an insight into the meaning of life that Jesus' history and my own make contact. "It is only the 'inner history' that ultimately matters."[20] The historian must remember that the past event is constituted by thought. His task is to think himself into the agents' thought. History is primarily the ongoing process of thought. Differently from the scientist's perception of natural facts, the historian is able to grasp thoughts because he himself is involved in the on-going process. He can revive the past by re-enacting the process of thought.[21] For Bultmann as for Collingwood, history is a rebirth of the ideas of the past in the mind of the historian. Past acts of thoughts survive and are able to be revived. However, as we have seen, that revival is not a passive surrender to another mind, but a critical appropriation of past thought. As Malet points out, Collingwood's critical rethinking of the past translated into Bultmann's language "means that we reach the past by disclosing those meanings of the past which answer to the tasks of the present."[22] Clearly indicating Bultmann's debt to Collingwood, Malet continues.

> The critique must not be made as from outside history but as from inside it. For if the conceptual systems of the past remain valid for later generations it is not in spite of their historical character but rather because of it. In our eyes the ideas they convey are things of the past, but that past is not dead. By understanding it we absorb it into our present thought; and by working up and critically examining this inheritance we are able to use it for our own advancement.[23]

To a great extent, it can be understood how Bultmann is able to appropriate Collingwood as justification for his existential understanding of history and demythologizing hermeneutic. However his a-historical emphasis on existential encounter with the meaning of the events of Jesus' life betrays an interpretation of the outside-inside distinction and re-enactment which exploits only one side of Collingwood's understanding of history. Historical evidence and objectivity receive little attention. This objection however receives a brief rejoinder. Bultmann seconds the view that historical knowledge relies on evidence, not statements. Evidence of the past exists in the present and provokes questions. Every present has a past and the imaginative reconstruction process has as its goal the reconstruction of the past of this present. In spite of this endorsement, Bultmann does not discuss the re-enactment theory in relation to the interpretation of concrete historical evidence. Rather the use of "the entire perceptible here-and-now as evidence for the entire past through whose process it has come into being"[24] appears to be concerned with an existential analysis of the human situation as such. While Collingwood's historical imagination, re-enactment, incapsulation and use of evidence include the results of a reflective analysis, they are much more directly linked to concrete historical remains which point to a particular past.[25]

At this point in the discussion Bultmann refers to Collingwood's approach under the label "existential". By this he means that the subject and object of historical science do not exist independently of one another.[26] The historian himself, as we have noted before, is a participant in history. For this reason historical investigation is never finished. The understanding of history and self-understanding are intimately linked. History is for human self-knowledge. By studying history we learn what man is capable of being and doing. Bultmann obviously is able to rest easy with Collingwood's anthropocentric view of history and antisubstantialist view of man. Man, for Collingwood, is essentially mind, and history is the life of mind. "But mind is something more than mere reason."[27] It is here that Bultmann adds an originality to his interpretation and places his own existential-eschatological stamp on the philosopher-historian. Since Collingwood defines thought as a reflective unity of willing and thinking, freedom, of course, becomes a central factor. A deliberate or reflective act is "an act which we not only do, but intend to do before doing it."[28] Thought includes intention and purpose. Bultmann quotes Collingwood: "The historian's thought must spring from the organic unity of his total experience, and be a function of his entire personality with its practical as well as its theoretical interests."[29]

From this, Bultmann appropriates *The Idea of History* as a support for his own existential interpretation of human historicity. He concludes that Collingwood understands thought not simply as an act of thinking, "but as an act of man in his entire existence, as act of decision." The decisional aspect of thinking and rethinking and its relation to the meaning or goal of history in Bultmann's eyes makes Collingwood a kindred spirit. Although admitting that Collingwood, as a philosopher-historian claims no eschatology, Bultmann is able to apply an eschatological interpretation.

> For every *now,* every moment, in its historical relatedness of course, has within itself a full meaning. The past from which every present springs is not a determining past, but a past offering to the present the problems which demand solution or development. . . . to ask for meaning in history is not allowable if one is asking for meaning in the sense of goal. The meaning in history is immanent in history because history is the history of mind . . . for Collingwood every present moment is an eschatological moment and . . . history and eschatology are identified.[30]

This reading of Collingwood is not without its critics. Jasper Hopkins remarks that Bultmann "seems to be offering a tendentious interpretation . . . by rendering his statements into the language of kerymatic theology."[31] Collingwood at one point at least is adamant that the historian has no evidence of the future. The future is and must remain a "closed book" to him. "History *must* end with the present because nothing else has happened."[32] However, if we go beyond a merely surface reading of the epilegomena to *The Idea of History* and employ a dialectical reading of Collingwood's approach to history, Bultmann's eschatological intepretation might have even more validity than he suspected. Such a reading will also provide the basis for responding to one of two criticisms Bultmann levels at Collingwood.

Bultmann claims that self-knowledge must be understood more profoundly than Collingwood has done. Self-knowledge certainly includes knowledge of present and past, but Bultmann asks does it not also include "responsibility over against the future."[33] Only when thought is understood to include an act of decision with responsibility toward the future, as Bultmann has done, is the historicity of human being truly grasped. "Genuine historicity means to live in responsibility and history is a call to historicity.'[34] A look at sources other than *The Idea of History* would indicate that Collingwood's understanding of mind and history is not without a future dimension. In spite of his own disclaimers as to the lack of evidence for the future, a closer look at his incapsulation theory would have indicated that evidence for the future does exist in present thought. The historian, as *An Autobiography* points out, does have the tools for constructing the foundations of the future. The philosophical study of history is not without its importance for praxis in the present which opens to the future.[35] In the last chapter we looked at Collingwood's conception of the present as a synthesis of past and future. Past and future are both immanent in and transcendent of the present. Both act on the present, the past in a more fixed determined way and the future in a more open, free way. This immanence-transcendence doctrine is drawn out of the discussion of absolute mind in *Speculum Mentis*.

Collingwood's philosophy of history with its dialectical progress builds up until the presuppositions of human thought correspond with the presuppositions of the absolute standpoint. At this point, history and philosophy, experience and thought, object and subject coincide. Access to *Speculum Mentis* and other writings would have provided Bultmann with a more solid basis for the eschatological thrust he reads in Collingwood. It would also have deflated his criticism of Collingwood's notion of self-knowledge as lacking a future dimension. As Rubinoff points out, the word "eschatological" does belong. "At this 'eschatological' moment the ideal limit of philosophy is reached, the unhappy consciousness is redeemed, the alienation of the self with itself is overcome, and we have finally reached a standpoint without presuppositons."[36] To be sure, such a standpoint can only be glimpsed in the present and signals the very end of history. In order to depict this, Collingwood has no recourse but to turn to religious language and imagery. In the beginning God created the universe with man, the spirit-filled being, as its center

> . . . Now man, by his misguided thirst for knowledge, partakes of that knowledge which is forbidden, namely error, or the human wisdom, which negates God's wisdom. This error deforms his own true, that is divine, nature, and the deformation takes the shape of banishment from the presence of God into the wilderness of the visible world. Having thus lost even the sight of God, the knowledge of what he himself ought to be, he cannot recover his lost perfection until he comes to know himself as he actually is. But not knowing himself as he ought to be, he cannot know himself as he is. His error is implicit just because it is complete. It can only become explicit if God reveals himself afresh, if the true ideal breaks in upon the soul clouded by error. This, in the fullness of time, is granted. Human nature sunk in error is confronted by the confutation of its own error, and thus, through a fresh dialectical process, redeemed.
>
> Now in this imagery there is one flaw, namely the transcendence of God. God standing aloof from the drama of human sin and redemption, a mere stage manager, is no true symbol of the absolute mind in its concreteness. But this is exactly where the truth of our religious imagery shines most brilliantly. It is God who accepts the burden of error, takes upon himself the moral responsibility for the fall, and so redeems not his creature but himself.[37]

Absolute mind, the content of Collingwood's "eschaton", is illustrated in terms that Bultmann would find very compatible, the drama of the fall and redemption.

A second criticism made by Bultmann can be disposed of more quickly. He remarks that Collingwood's definition of history as the history of human actions is too "one-sided." By this he means that history is not only what past agents have done but also what happens to them. Bultmann's point here is that humans are responsible for their reactions as well as actions. Behavior or conduct in the face of natural events also provokes decisions. The classic case for him is the thunder-clap which sent Luther into the monastery. Such events are also part of history.

In response, it can be said that Collingwood too would admit the thunder-clap to the annals of history. However, he indicates that such events become historical when they are understood as affecting the course of human affairs. Collingwood's position on this question is very close to Bultmann's.

> Some 'events' of interest to the historian are not actions but the opposite, for which we have no English word: not *actiones* but *passiones,* instances of being acted upon. Thus the eruption of Vesuvius in A.D. 79 is to the historian a *passio* on the part of the people affected by it. It becomes an 'historical event' in so far as people were not merely affected by it, but reacted to this affection by actions of various kinds. The historian of the eruption is in reality the historian of these actions.[38]

Bultmann's two criticisms of Collingwood mirror a reading limited to *The Idea of History*. Although Collingwood does not attempt a complete analysis of the self, his understanding of history is not without a future dimension. Also his emphasis on human affairs as the subject of history does not permit the narrow interpretation Bultmann offers. His limited vision is the cause of a one-sided use of Collingwood. That side obviously is the "inner", personal and "existential" approach to knowing the past. Nevertheless, the use made of Collingwood was seminal and provocative. The Oxford don, now clad in the gown of a Marburg theologian, provides a critical response to nineteenth century positivistic and mechanistic conceptions of history, a theory congenial to the "existential" view of history[39] and a step beyond the psychological hermeneutic of Dilthey.

At this point, it may not be out of order to offer some tentative criticisms about Bultmann's use of Collingwood's philosophy of history. First, Bultmann embraces the outside-inside distinction in historical events and, by aligning that distinction with the German distinction between *Historie and Geschichte,* helps to enfranchise it into theology. In practice, however, form-criticism abidges the importance of the "outside" of history, the critical weighing of text, testimony and evidence for ascertaining historical truth. This is apparent from the scant historical weight Bultmann attaches to the synoptic gospels. In chapter V, we referred to Bultmann's treatment of the crucifixion as illustrating the outside-inside distinction. The resurrection accounts also offer the possibility of employing that methodological device, but Bultmann's treatment of these accounts exemplifies once more the onesidedness of his use of that distinction. With the resurrection "outer" history pales into insignificance. "Indeed, faith in the resurrection is really the same thing as faith in the saving efficacy of the cross. . . ."[40] Thinking oneself into the meaning of the risen Lord means accepting faith in the preached Christ. The empty tomb and appearances play no historical role. "An historical fact which involves a resurrection from the dead is utterly inconceivable!"[41] The resurrection presents in mythological form the "inner" meaning of the crucifixion as God's opening of man to a new self-understanding and existence. This is one way of handling the obvious and perhaps insurmountable difficulties in the resurrection narratives and other moments of Jesus' life, but it is clearly a limited application of Collingwood. The interpretation of historical evidence in the form of a text and testimony would require, according to Collingwood, much more attention than Bultmann is prepared to lend to it.

Second, although Bultmann enthusiastically endorsed the re-enactment theory, he filters it through existential and kerymatic language, identifying thought with an "act of decision" and therefore claiming re-enactment as a philosophical justification for his own idea of existential encounter with the "cause" or "work" of Jesus. This claim does have some validity, since Collingwood's philosophy, in spite of its definite idealism, does not preclude an existential interpretation.[42] However Bultmann makes little attempt to analyze the metaphysics of re-enactment and fails to grasp it as a process made operative and confirmed by a detailed interpretation of historical evidence. Re-thinking, for Bultmann, appears to be a retrieval of the past based on an existential analysis of the present. This accounts for one-half of Collingwood's theory. For him, such an existential analysis of the human situation provides the opening question for historical investigation. However, re-enactment of a particular past thought is possible because the thought lives on in the present and is mediated through observable evidence. In his use of the outside-inside distinction and the re-enactment theory, Bultmann would seem to be guilty of what Collingwood refers to as the fallacy of the false disjunction, which is "the principle that when a generic concept is divided into its species there is a corresponding division of its instances into mutually exclusive classes."[43] Without any pretense of ending the debate as to whether Bultmann too greatly dichotomizes *Historie and Geschichte* and widens the gap between the Jesus of history and the Christ of faith, a false disjunction is clearly present in his understanding of Collingwood. As Harvey and Ogden have shown, Bultmann acknowledged throughout his career a basic continuity between the events of Jesus' life and the preached Christ.[44] His early works especially manifest a respect and talent for the critical historical method and its task of reconstruction.[45] However that is not the point here. Of concern to us is that Bultmann does not see the close relationship Collingwood saw between the reconstructive task and the interpretative task. As a matter of fact, such reconstruction is ultimtely considered unnecessary and even irrelevant. Ogden states:

> Bultmann holds . . . that while such a process [of critical historical reconstruction] is possible, it is hardly necessary. For, 'the crucified one is not at all proclaimed in the New Testament in such a way that the meaning of the cross would be disclosed from his historical life as reproduced by historical research.'[46]

Collingwood's approach would much more closely relate Christian faith and historical event. This is not, however, to suggest that he would claim that historical research could prove faith, or that faith is dependent on such research. Rather an incarnational religion means that full import must be given to human history as the *locus* of faith.⁴⁷ The understanding of Christian faith in the present, runs parallel with the ongoing reconstruction, however tenuous and open to correction, of the history in which that faith was definitvely manifest. The past in such an approach is much more than a mere "dass". It is a reconstructed and yet a living presence.

Finally, in a more positive vein, a link might be forged between Bultmann's view of history, as influenced by Collingwood, and his stance in the face of two groups of critics. On the one hand some followers accuse him of historical skepticism and claim the support of the new historiography as opening the way to the authentic selfhood of Jesus. James Robinson, speaking for such "new questers" as Käsemann, Bornkamm, Fuchs, Ebeling and other, asserts that their approach is better able to establish continuity between Jesus and the kerygma. One of the principal sources for the new historiography, and one whom Robinson names in support, is R. G. Collingwood. Rather than the chronologizing and categorizing of the old quest, "the historian's task was seen to consist in understanding those deep-lying intentions of the past by involving one's selfhood in an encounter in which one's own intentions and views of existence are put in question, and perhaps altered or even radically reversed."⁴⁸

The new questers' emphasis on the history of Jesus would have pleased Collingwood, as would their attempt to get to the "inside" of the Jesus event. In one of his few references to the study of the New Testament, as we have seen above, he claims it imperative "to study the mind of Jesus from within."⁴⁹ It is important to note however, that in light of our analysis, the new quester's manner of reaching the inside would not have met with his approval. Historian Paul Merkley points out that the outside-inside distinction "is the one sample of Collingwood's very special vocabulary which seems to get into every one of the New Quester's books."⁵⁰ In spite of the use of Collingwood's terminology, there is no detailed analysis of his approach to history. There is also a tendency to push Bultmann's existential interpretation beyond a meaningful relation to Collingwood's stated views. Penetrating to the "inside" of history, in spite of statements to the contrary,⁵¹ smacks of biographical or psychological recovery of the selfhood of Jesus. Various notions are put to this task: language, conduct, authority, faith and openness to transcendence. Modern historiography's task is "to grasp such acts of intention, such commitments, such meaning, such self-actualization; it is the task of modern biography to lay hold of the selfhood which is therein revealed."[52] The resource for such an approach might perhaps be Dilthey, but certainly not Collingwood. Selfhood, personality and biography are not ingredients to the re-enactment theory of history. Documents and potsherds can tell us much about the thoughts and intentions of past agents, but little about personality and selfhood. In fact, Collingwood issued an explicit warning about the incompatibility of biography and history.

> Of everything other than thought, there can be no history. Thus a biography, for example, however much history it contains, is constructed on principles that are not only non-historical but anti-historical. . . . At its best, it [biography] is poetry; at its worst, an obtrusive egotism; but history it can never be.[53]

Indeed, a strong statement and one not without difficulties. We quote it here not to claim that the new questers are writing biographies of Jesus. On the contrary, they are at pains to distance themselves from the liberal lives of Jesus. Nevertheless their approach opens them to the charge of seeking the "inner life" or personality of Jesus in a fashion reminiscent of their nineteenth century predecessors.[54] If our understanding of Collingwood has validity, he would not recognize his own philosophy of history in an approach which claims to gain access to the selfhood of Jesus by allying to historical research categories such as "existential openness," "intuitive encounter" and even "Easter faith."[55]

Bultmann, in spite of problems of interpretation, remains a more faithful interpreter of re-enactment. He avoided making undue demands on the science of history and sought out the work or ideas of Jesus. His lack of interest in personality and selfhood was most compatible with the re-enactment theory.

As the new questers criticize Bultmann for moving too close to historical skepticism, critics from a different direction assert that he ties faith too closely to a historical stake. Schubert Ogden, for example, agrees with Buri that when Bultmann appeals to the unique event of Jesus Christ, he is "falling back into mythology"[56] and not being consistent with his own demythologization thesis. However, in holding to a concrete historical event as the basis for faith, Bultmann again stays within the Collingwood ambit of history. Philosophically, Collingwood and Ogden would have some affinity.[57] Obviously, however, Collingwood places more weight on the historical past and more confidence in the ability of modern historical science to reconstruct that past. Unknown to Bultmann, he could have called upon Collingwood for support in his response to the position of Buri and Ogden. In his first book Collingwood wrote:

> The whole value of an example is lost unless it is historical. If an athlete tries to equal the feats of Herakles, or an engineer spends his life trying to recover the secret of the man who invented a perpetual-motion machine, they are merely deluding themselves with false hopes if Herakles and the supposed inventor never lived. The Good Samaritan's action is the kind of thing that any good man might do; it is typical of a kind of conduct which we see around us and know to be both admirable and possible. But if the life of Jesus is a myth, it is more preposterous to ask a man to imitate it than to ask him to imitate Herakles. Any valid command must guarantee the possibility of carrying it out; and the historical life of Jesus is the guarantee that man can be perfect if he will.[58]

In summary, then, it is clear that Bultmann finds in Collingwood an intellectual ally. He explicitly accepts the outside-inside distinction and the re-enactment theory and implicitly, at least, the theories of historical imagination and incapsulation. However, his failure to analyze them fully leads to a one-sided exploitation. Not being familiar with Collingwood's notion of overlap, he separates too greatly inner and outer history. Collingwood understood the two dimensions of history as convex and concave. Had Bultmann realized this, he would have been able to link more closely the historical task of reconstruction with the hermeneutical task of interpretation. Such a linkage would make clearer the relation of revelation to historical signs. His eventual downgrading of historical evidence, the "outside" of rethinking, is explainable by many practical reasons spanning the period between the wars. His Heideggerian emphasis on historicity pushed him to identify history and historicity and not allow pastness its full impact. There is much food for thought in speculating on the outcome of bringing together a fully developed analysis of Collingwood's critical-scientific historiography with its positing of an event in order to explain evidence and Bultmann's demythologizing hermeneutic. The spark for a radically de-mystified and historical Christology would be ignited.

Despite a limited reading and existential interpretation, Bultmann's views on the notion of history and historical research[59] receive much of their philosophical underpinnings from Collingwood. It is clear that his treatment of the eschatological movement as present, the relation of time to eternity and the very nature of *Geschichte* all bear the Collingwood imprint.

Wolfhart Pannenberg

Our second illustration is Wolfhart Pannenberg. Although strongly influenced by Bultmann, his theology moves in an historical direction and may be read as a reaction against Bultmann and the theology of the word. He eschews the *Historie-Geschichte* distinction as a theological escapism. He seeks to free theology from what he considers a ghetto mentality and to expose it to the pluralistic city of science and history. Christianity is the product of historical events, and therefore the only honest method of settling many theological problems is by the proper employment of the scientific methods of modern historical inquiry.

A complete analysis of Pannenberg's theology is not possible here. We will confine ourselves to two major areas: first, we shall offer some general remarks about the importance of history and hermeneutics to this thought; and second, we shall discuss his dependence on Collingwood for the understanding of historical methodology.

In spite of what at times appears to be uncritical fundamentalism, Pannenberg's understanding of revelation as history attempts to take into account the contemporary problematic involving confessional teaching, history and hermeneutics. Since the reformation, gaps have opened between our present meanings and those of the New Testament witnesses, and between the biblical texts and the events to which they refer.[60] Pannenberg's sets out to close both gaps and thereby indicates the mutual dependence of history and hermeneutics. His handling of the hermeneutical task owes much to Gadamer. For the historical task of reaching behind the texts to event, he employs Collingwood's methodology. In a convergence of the two tasks, Pannenberg introduces his notion of universal history. The event behind the text does not surface with any degree of meaning when understood as an isolated fact. The event and its meanings are known "only within universal continuities of events and of meanings, i.e., only within the horizon of universal history, which, incidentally, also embraces the present era of the investigator."[61]

Before looking at the notion of universal history, let us briefly examine Pannenberg's understanding of the hermeneutical task, that is the task of bridging the gap between our time and the text's. Pannenberg is not satisfied with past efforts at accomplishing that task. Bultmann's existential hermeneutic, like Schleiermacher's and Dilthey's psychological hermeneutic, restricts the content of a text from the past to questions concerning human existence; "absolutely everything becomes relevant, but only *as* the possibility of an understanding of human existence."[62] Pannenberg finds this approach too constricting. While the New Testament deals with the understanding and meaning of human existence, it is also concerned with the understanding and meaning of God. He has much sympathy for Gadamer's movement beyond the existential interpretation to the linguisticality of understanding. While Gadamer's descriptive metaphors of "fusion of horizon" and "conversation" are to some extent compatible with Pannenberg, they are not broad enough in his opinion to correspond with the hermeneutical process.

> The hermeneutical process is certainly articulated in language. But this is much more a matter of the creative formation of language by the interpreter than of being called by a "thou". The text does not "speak," but rather the interpreter finds a linguistic expression which combines the essential content of the text with his own contemporary horizon. It is always a matter of formulating an assertion [Aussage]. And here we reach the point at which we can no longer follow Gadamer.[63]

The step from hermeneutics to history is deliberate and decisive. Adding an emphasis to Gadamer, Pannenberg makes the historical inquiry, that seeks out the event, the focal point of this theology. Gadamer's devaluing of assertion (statement) with its necessary objectification of language is the major point of Pannenberg's critique. Although Gadamer's critical view of the statement is rightly directed at the attempt to separate what is said from what is unsaid, this position does not allow the element of objectification as a basic element of language itself. Gadamer and Pannenberg agree that background is important, but for the latter "background can only be fully understood when it becomes explicit, that is, when it is the subject of assertions."[64] The reconstruction of the alien horizon, according to Pannenberg, involves objectification. Gadamer excludes the objectifying function of the statement. And, for Pannenberg, in terms of the current discussion of the hermeneutical task in theology:

> . . . it is this exclusion which gives rise to the equally problematic affinity of Gadamer's hermeneutic with a theological "hermeneutic of the language-event" which attempts to relieve the interpretation and current appropriation of the biblical texts of the awkward problems associated with the historical facticity of the events transmitted by tradition and to reduce them to their existential relevance for present-day man.[65]

While accepting much of Gadamer's hermeneutical theory, Pannenberg insists much more strongly on the reconstructive task of the historical consciousness. History and hermeneutics, reconstruction or, as Pannenberg often calls it, "reproduction," and understanding cannot be isolated from one another.

In developing his own position which involves a full-blown theology of history, Pannenberg makes ample use of modern scientific historiography. Both his theology of history and scientific historical method are woven together into a universal history made possible by belief in God the creator who mediates all understanding of reality through the historical process. Revelation takes place in the historical acts of God, and is only fully understood at the end of "revealing history". We are, however, afforded a glimpse of that end in the fate of Jesus, since his fate is the anticipation of all that is human.[66] A number of points here link Pannenberg with Collingwood. In spite of Collingwood's criticism of medieval historiography[67] with its heavy and direct reliance on God and providence, his understanding of God as an absolute presupposition for history, freedom and the future[68] appears to be compatible with Pannenberg's understanding of God as the totality of all history. Also, as we shall see below, Pannenberg uses Collingwood's doctrine of the historical imagination for his projection of the totality: a universal history. Although Collingwood does not use the term often and would not allow such a grandiose vision of history as a whole, universal history is for him the "historian's conception of history as such."[69] This conception projects a grasp of history which intertwines fact and interpretation, and shows the interrelationship of past, present and future. Collingwood's constant plea that history be rewritten by every generation, and the element of progress in the historical process necessarily include a future dimension. Reenactment of past thought and the incapsulation theory, discussed in Chapter VI, find close parallels in Pannenberg's history as the transmission of traditions which is "a hermeneutical process involving the ceaseless revision of the transmitted tradition in the light of new experiences and new expectations of the future."[70]

After these rather general comments, it is time to move on to those elements of Pannenberg's theology of history which bear the mark of the direct influence of Collingwood. Our contention here is that Pannenberg's understanding of critical historical methodology is heavily indebted to Collingwood's *The Idea of History*. While the ideas of the two men touch at many points, we will concentrate on two central issues: first, the image of totality in universal history based on the historical imagination, and, second, the use of the critical historical methodology in New Testament study. Both issues are highlighted in Pannenberg's treatment of the Resurrection.

Pannenberg contributes an important insight to the discussion of historicity and the scriptures. He maintains that, before the New Testament can be demythologized, it must be "depositivized".[71] Revelation cannot depend on some authority "which suppresses critical questioning and individual judgement." He draws on Collingwood's criticism of nineteenth century historiography as a collection of isolated facts separated from interpretation. Rather for Pannenberg, certain assumptions must first be put forth to establish the wholistic nature of history. He bases these assumptions on the biblical view of history.

> The universal-historical theme of modern philosophy of history was inherited from Jewish Apocalyptic and Christian theology of history. The difficulty of speaking of a goal of history as a whole makes it questionable whether universal history can be understood as a unity without the biblical ideas of God.[72]

The Bible provides the opportunity to understand history as a whole, with its beginning, middle and end. In this sense biblical theology is a hermeneutic of all of human life. This is a key notion for Pannenberg. For this reason the historical roots of the universality of theology must be retrieved. In discussing Israel's role in the origins of history, Pannenberg relies on Collingwood with whom he has some disagreement. He states: "According to Collingwood, it was not Israel but the Greek Herodotus who discovered history."[73] But according to Pannenberg, Collingwood here means by history the "methodical determination of past events—not *Geschichte* but precisely *Historie*." The complaint here is that Herodotus, with the Greek substantialist approach to history, was concerned with constructing monuments to the bygone past, but was not concerned with historical change as such, and therefore did not really contribute to a new understanding of reality. It was Israel rather who "finally drew the whole of creation into history."[74] Collingwood's own position in *The Idea of History*, in spite of some confusion, is in agreement. The Greeks were responsible for history as a form of research, yet history as universal and apocalyptic is most certainly the product of the Judeo-Christian tradition, especially the doctrine of creation.[75]

It is this image of history as a totality based on God the creator which Pannenberg places into a wider historical methodology by drawing on Collingwood's doctrine of the historical imagination. He begins his historical hermeneutic of the Bible with an imaginative projection supported by Collingwood's teaching about absolute presuppositions and the use of evidence. The evidence, under examination, may alter or even eliminate the projection. "The point of departure for historical work is constituted by a spontaneous pre-projection of nexuses of meaning which then are tested against observation of all the available individual details, and confirmed or modified in accord with each of these."[76] Not only is a notion of universal history necessary for understanding historical events but also the historian's imaginative projected picture influences his interpretation and judgement of historical events.

Pannenberg's pre-projection of a "totality" is neither fundamentalistic nor naive. He does not claim that the bible contains no mythology nor that the historian can somehow bring back the past as it actually was. The starting point for historical research is the historical imagination's conception of a unity, a unity which allows for contingency, yet at least in retrospect, provides for continuity. Research into historical particulars presupposes an outline of history as a totality. Pannenberg cites Collingwood's analogy for history as criminal investigation. Details provide the detective with information for or against his conjecture of the crime. Likewise, "documents accessible to the modern historian are indicators for or against the historian's spontaneously projected model of the event."[77]

The importance of the historical imagination's ability to grasp the universal-historical horizon cannot be over-estimated in Pannenberg's theology. The historical imagination is the answer to what he refers to as the central question for the debate between history and theology: "how is the conception of a unity of history possible?"[78] The imaginative projection provides the means of bringing together fact and interpretation, as well as the framework for the "cognitive value of the historical projection," a point which Pannenberg thinks Collingwood overlooked. Familiarity with a wider segment of Collingwood's writings on incapsulation, rethinking and evidence would have indicated that this point was indeed of great importance for Collingwood. On the other hand, Pannenberg's emphasis on the poetic value of his projection indicates a deviation from Collingwood and from the scientific historical method. Pannenberg's emphasis is clear.

> To be sure, the historian with his own historical location belongs together with the effects of the event he is investigating. But despite this "subjective conditioning" of his viewpoint he cannot change his picture of the course of history in any way he pleases without thereby surrendering

the cognitive value of historical projection. If the historian does not want to lose sight of his own involvement in the event he describes, but on the other hand also does not want to surrender the cognitive claim of his historical projection, then he can only interpret this projection as a spontaneous reproduction of a previously given unity of history, which, to be sure, only becomes conscious of itself in this reproductive act.[79]

The above clearly entails much more "poetically" than Collingwood intended for the picture produced by the historical imagination. Pannenberg's projection is too controlling. For Collingwood, the historical imagination was more flexible, and not simply a projection of universal hypotheses to be corraborated by evidence.

Following up on the idea of history as imaginative reconstruction, Pannenberg applies Collingwood's method. He avoids the traps of applying the approach in its extremes, as on the one hand, the collection of evidence and on the other, a form of intuition. Thinking oneself, with one's own horizon, into the horizon of a past context is, as we have seen, a process which is the result of carefully collecting and interpreting evidence and thinking through the events (processes) which they presuppose. Collingwood, according to Pannenberg,

> Avoids the problematical assumption that intuition is an independent source of historical knowledge alongside historical observation of the particulars. By referring the imagination to verification by detailed investigation, he avoids the danger of a dualism between the two, such as is expressed in theology in the dualism between the revelatory-historical and historical-critical formulations of the question.[80]

Collingwood's approach to history turns out to be exactly the methodological tool Pannenberg needs to shore up the foundation for his historicizing exegesis. The approach, as we have seen, allows for both contingency and individuality, and yet does not deny continuity. Such fundamental characteristics of the historical are focal for grasping the meaning of biblical events. The understanding of reality as contingent yet continuous gains clarity in the events of Jesus' life which disclose an understanding of the world as an historical-redemptive process. Pannenberg's view of this process is obviously different from the usual understanding of redemption-history thinking in that, in principle at least, his approach calls for historical verification. However, such verification by no means implies verification in any positivistic sense of apodicticity. He is rather employing Collingwood's understanding of history as the imaginative reconstruction of the past event inductively built up from evidence and testimony found in the present. Verification here is the ongoing mutual confirmation process carried out by the interaction between the picture produced by the historical imagination and the available evidence. Pannenberg, like Collingwood, is concerned with historical detail and inference. The event and its meaning is a projected construction, in principle at least, always open to further findings. It may be mentioned here that although this qualifier is always included by Pannenberg, an obvious difficulty is that the projected image is too controlling and at times appears impervious to evidence. Concerning historical verification and revelatory history, Pannenberg makes it clear that he is not claiming that redemptive-historical thinking could be read directly from historical evidence. Indeed using Collingwood's approach, such a reading could not be gleaned from any historical projection. A theological understanding of history could never meet a strictly positivistic requirement that the continuity between faith and history be derived from the simple observation of particulars. If such a conception were the only available approach to history, Pannenberg states, theology would be forced to retreat to a "supra or primal history". He hastens to add however that

> This situation has been fundamentally changed by Collingwood's proof that this positivistic demand is inappropriate to the historical object as such A verification through subsequent testing by observation of the particulars may unreservedly be expected of a theological projection of history. Its ability to take into account all known historical details would be the positive criterion of its truth; the proof that without its specific assertions the accessible information

would not be at all or would be only incompletely explicable, can be used as a negative criterion.[81]

Christian faith, taking radically serious the incarnation, must seek not a proof but "intellectual confirmation" in history. Theology must absorb what is true in the "immanent" understanding of events. "It may not supplant historical investigation by supernaturalistic hypotheses".[82] Pannenberg finds that confirmation in Collingwood's method. He writes: "The theological fruitfulness of Collingwood's historical epistemology is easy to see."[83]

In obvious contrast to Bultmann, Pannenberg applies Collingwood's historical methodology to the resurrection. He places enormous weight on the historicity of the resurrection, and, at least in his earlier writings, makes it determinative of his whole theology.[84] Rather than faith being the basis of the resurrection, resurrection understood as an historical event is the basis for faith. This, according to Pannenberg, is Paul's position in I Corinthians 15. He does not hesitate to use the word "proof". "The proof Paul gave us was for his time a historical proof, a firsthand proof beyond doubt."[85] Of course such a proof cannot be tested in the present. But secondhand proofs can be validated by means of the critical historical method. Pannenberg's approach begins with the assumption that resurrection cannot be ruled out before-hand. Again a contolling factor seems operative here. The possibility of resurrection is a by-product of Pannenberg's anthropology. Humans cannot understand themselves without a conception of resurrection. "That man has to seek for his final destination beyond death is based on the specifically human structure of existence, on the so-called openness to the world."[86] However if the contingencies of history are overruled by theories of historical explanation which render certain occurrences impossible, then understanding the resurrection as historical is impossible. He opposes historians, "who begin dogmatically with a narrow concept of reality according to which 'dead men do not rise'." [87] Pannenbrg is not speaking of a resuscitated body nor just a "random miracle." He readily admits that the expression resurrection has a "metaphysical character" However, he relates the expression to the daily experience of rising from sleep.[88] What is essential for an historical investigation of the narratives is the projected image, the possibility of resurrection. The historical investigation begins with a detailed and careful examination of the traditions of the appearances and the empty tomb.[89]

Along with the detailed interpretation of the texts, the historian-theologian must also think himself into the apocalyptic context of the time. St. Paul's understanding of the resurrection as a radical transformation was not simply the product of impressions made on him by his experiencing of Jesus as risen. "Even the understanding of the qualitative differences between the resurrection life as imperishable and the present life as perishable has Jewish parallels.[90] In short, rather than unexpected, the resurrection was expected and longed for.[91] Thinking back into that context and examining the texts disallow the existential interpretation that the resurrection stories are merely the faith products of the Christian community. Historical research forces us to acknowledge an historical event which the historian may validly if metaphorically reconstruct as resurrection. The resurrection is an historical event in the sense that it best explains the available evidence concerning the origins of Christianity.

> If the emergence of primitive Christianity, which apart from other traditions, is also traced back by Paul to appearances of the resurrected Jesus, can be understood in spite of all critical examination of the tradition only if one examines it in the light of the eschatological hope for a resurrection from the dead, then that which is so designated is a historical event, even if we do not know anything more particular about it.[92]

Although Pannenberg does not mention Collingwood directly in connection with his treatment of the resurrection accounts, the resurrection is for him the *locus classicus* for applying the outside-inside theory of history. As Galloway indicates, "The inside of an event or fact is the meaning it has within its total context for those whose experience it touches."[93] He proceeds to point out that for Pannenberg, as for Collingwood, meaning must be *for somebody* and can be extracted from events because it does not inhere as some ghostly existence but precisely as interpretation, motives or thoughts. The "outside" of the event or fact lives on in texts and evidence. The "inside" continues on as part of a living tradition.

> The natural events that are involved in the history of a people have no meaning apart from the connection with the traditions and expectations in which men live. The events of history speak their own language, the language of facts; however, this language is understandable only in the context of the traditions and expectations in which the given events occur.[94]

Pannenberg's refusal, even in such a controversial instance as the resurrection of Jesus to separate fact from interpretation, is symbolic of his view of historicity. He weaves a pattern of happening out of the evidence and, based on his version of the whole, unearths the meaning inherent in the event. Meaning is given in the nexus of events. The historian-theologian gets to that meaning by thinking back into that nexus and "reproducing" it. Of course, as we have seen, the specific meaning of the resurrection is not totally alien according to Pannenberg, because of his view of man and because it has been kept alive in the tradition flowing from the scriptures.

By a careful reading of the appearance narratives and the stories of the empty tomb, bolstered by an anthropology which hopes for and, practically speaking, demands life beyond the grave, and an apolocyptic background for such a hope, Pannenberg posits an historical resurrection which best explains the available evidence. Even from this brief sketch, it is apparent that Pannenberg has equated his own "history of transmission of tradition," complete with its eschatological emphasis, with critical historical method. The resurrection is an historical reality because it fulfills the pre-requisites for sound historical method. First, it is a "reproduced" event which provides the "best explanation" for the available evidence. Second, it is part of a passed-on living tradition, stretching backward to Jewish apocalyptic hope and foreward to modern man's "openness to the world." Third, it is guaranteed by a philosophical analysis of human existence which relates resurrection to present experience. And fourth, it is given a covering metaphorical expression understandable to both past and present. The resurrection of Jesus as the "prolepsis" of human destiny which has occured within history functions like a key to history. The same method may be applied to all historical events.[95]

Pannenberg has done an invaluable service for Christian theology in forcing it to reexamine its historical roots and pay attention to the obvious, the linkage between Christian faith and history. It seems fairly apparent that his emphasis on objectification and historical method in relation to the resurrection is overstated. This is indicated by developments in his most recent writing. His use of the historical method has evoked much criticism. He has been accused of justification by historical method, substituting history for the Holy Spirit, and quite simply of maintaining too high a trust level in his acceptance of modern historical method. Since Pannenberg has already responded to many of these criticisms, they will not be taken up here.[96]

A brief comment may be inserted about Pannenberg's argument for the historicity of the resurrection. Herbert Burhenn has convincingly argued that, while Pannenberg's treatment of the appearance narratives and the empty tomb is not without historical cogency, his defense of the historicity of the resurrection clearly goes beyond historical method. First, Burhenn questions whether the evidence does point to a historical event of resurrection or whether the historian is not compelled to admit an insufficiency of evidence. In the background of Pannenberg's approach is the position that the historian is almost compelled to account for the origins of Christianity. While this remains an important and necessarily somewhat open question for the historian, according to Burhenn, he must admit that based only on historical method, another account beside an historical resurrection might be a better explanation of the evidence. Secondly, he points out, as should be apparent from the above discussion, that Pannenberg's argument is more philosophical and theological than it is historical. Although his arguments are real historical arguments, and this is Pannenberg's contribution, his conclusions "are no longer simply historical."[97] The outcome of his argument is pre-controlled by his view of divine action in history. In spite of his disclaimers, he ends up resorting to some form of metahistory.

At this point some concluding remarks are in order concerning Pannenberg's use of Collingwood. On the positive side, it can be said that more than any other theologian, Pannenberg has exploited the methodological side of Collingwood's philosophy of history. Three factors stand out. First, he has clearly understood the implications of Collingwood's critique of historical positivism.[98] This allows him to integrate fact and interpretation, which amounts to realizing the subjective element in historical reconstruction without severing ties to the historical event. Secondly, he has creatively appropriated Collingwood's notion of historical imagination as a pre-projection around which history is construted Thirdly, he accepts the notion and its implications that the text is a piece of evidence which when interrogated and interpreted allows for and even calls for the reconstruction of an event. In theory, at least, he claims to be wiling to let the evidence lead where it will.[99]

On the negative side, points two and three above clearly indicate the misunderstandings in Pannenberg's application of Collingwood. While sensing the profound importance of the imagination for the reconstruction of a past continuous with the present, Pannenberg has trespassed the legitimate parameters even in the most creative interpretation of Collingwood's doctrine. Historical imagination explains history in its quality as an innate and a priori capacity of the mind and calls for interpolation. The projected picture and interpolations are always closely tied to evidence. The imaginative picture points to the possibility of history as such, not to a specific understanding of history as a whole, as Pannenberg conceives it. No matter how much Collingwood's doctrine may be stretched, it could never be used to maintain that the historian has the ability to lay hold of a universal historical horizon. Although Collingwood places great importance on God as an absolute presupposition for history, he does not accept a notion of universal history understood as a vision of history as a whole. As a matter of fact, he would consider such a position an outlandish departure from scientific historical method. This would seem to be behind his criticisms of such sweeping views of history as Augustine's, Spengler's and Toynbee's.

In sum, it has been argued that Pannenberg stretches historical imagination beyond recognition and justifies far more than Collingwood allows. Concerning evidence, Pannenberg sets out to use it in a scientific manner and, to a great extent, achieves his intent. However, although he qualifies the history that rests on that evidence as a provisional reproduction, his approach appears to be overly guided by a pre-projected image and controlled by philosophical and theological assumptions. Certainly Pannenberg seeks to take seriously the notion of text as evidence for event, yet, his conclusions couched perhaps in too objectifying terms, appear to end up as spontaneous reproductions based on a faith position. This might be as it ought to be, and Pannenberg himself would claim that the historical method necessarily includes more than history.[100] For such a contention he might also call on Collingwood for support. However, by allowing the projection to exercise such control, he fails to see the importance of his own philosophical and faith assumptions. The resurrection might well be the key to history, but it is not clear from the historical method alone that it should also be called an historical event.

Contrary to Bultmann, Pannenberg employed Collingwood methodologically without fully understanding his notion of history as such: human actions done in the past, and understood in the present by reconstructing thoughts, motives and purposes. In Pannenberg's view of revelation and theology as history, history is *theonomous*, rather than *autonomous* which is the way Collingwood understood it. History and theology are collapsed into one another.

Pannenberg's methodological use of Collingwood is weakened in spite of its strengths, in that he seems overly tied to a "critical" model of history. Although at various points he comes close to the model Collingwood refers to as "scientific," he never fully moves into it. His use is also made somewhat ambiguous because he comes dangerously close to grasping the method as an attempt at historical explanation.[101] In contrast, as we have seen, the primary concern of the imaginative reconstruction by rethinking is not explanation but understanding and interpreting.

In conclusion, Pannenberg makes selective use of Collingwood, and ends up expecting too much from the historical method. It is obvious that his contribution is striking and somewhat unique in that he has shown the intertwining of understanding and reconstruction in grasping the meaning of biblical history. It must also be said that he has to a great extent applied the historical method correctly. However, it is only in his later writings that he seems to realize the importance of his own "tacit assumptions" which control the outcome of his theological-historical endeavors. In *Theology and the Philosophy of Science* he does not reject his earlier stance, but he edges away from an over-dependence on an overly objective view of history and historical method. There, resurrection as history does not play a role. Historical method is placed within a much wider context of scientific method as articulated by Karl Popper. This later book worked out in dialogue with Popper, Dilthey and Gadamer does a great deal to explain much of what is left unsaid in the earlier Pannenberg.[102] His working out of the relationship between history and hermeneutic in his theological method is still unfolding.

Conclusion

While the theological use of Collingwood has been extensive, it has not always been deep. Theologians have selectively chosen those aspects of his thought which support their own theological positions They have failed to grasp the distinction and the interrelation between what may be called the objective aspect of historical understanding—the method and its subject—and the subjective aspect—the theoretical a priori of history itself.

The diversity of application may be seen in the almost diametrically opposed ways in which Bultmann and Pannenberg use Collingwood. Both align themselves to his attempt to get to "real" history by imaginatively thinking themselves into the meaning of the past event. However, Bultmann emphasizes the idea of history itself as past human affairs which vibrate in the present. He pays little attention to Collingwood's historical method. He reads him as supportive of his own existential approach to history. Pannenberg, in contrast, has used Collingwood methodologically and fails to take full account of history as past human actions. While one uses the Oxford idealist to free the New Testament from the demands of history, the other sees him as a means of radically historicizing the biblical events. Their respective treatments of the resurrection provide the most graphic example. [103]

But if Bultmann and Pannenberg err in their use of Collingwood, they err creatively. However, from their erring creativity distortion follows. Collingwood's name is taken in vain. On the one hand, history is pushed out of the picture for the sake of an existential encounter with Christ; on the other hand, New Testament history is objectified to a point beyond the reach of historical method. In a sense history and hermeneutic are linked in rethinking. But each theologian refashions rethinking in his own image moving respectively toward a subjective encounter or an objective reproduction.

Although not a theologian, Collingwood was both a believer and a scientific historian. Rather than extracting from his writings justification for themselves and their work, theologians ought to use a more balanced understanding of his approach to history and hermeneutics. Then they might find themselves with something better to do than to perform a series of "salvage operations" in their attempts "to reconcile the ethic of critical historical inquiry with the apparent demands of Christian faith."[104]

NOTES

1. Walter Schmithals, *An Introduction to the Theology of Rudolf Bultmann* (London: SCM Press, 1968), p. 243.

2. Ted Peters, "Truth in History: Gadamer's Hermeneutics and Pannenberg's Apologetic Method", *Journal of Religion* 58 (1975): 44–56.

3. James C. G. Greig, "Some Aspects of Hermeneutics: A Brief Survey", *Religion* 1 (1971):131.

4. Norman Sykes, "Some Current Conceptions of Historiography and their Significance for Christian Apologetic," *Journal of Theological Studies* 50 (1949): 32.

5. Hartt, Review of *Faith and Reason*, p. 282. As we have indicated in the introduction above, Hartt is both cynical and critical about much of the theological appropriation of Collingwood. This chapter illustrates that there is some validity to his criticism.

6. Collingwood has influenced many and diverse theologians. For a sampling of that influence cf. Sykes, "Current Historiography", 24–37; T. A. Roberts, *History and Christian Apologetic* (London: SPCK, 1960) pp. 1–21; Alan Richardson, *History Sacred and Profane* (Philadelphia: Westminster Press, 1964), pp. 162–66, 184–94; John Navone, *History and Faith in the Thought of Alan Richardson* (London: SCM Press, 1966), pp. 42–43, 50; Paul M. Van Buren, *The Secular Meaning of the Gospel* (New York: Macmillan (1963), pp. 109–17. See above ch. V, fn. 31. Bultmann, the *New Questers*, and Pannenberg will be discussed in this chapter.

Bultmann's use of Collingwood in *History and Eschatology* (1955) is the point of insertion into theological hermeneutics. However, further historical research might well indicate much earlier links through B. H Streeter, R. H. Lightfoot and C. H. Dodd. Syke's article (mentioned above) originally read to the Oxford Society of Historical Theology on May 13, 1948, and S. G. F. Brandon, "Modern Interpretations of History and their Challenge," *Modern Churchman* 39 (1949): 238–52, indicate some of the points of contact which predate Bultmann's use. See also Patrick, *Magdalen Metaphysicals*, pp. 77–108.

7. Rudolf Bultmann, *Jesus and the Word*, trans. Louise Pettibone Smith and Erminie Huntress Lantero (New York: Charles Scribner's, 1958), p. 4.

8. Ibid., p. 8.

9. Ibid., p. 9.

10. Rudolf Bultmann, "New Testament and Mythology," *Kerygma and Myth: A Theological Debate*, ed. Hans Werner Bartsch; trans. rev. ed., Reginald H. Fuller (New York: Harper Torchbooks, 1961), pp. 1–44. As we have seen above, Collingwood's intellectual

journey was not dissimilar. He worked at history and archeology and only later in A and IH presented a theoretical explanation of what he had long been doing.

11. Rudolf Bultmann, "The Problem of Hermeneutics," in Rudolph Bultmann, *Essays Philosophical and Theological*, trans. James C. G. Greig (London: SCM Press Ltd, 1955), pp. 234–61.

12. Bultmann, *History and Eschatology*, esp. pp. 130–37. For a recent but limited treatment of Bultmann's use of Collingwood, see Anthony C. Thiselton, *The Two Horizons: New Testament Hermeneutics and Philosophical Description*. (Grand Rapids: Eerdmans, 1980) pp. 240–245. For an excellent analysis of this study, see the review of Louis Brodie in *Thomist* 45 (1981): 480–486.

13. Bultmann, "Problem of Hermeneutics," pp. 234–40.

14. Schmithals, *Theology of Bultmann*, pp. 236–37.

15. Rudolf Bultmann, *Jesus Christ and Mythology* (New York: Charles Scribner's Sons, 1958), p. 56. The questions of preunderstanding and Bultmann's approach to hermeneutics involve the important difference between *Existenzial* and *Existenziell*. For discussion of that issue see: Bultmann, "Problem of Hermeneutics", pp. 235–36, fn. 2; cf. John Macquarrie, An Existentialist Theology: A Comparison of Heidegger and Bultmann (New York: Macmillan, 1955), pp. 33–35.

16. Bultmann, *Jesus Christ and Mythology*, p. 84.

17. Bultmann, *History and Eschatology*, p. 130.

18. Ibid., pp. 130–35.

19. See Martin Kähler, *The So-Called Historical Jesus and the Historic Biblical Christ*, trans., ed. Carl E. Braaten (Philadelphia: Fortress Press, 1964).

20. William G. Doty, *Contemporary New Testament Interpretation* (Englewood Cliffs: Prentice-Hall Inc., 1972), p. 22.

21. Bultmann, *History and Eschatology*, p. 131.

22. André Malet, *The Thought of Rudolf Bultmann*, trans. Richard Strachan, preface by Rudolf Bultmann (Garden City: Doubleday, 1971), p. 78.

23. Ibid., p. 78; cf. Bultmann, *History and Eschatology*, pp. 131–32.

24. Bultmann, *History and Eschatology*, p. 132; cf. IH, p. 247.

25. Bultmann often seems to be speaking of evidence, as evidence of the human condition as such, and not as evidence of a particular past. This would appear to be close to Gordon Kaufman's understanding of the evidence used for the construction of myth discussed above at the end of Chap. V.

26. Bultmann, *History and Eschatology*, p. 133. Many theologians, including John

Macquarrie, James Robinson and Hugh Anderson, have followed Bultmann in applying the tag "existential" to Collingwood.

27. Bultmann, *History and Eschatology*, p. 134.

28. Ibid., p. 135.

29. Ibid.; cf. IH, p. 305.

30. Bultmann, *History and Eschatology*, pp. 135–36; cf. Greig, "Some Aspects of Hermeneutics," 142.

31. Hopkins, "Bultmann on Collingwood," 288.

32. IH, p. 120.

33. Bultmann, *History and Eschatology*, p. 136.

34. Ibid.

35. A, pp. 89–106, 147–67; cf. Rubinoff, "Religion and the Rapprochement," pp. 79–112.

36. Rubinoff, *Reform of Metaphysics*, p. 292.

37. SM, p. 303; cf. RP, pp. 191–211 and "The Devil" in *Faith and Reason*, ed. Rubinoff, pp. 212–33; Rubinoff, "Religion and the Rapprochement," pp. 100–03.

38. A, p. 128, fn. 1; cf. Hopkins, "Bultmann on Collingwood," pp. 231–32.

39. A. O. Dyson, *The Immortality of the Past* (London: SCM Press, 1974), pp. 83–84 states that Bultmann, along with others is seeking confirmation "of his own theological approach in a congenial historical theory (if it is in fact a *historical* theory)."

40. Bultmann, "New Testament and Mythology", p. 41; cf. Hugh Anderson *Jesus and Christian Origins* (New York: Oxford University Press, 1964), pp. 205–11.

41. Bultmann, "New Testament and Mythology," p. 39.

42. See for example, Mink, *Mind, History and Dialectic*, pp. 7–12.

43. EPM, p. 49. See Stevenson, *History as Myth*, pp. 82–83. The question as to whether too great a disjunction dominates all of Bultmann's approach is too large to be treated here. Cf. Macquarrie, *Scope of Demythologizing*, pp. 58–100, 245–48; Van A. Harvey and Schubert M. Ogden, "How New is the 'New Quest of the Historical Jesus'?" in *The Historical Jesus and the Kerygmatic Christ*, trans and ed. by Carl E. Braaten and Roy A. Harrisville (New York: Abingdon Press, 1964), pp. 197–242.

44. Harvey and Ogden "How New is New Quest," pp. 210–11.

45. See especially Bultmann, *Jesus and the Word;* Idem, *Primitive Christianity in its Contemporary Setting*, trans. R. H. Fuller (New York: Meridian Books, 1956).

46. Schubert M. Ogden, *Christ Without Myth* (New York: Harper & Row, 1961), p. 83.

47. RP, pp. 73–88; see Stevenson's critique *(History as Myth* p. 84) where the false disjunction in Bultmann can also be read as a criticism of Bultmann's use of Collingwood. "In terms of our own analysis, this introduction of the False Disjunction assumes that critical historical knowledge has an independent status, which in fact it does not possess; and it also falsifies the dynamics of historical knowledge by obscuring the intimate relationship between existential, historical interpretation in the "now" of decision, and the content of the past in relation to which decision is made. Whenever this disjunction appears, it manifests itself in the most dubious ways, as, for example, when Bultmann affirms that faith must be held apart from history in its *historisch* aspect because God 'can only be believed upon in defiance of all outward appearance,' and that this 'is in fact a perfect parallel to St. Paul's and Luther's doctrine of justification by faith alone apart from the works of the Law.' Bultmann's position, in other words, is that history (Historie) like sin and good works, looks to the past; while eschatological history looks to and lives from the future. But this is just the disjunction which, we have maintained, violates the nature of historical existence and knowledge."

48. Robinson, *New Quest*, p. 39.

49. RP, p. 78.

50. Merkley, "New Quests for Old," 205; cf. Nicol, "History and Transcendence," p. 88. Since Collingwood's name is often linked with the new questers, a systematic treatment of their use of him was originally envisioned for this study. However, a reading of the key statements of Robinson, Käsemann, Bornkamm, Fuchs and Ebeling suggests the use of ideas bearing resemblance to Collingwood's but not critical exposition of those ideas. There appears to be no detailed treatment of Collingwood by any writers connected with the so-called new quest for the historical Jesus. The only direct use made of Collingwood is Robinson's, *New Quest*, pp. 31, 42, 71. Even here however, the position is left general and unexamined; cf. Biehl, "Zur Frage" pp. 69–76. Appropriation of Collingwood's name seems totally dependent on Bultmann's treatment. Merkley, in a caustic critique of the new quest, claims that their enthusiasm for Collingwood "is based upon an egregious misinterpretation of his famous distinction between the 'inside' and 'outside' of 'events.'" (p. 205). Merkley unfortunately includes Pannenberg in his critique and fails to note that Pannenberg attempts a more serious and probing application of Collingwood. Harvey and Ogden, "How New is New Quest," p. 240, fn. 118, criticize Robinson's appeal to the hermeneutics of Collingwood and Dilthey. See also, Rudolf Bultmann, "The Primitive Christian Kerygma and the Historical Jesus," in *Historical Jesus and Kerygmatic Christ*, eds. Carl Braaten and Roy A. Harrisville (New York: Abingdon Press, 1964), pp. 15–42.

51. Günther Bornkamm, *Jesus of Nazareth*, tr. Irene and Fraser McLuskey with James M. Robinson (New York: Harper and Row, 1960), pp. 24–25.

52. Robinson, *New Quest*, p. 68.

53. IH, p. 304; cf. Merkley, "New Quests for Old," p. 208.

54. Harvey and Ogden, "How New is New Quest," p. 234.

55. Anderson, *Jesus and Christian Origins*, p. 181 criticizes the new quester's claims and

places some of the blame on the "existential approach to history" which he lays at the feet of Dilthey, Heidegger and Collingwood. However, it is obvious that Collingwood's philosophy of history and historical method can only be labelled existential if accompanied by many qualifiers.

56. Ogden, *Christ Without Myth*, p. 107.

57. See above ch. 3, fn. 57; see also Mink, *Mind, History and Dialectic*, p. 6 for the influence of Whitehead on the later Collingwood.

58. RP, p. 86. For Ogden's position see *Christ Without Myth*, pp. 111–26. Ogden's reluctance to relate a "possibility in principle" to a "possibility in fact," the "*geschichthich*" with the "*historisch*" contrasts sharply with Collingwood's "concrete universal" where the universal can only be grasped in individual being or history; cf. Norman J. Young, *History and Existential Theory* (Philadelphia: Westminster Press, 1969), pp. 111–18.

59. Bultmann's "Exegesis without Presuppositions?" reflects clearly Collingwood's approach, not only by manifesting the importance of presuppositions but also the need to rethink the past. "But even a free decision does not happen without a cause, without a motive; and the task of the historian is to come to know the motives of actions" (p. 291).

60. See above chap. 1, fn. 4.

61. Pannenberg, *Basic Questions* 1: 125–28.

62. Ibid., 1: 109.

63. Ibid, 1: 123–24.

64. Geoffrey Turner, "Wolfhart Pannenberg and the Hermeneutical Problem," *Irish Theological Quarterly* 39 (1972): 117.

65. Pannenberg, *Theology and Philosophy of Science*, p. 169; cf. Idem, *Basic Questions* 1: 125–28.

66. For a summary of Pannenberg's views on revelation see his "Dogmatic Theses on the Doctrine of Revelation" in *Revelation as History*, eds. Wolfhart Pannenberg, Rolf Rendtorff, Trutz Rendtorff and Ulrich Wilkens, trans. David Granskow (London: Macmillan, 1968), pp. 125–28.

67. IH, p. 54.

68. See EM, pp. 185–90, 290–95 and IH, pp. 315–20.

69. IH, p. 104.

70. Pannenberg, "Foreward" to *Basic Questions*, I: xviii. He points out that the "history of the transmission of tradition" alters his earlier position of history as "event suspended between promise and fulfillment"; cf. E. Frank Tupper, *The Theology of Wolfhart Pannenberg* (Philadelphia: Westminster Press, 1973), pp. 102–07. Here Tupper presents a summary of the "history of the transmission of traditions." Although Collingwood

would have difficulties with Pannenberg's universal history, his notions of the rethinking process and incapsulation as presented in A prove supportive of "transmission of traditions", and the unity of the future as creative of present and past. See Wolfhart Pannenberg, *Theology and the Kingdom of God* (Philadelphia: Westminster Press, 1969), p. 61. Unfortunately Pannenberg seems only to be conversant with IH.

71. Wolfhart Pannenberg, "Response to the Discussion," in *New Frontiers in Theology* vol. 3: *Theology as History* eds. James M. Robinson and John B. Cobb, Jr. (New York: Harper & Row, 1967), pp. 228–29; cf. Turner, "Pannenberg and Hermeneutical Problem," 114.

72. Pannenberg, *Basic Questions* 1:12.

73. Ibid., 1: 21.

74. Ibid.

75. IH, pp. 49–52. It is Collingwood's position that history as the "historical understanding of reality" arose out of the biblical experience; see Stevenson, *History of Myth*, p. 33.

76. Pannenberg, *Basic Questions*, 1: 199; cf. Tupper, *Theology of Pannenberg*, pp. 97–98.

77. Pannenberg, *Basic Questions*, 1: 70.

78. Ibid., p. 68.

79. Ibid., 1: 71–72.

80. Ibid., 1: 70, n. 138.

81. Ibid., 1: 78.

82. Ibid., 1: 79.

83. Ibid., 1: 72.

84. The numerous problems and critique of Pannenberg's treatment cannot be adequately covered here. Principle sources are: Wolfhart Pannenberg, *Jesus-God and Man*, trans. Lewis L. Wilkins and Duane A. Priebe (Philadelphia: Westminster Press, 1968), pp. 88–106; "Did Jesus Really Rise from the Dead," *Dialog* 4 (1965): 128–35. Helpful commentaries include: Herbert Burhenn, "Pannenberg's Argument for the Historicity of the Resurrection," *Journal of the American Academy of Religion* 40 (1972): 368–79; Daniel P. Fuller, "The Resurrection of Jesus and the Historical Method," *Journal of Bible and Religion* 34 (1966): 18–24; Ted Peters, "The Use of Analogy in Historical Method," *Catholic Biblical Quarterly* 35 (1973): 475–82; Robert North, "Pannenberg's Historicizing Exegesis,"*The Heythrop Journal* 12 (1971): 377–400; Carl E. Braaten, *New Directions in Theology Today*, vol. 2: *History and Hermeneutics* (Philadelphia: Westminster Press, 1966), pp. 91–102.

85. Pannenberg, "Did Jesus Really Rise," pp. 128–31.

86. Ibid., p. 131; cf. Wolfhart Pannenberg, *What is Man?*, trans. Duane A. Priebe (Philadelphia: Fortress Press, 1972).

87. Pannenberg, *Jesus*, p. 109; Idem, *Theology and Philosophy of Science*, pp. 145–47. Pannenberg appears to be defending miracles at the expense of the historical method, his position however is more complicated and sensitive to that method. For example he claims to accept the principle of historical analogy but adds his own criticism about its limits. He is critical of positivist historians' use of analogy and their failure to realize its limits. He wants to protect the contingency of individual events and leave room for the new and unexpected. With the intention of making historical space for the resurrection, he replies to his critics. "My criticism is not directed against the critical use of the principle of analogy, which is basic to the critical historical method. This use is merely restricted. The instrument of analogy gains precision, if judgements about the historicity or nonhistoricity of events asserted in the tradition are based only on *positive* analogies between the tradition which is being studied and situations known elsewhere, but not on the *lack* of such analogies." Pannenberg, "Response to the Discussion," pp. 264–65, n. 75. Cf. Fuller, "Resurrection" 21–24 and Peters, "Use of Analogy" 475–82.

88. Pannenberg, *Jesus*, p. 74; "Did Jesus Really Rise," 129.

89. Pannenberg, *Jesus*, pp. 105–06. Analyzing Pannenberg's treatment of the biblical texts would bring us far beyond our immediate task. Burhenn, "Historicity of Resurrection", 370, handily summarizes his historical treatment in two theses: "(1) no coherent or plausible naturalistic account can be given of the transition from Jesus' death to the activity and message of the primitive church; (2) the best explanation of this transition is one which refers to "real" appearances (i.e. with extrasubjective basis) of the resurrected Lord and to a "really" empty grave."

90. Pannenberg, *Jesus*, p. 81.

91. Pannenberg qualifies this indicating that the hoped for resurrection was of a general nature and not necessarily individual. See "Did Jesus Really Rise?" 130–31.

92. Pannenberg, *Jesus*, p. 98.

93. Allan D. Galloway, *Wolfhart Pannenberg* (London: Allen and Unwin, 1973), p. 39.

94. Pannenberg, "Doctrine of Revelation," pp. 152–53; cf. Galloway, *Pannenberg*, p. 39.

95. Tjalve, "Collingwood og Theologerne," p. 7. Overall Tjalve rejects the interpretation of Collingwood offered by Pannenberg, Sykes and Van Buren. He believes Bultmann has best understood and applied Collingwood.

96. Pannenberg, "Response to Discussion," pp. 221–76.

97. Burhenn, "Historicity of Resurrection," p. 378. See also North, "Historicizing Exegesis", p. 396–400.

98. Pannenberg accepts the critique but the question can be raised as to whether he has moved far enough on the basis of that critique. His understanding of revelatory history seems to fit into Collingwood's category of "critical" history. He consistently uses

the term "critical-historical method." Collingwood calls his own approach, "scientific history," and considers "critical" history as not too far removed from "scissors and paste" history (IH, pp. 258–60 and 274–82). In critical history documents are viewed as sources containing statements. Such statements may be used to support historical hypothesis. Scientific history, on the other hand, contains no ready-made statements. All statements are treated as evidence which evoke meaning. Pannenberg's position remains somewhat ambiguous since he uses both approaches. However, his constant use of the term "critical" may betray something of his overly objective approach to revelation and history and indicates a subtle dependence on Dilthey who never really left the positivist model of history. See *New Catholic Encyclopedia*, A, 1967, ed., s.v. "Dilthey, Wilhelm," by P. L. Hug. Pannenberg's ambiguity in this and his movement at times closer to Collingwood's model is indicated in the next footnote.

99. Wolfhart Pannenberg, *Faith and Reality*, trans. John Maxwell (Philadelphia: Westminster Press, 1977), p. 71. In this small book, Pannenberg, again endorses the historical method and indicates his agreement with Collingwood's analogy of historical research to criminal investigation. He also indicates an open-endedness to history. "The conclusions of such historical research are never completely incontestable. They are always more or less probable and can be changed by new discoveries and new approaches to the problem. Nevertheless, historically-assured certainty is the greatest certainty we can ever have of past events. If Christian faith presupposes information about events of a distant past, it can gain the greatest possible certainty about those events only by historical research."

100. See, Peters "Truth in History", p. 52–53, fn. 66, where he refers to Burhenn's, "Historicity of Resurrection", as "the only convincing critique of Pannenberg's proof. . . ." Burhenn claims that the arguments Pannenberg offers are not specifically historical. Peters adds, "Pannenberg recognizes this fact and claims that the presuppositions of historical-critical method preclude a genuine evaluation of the evidence regarding Jesus' resurrection."

101. In this Pannenberg appears to follow a line similar to Richardson's use of Collingwood. See Richardson, *History Sacred and Profane*, pp. 197–200 and Anthony Hanson, "Alan Richardson and his Critics in the Area of Hermeneutics," in *Theology and Change: Essays in Memory of Alan Richardson* (London: SCM Press, 1975), pp. 39–40.

102. See, Pannenberg, *Theology and Philosophy of Science*. For an excellent analysis and evaluation of this work see Edmund J. Dobbin, "Seminar on Foundations: Pannenberg on Theological Method" Catholic Theological Society of America, *Proceedings of the Thirty-Second Annual Convention* 32 (1977): 202–20. "Scientific Method as it emerges from Pannenberg's dialogue with Popper then is: the systematic elaboration and critical corraboration of hypotheses in the light of the available evidence. This method, while recognizing the need for presuppositions in all interpretation, presupposes that there are no dogmatic or self-evident truths unassailable in principle by critical examination," (p. 205). History is a critical science in this sense. Dilthey is indicated as Pannenberg's source for "the central idea of his own thought, i.e. Dilthey's contextual definition of meaning. For Dilthey meaning is always a relationship between a whole and its parts. As experienced by human beings meaning is the very structure of life. Human life is a system of interrelated experiences, open to itself, essentially historical, and forming a whole which at any given moment is not yet given." (p. 207). Dobbin concludes this section of his paper with a dialogue with Gadamer. "In contrast with Gadamer, then, Pannenberg presents the hermeneutical event of interpretation as a methodical event of

construction, consciously controlled to a high degree by the interpreter. Pannenberg of course recognizes tacit factors involved in this process." (pp. 210–11). With hind-sight afforded by *Theology and the Philosophy of Science* it can be seen that Pannenberg's use of Collingwood's method is strongly affected by a contextualist definition of meaning and a critical rationalist view of science as the testing of hypothesis against data.

103. Perhaps the best use of Collingwood's understanding of history and historical method as applied to the events of Jesus' life and especially the resurrection is that of Kaufman, *Systematic Theology*, for his treatment of the resurrection see, pp. 411–34.

104. Harvey, *Historian and the Believer*, p. 246.

CONCLUSION

It will not be necessary to summarize here the findings that have emerged from this study. We would rather like to conclude by critically correlating Collingwood's contribution to hermeneutical theory with recent attempts at solving problems that are encountered by anyone who seeks to translate biblical meanings into the fabric of a later time. This might be an appropriate way to take leave of our task and set the stage for tasks still to come.

The problem of hermeneutics for the Christian theologian is the translation of meaning of the biblical message to a highly secular and post-industrial world which, ironically, is acutely aware of its own historicity and yet anti-historical. Attempts at solving this problem have appeared in various guises. The recent history of biblical theology, however, indicates that the paradigm of that discipline has been the descriptive task which sets it off from the more properly hermeneutical task being assigned to systematic theology. Biblical theology understood in this strictly descriptive, "historical" sense quite frankly opts for finding a meaning-meant-then and leaves a meaning that can be meant now to a subsequent interpretative step in theology. Stendahl's position, for example, appears to be that anything beyond such a descriptive approach detracts from the respect which is due the historicity of the biblical message, divorces the interpreter from the challenge of the original text and makes the next, hermeneutical step impossible.[1] The presumption here is that the past can somehow be apprehended without interference from the present. A sharp dichotomy is drawn between past and present, normative and interpretative, historical and hermeneutical.

From a philosophical and methodological perspective, Collingwood's contribution serves to expose such neat distinctions as illusory and casts a completely different light on the nature of biblical theology. In his "scientific" history, the descriptive task and the hermeneutical task go on together. There can be no historical reconstruction without translation of meaning and, to a great extent, translation of meaning involves a reconstruction of it. The historical process that reaches a "then" is a hermeneutical process that is controlled by a "now". But the "now" in such an historical-hermeneutical approach is clearly exposed as the processive offspring of a "then". The architecture of Stendahl's dichotomy between the descriptive and the hermeneutical tasks falls apart.

We have examined how Bultmann and Pannenberg grapple with the translation of meaning into the present. Both employ Collingwood in that task. However in each case the hermeneutical process is adversely affected by a dated understanding of history. Bultmann and Pannenberg are dependent on a pre-Collingwood "critical" model of history, which remains precariously close to an objective-positivist model. Although they creatively and effectively apply various elements of Collingwood's approach, neither Bultmann's existential encounter with the "inside" of history nor Pannenberg's "reproduction" of the "outside" of history expresses adequately the implications of his theory of history for hermeneutics. Sharp dichotomies between the outside and inside of history, the existential and the historical, and faith and history distort their visions of the event of understanding and translation. In summary, it can be said that the attempts made at resolving the translation problem have this in common: they rely heavily on dichotomies, on unilateral emphasis and on exclusive claims.

While distinctions and dichotomies serve a useful role in analysis, for the task of synthesis which understanding and translation is, they must be overcome. It is precisely here that Collingwood's contribution is of immense help. His investment in historical method yields a hermeneutical dividend.[2] The fruit of the controversial re-enactment and incapsulation theories is the intricate interweaving of the historical and hermeneutical processes. It seems obvious that reconstruction of the past demands understanding in the present, but if our interpretation of Collingwood has validity, the reverse is also true. In order to understand an expression from the past, one must engage in reconstruction of that past itself. The re-enactment theory describes how the mind, when confronted with an expression of the past, sets about constructing a past context and meaning, but always in the wider context of later happenings and present meanings. Re-enactment of past thought by interpreting evidence entails both reconstruction and translation of meaning.

The question of the translation of meaning and its importance for theology in its biblical, historical and systematic forms is of course far from settled. However Collingwood's linking of the historical and the hermeneutical in the re-enactment theory contributes to what is required both to advance the state of the question and to transcend some rigid and false dichotomies. Inflexible barriers between the descriptive and the hermeneutical, the contextual and textual, are awarded the same fate as the false dichotomy between the outside and inside of history. Biblical, historical theology is hermeneutical; systematic, hermeneutical theology is historical. Not only does hermeneutics prohibit an abstract separation of meaning "then" from meaning "now", sound "scientific" history based on the very historicity of understanding does the same.[3]

Collingwood's contribution does not provide a new hermeneutical orthodoxy. On the contrary, his theory of how the past is known upsets the comfort found in the all too neat current orthodoxies. Nonetheless, his contribution strongly supports recent efforts to move hermeneutics to a next step. Neither contextualism, with its grounding in original intention and the past as such, nor textualism, with its insistence on the autonomy of the text in the present, allows meaning in the fullest sense, with its confluence of past, present and future, to emerge. He brings us beyond the context-text split and, understood hermeneutically, should be located as a key precursor for the next integrative step in the ascent of hermeneutics pioneered by Gadamer. The "fusion of horizons" and reenactment both attempt to transcend rigid dichotomies in describing what happens when past and present put each other to the question.[4] Collingwood also provides clarifying insights for Gadamer's integrative effort in that his approach emphasizes the historical method, and clearly articulates the relation between the interpretation of texts and reconstruction of the historical past within the functioning of the historically effective consciousness.

In obedience to the dialectic of question and answer, it might be in order to conclude by adverting to some of the work that remains to be done. Influenced by his reading of Marx, Collingwood moved in his later years toward a *rapprochement* between theory and practice. He may have much to contribute to the current attempt at determining what is to be the role of praxis in the emergence of interpretation. His theory of history would call for an interpretation that reacts adversely to an isolated word theology and strongly favors social implications.[5] Other areas of inquiry where Collingwood is relevant are the functioning of mythic consciousness and the conception of theology as story.[6] In both cases religious meanings are constructed out of one's own personal or communal history. Finally, further study of Collingwood's incapsulation theory should offer considerable help toward understanding the development of dogma as the ongoing transmission of meanings within a tradition.

NOTES

1. Stendahl, "Biblical Theology," p. 425; cf. Roy A. Harrisville, "Introduction" to Peter Stuhlmacher: *Historical Criticism and Theological Interpretation of Scripture*, trans. Roy A. Harrisville (Philadelphia: Fortress Press, 1977), p. 9.

2. It is somewhat ironic that Collingwood's only book dealing principally with religion, *Religion and Philosophy* does not constitute the bulk of his contribution to religion and theology. That contribution had to wait for his later writings in the philosophy of history with their overtones for hermeneutical theory.

3. Cf. Ommen, *Hermeneutic of Dogma*, pp. 231–32. Ommen adds that the "final unity" in theology does not deny the need for what Lonergan calls "functional specialization" allowing for historical theology and "mediating theology."

4. Nicol, "History and Transendence", p. 85 claims that Gadamer's statement, "Genuine historical *(historisches)* thinking must always operate in critical awareness of its own historicality *(Geschichtlichkeit)*," provides a succinct summary of what Collingwood means by an imaginative and critical re-enactment of past thought in the present. That statement illustrates the essentially dialogial and dialectical nerve of history discussed in this study. See above, the conclusion to chap. VI.

5. Cf. A, pp. 147–67; Rubinoff, "Religion and Rapprochement"; Thomas F. O'Meara, "Bultmann and Tomorrow's Theology", in *Rudolf Bultmann in Catholic Thought*, eds. Thomas F. O'Meara and Donald M. Weisser (New York: Herder & Herder, 1968), pp. 244–49.

6. See above, the conclusion to chap. V; cf. James B. Wiggins, *Religion as Story* (New York: Harper & Row, 1975); John Shea, "Theology as Autobiography", *Commonweal* 105 (June 16, 1978): 358–62; IDEM, *Stories of God: An Unauthorized Biography* (Chicago: Thomas More Press, 1978).

SELECTED BIBLIOGRAPHY

Primary Sources
R. G. Collingwood

Books

Archaeology of Roman Britain. London: Methuen, 1930.

Autobiography. London: Oxford University Press, 1939.

Essay on Metaphysics. Oxford: Clarendon Press, 1940.

Essay on Philosophical Method. Oxford: Clarendon Press, 1933.

First Mate's Log. London: Oxford University Press, 1940.

Idea of History. Edited by T. M. Knox. Oxford: Clarendon Press, 1946.

Idea of Nature. Edited by T. M. Knox. Oxford: Clarendon Press, 1945.

New Leviathan. Oxford: Clarendon Press, 1942; Reprinted New York: Thomas Y. Crowell, 1971.

Outlines of a Philosophy of Art. London: Oxford University Press, 1925. Reprinted in *Essays in the Philosophy of Art.* Edited by Alan Donagan. Bloomington: Indiana University Press, 1946.

Principles of Art. London: Clarendon Press, 1938.

Religion and Philosophy. London: Macmillan Co., 1916; partially reprinted in *Faith and Reason.* Edited by Lionel Rubinoff. Chicago: Quadrangle Books, 1968.

Roman Britain. Oxford: Clarendon Press, revised edition, 1934.

Roman Britain and the English Settlements. With J. N. L. Meyers. Oxford: Clarendon Press, 1924.

Speculum Mentis or The Map of Knowledge. Oxford: Clarendon Press, 1924.

Articles & Pamphlets

"Are History and Science Different Kinds of Knowledge?" *Mind* 31 (1922): 443–51. Reprinted in *Essays in the Philosophy of History*, pp. 23–33. Edited by William Debbins. Austin: University of Texas Press, 1965.

"Can the New Idealism Dispense with Mysticism?" *Proceedings of the Aristotelian Society*, Supplement 3 (1923): 161–75. Reprinted in *Faith and Reason*, pp. 270–82. Edited by Lionel Rubinoff. Chicago: Quadrangle Books, 1968.

"Croce's Philosophy of History." *Hibbert Journal* 19 (1921): 263–78. Reprinted in *Essays in the Philosophy of History*, pp. 3–22. Edited by William Debbins. University of Texas Press, 1965.

"Devil." In *Concerning Prayer.* Edited by B. H. Streeter et al. London: Macmillan, 1916. Reprinted by *Faith and Reason*, pp. 212–33. Edited by Lionel Rubinoff. Chicago: Quadrangle Books, 1968.

"Economics as a Philosophical Science." *International Journal of Ethics* 36 (1926): 162–85.

Faith and Reason. London: Ernest Benn, 1928. Reprinted in *Faith and Reason*, pp. 122–47. Edited by Lionel Rubinoff. Chicago: Quadrangle Books, 1968.

"Fascism and Nazism." *Philosophy* 15 (1940): 168–76.

"Form and Content in Art." *Journal of Philosophical Studies* 4 (1929): 332–45. Reprinted in *Philosophy of Art*, pp. 211–32. Edited by Alan Donagan. Bloomington: Indiana University Press, 1946.

"Historical Imagination." Oxford: Clarendon Press, 1935. Reprinted in *Idea of History*, pp. 231–49. Edited by T. M. Knox.

Human Nature and Human History. London: H. Milford, 1936. Reprinted in *Proceedings of the British Academy* 22 (1937): 97–127 and *Idea of History*, pp. 205–31. Edited by T. M. Knox.

"Limits of Historical Knowledge." *Journal of Philosophical Studies* 3 (1928):

213–22. Reprinted in *Essays in the Philosophy of History,* pp. 34–56. Edited by William Debbins. Austin: University of Texas Press, 1965.

"Nature and Aim of a Philosophy of History." In *Essays in the Philosophy of History.* Edited by William Debbins. Austin: University of Texas Press, 1965.

"On the So-Called Idea of Causation." *Proceedings of the Aristotelian Society* 38(1937–38): 85–112.

"Oswald Spengler and the Theory of Historical Cycles." *Antiquity* 1 (1927): 311–25. Reprinted in *Essays in the Philosophy of History,* pp. 57–75. Edited by William Debbins. Austin: University of Texas Press, 1965.

Philosophy of History. London: G. Bell, 1930. Reprinted in *Essays in the Philosophy of History,* pp. 121–39. Edited by William Debbins. Austin: University of Texas Press, 1965.

"Philosophy of Progress." *Realist* 1 (1929): 64–77. Reprinted in *Essays in the Philosophy of History,* pp. 104–20. Edited by William Debbins. Austin: University of Texas Press, 1965.

"Place of Art in Education." *Hibbert Journal* 24 (1926): 434–48. Reprinted in *Essays in the Philosophy of Art.* Edited by Alan Donagan. Bloomington: Indiana University Press, 1946.

"Plato's Philosophy of Art." *Mind* 34 (1925): 154–72. Reprinted in *Essays in the Philosophy of Art.* Edited by Alan Donagan. Bloomington: Indiana University Press, 1946.

"Political Action." *Proceedings of the Aristotelian Society* 29 (1928–29): 155–76.

"Present Need of a Philosophy." *Philosophy* 9 (1943): 262–65.

"Reason is Faith Cultivating Itself." *Hibbert Journal* 26 (1927): 3–14. Reprinted in *Faith and Reason,* pp. 108–21. Edited by Lionel Rubinoff. Chicago: Quadrangle Books, 1968.

"Religion, Science and Philosophy." *Truth and Freedom* 2 (1926): Reprinted in *Faith and Reason.* Edited by Lionel Rubinoff. Chicago: Quadrangle Books. 1968.

Ruskin's Philosophy. Kendal: T. Wilson, 1922. Reprinted in *Essays in the Philosophy of Art.* Edited by Alan Donagan. Bloomington: Indiana University Press, 1946.

"Sensation and Thought." *Proceedings of the Aristotelian Society* 24 (1925–26): 55–76.

"Some Perplexities about Time: With an Attempted Solution." Proceedings of the Aristotelian Society 26 (1925–26): 135–50.

"Theory of Historical Cycles." *Antiquity* 1 (1927): 435–56. Reprinted in *Essays in the Philosophy of History*, pp. 76–89. Edited by William Debbins. Austin: University of Texas Press, 1965.

Three Laws of Politics. London: Oxford University Press, 1941. Reprinted in *The New Leviathan*, pp. 184–91.

"What is the Problem of Evil?" *Theology* 1 (1920). Reprinted in *Faith and Reason*, pp. 148–58. Edited by Lionel Rubinoff. Chicago: Quadrangle Books, 1968.

Anthologies

Donagan, Alan, editor. *Essays in the Philosophy of Art by R. G. Collingwood.* Bloomington: Indiana University Press, 1946.

Debbins, William, editor. *Essays in the Philosophy of History by R. G. Collingwood.* Austin: University of Texas Press, 1965.

Rubinoff, Lionel, editor. *Faith and Reason: Essays in the Philosophy of Religion by R. G. Collingwood.* Chicago: Quadrangle Books, 1968.

Secondary Sources

Books

Achtemeier, Paul J. *An Introduction to the New Hermeneutic.* Philadelphia: Westminster Press, 1969.

Albright, W. F. *History, Archaeology and Christian Humanism.* New York: McGraw-Hill, 1964.

Anderson, Charles C. *Critical Quests of Jesus.* Grand Rapids: William B. Eerdmans, 1969.

Anderson, Hugh. *Jesus and Christian Origins.* New York: Oxford University Press, 1964.

Ayer, Alfred Jules. *Language, Truth and Logic.* London: Gollancz, 1947.

———, *Philosophy in the Twentieth Century.* New York: Vintage Books, 1984.

Barbour, Ian G. *Issues in Science and Religion.* New York: Harper Torchbooks, 1971.

Barth, Karl. *The Epistle to the Romans.* 6th ed. Translated by Edwin C. Koskyns. London: Oxford University Press, 1933.

Bateson, Gregory. *Steps to an Ecology of Mind.* San Francisco: Chandler, 1972.

Betti, Emilio. *Teoria generale della interpretazione,* 2 Vols. Milan: Giuffre, 1955.

Bianchi, Eugene C. and Ruether, Rosemary Radford. *From Machismo to Mutuality: Woman-Man Liberation.* New York: Paulist Press, 1976.

Bornkamm, Günther. *Jesus of Nazareth.* Translated by Irene & Fraser McLuskey with James M. Robinson. New York: Harper & Row, 1960.

Braaten, Carl E. *New Directions in Theology Today.* Vol. 2: *History and Hermeneutics.* Philadelphia: Westminster Press, 1966.

Bradley, F. H. *The Presuppositions of Critical History.* Introduction & Commentary by Lionel Rubinoff. Chicago: Quadrangle Books, 1968.

Bultmann, Rudolf. *Essays Philosophical and Theological.* Translator James C. G. Greig. London: SCM Press, 1955.

———. *Existence and Faith: Shorter Writings of Rudolf Bultmann.* Translation & Introduction by Schubert M. Ogden. New York: Meridian Books, 1960.

———. *History and Eschatology: The Presence of Eternity.* New York: Harper Torchbooks, 1957.

———. *Jesus Christ and Mythology.* New York: Charles Scribner, 1958.

———. *Jesus and the Word.* Translated by Louise Pettibone Smith and Erminie Huntress Lantero. New York: Charles Scribner, 1958.

———. *Primitive Christianity in its Contemporary Setting.* Translated by R. H. Fuller. New York: Meridian Books, 1956.

———. and Five Critics. *Kerygma and Myth: A Theological Debate.* Edited by Hans Werner Bartsch. Revised edition translated by Reginald H. Fuller. New York: Harper Torchbooks, 1961.

Butterfield, Herbert. *Christianity and History*. London: Belt, 1949.

——— . *Man and His Past: The Study of the History of Historical Scholarship*. Cambridge: Cambridge University Press, 1955.

Carr, Edward Hallet. *What Is History?* New York: Vintage Books, 1961.

Casserly, J. V. Langmead. *The Christian in Philosophy*. London: Faber & Faber, 1949.

——— . *Toward A Theology of History*. New York: Holt, Rinehart & Winston, 1965.

Childs, Brevard S. *Memory and Tradition in Israel*. Naperville: Alec R. Allenson, Inc., 1962.

Connolly, James M. *Human History and the Word of God*. New York: Macmillan, 1965.

Coreth, Emerich. *Grundfragen der Hermeneutik: Ein philosophischer Beitrag*. Freiburg in Br.: Herder, 1969.

Croce, Benedetto. *An Autobiography*. Translator R. G. Collingwood. Oxford: Clarendon Press, 1927. Reprinted Freeport, N.Y.: Books for Libraries Press, 1970.

——— . *History as the Story of Liberty*. Translator Sylvia Sprigge. New York: W. W. Norton, 1941.

——— . *The Philosophy of Giambattista Vico*. Translator R. G. Collingwood. London: Latimer, 1913. Reissued by Allen and Unwin in the Library of Philosophy series.

D'Arcy, M. C. *The Meaning and Matter of History: A Christian View*. New York: Farrar, Straus and Co., 1959.

Dilthey, Wilheim. *Dilthey's Philosophy of Existence*. Translator William Kluback and Martin Weinbaum. New York: Bookman Associates, 1957.

——— . *Pattern and Meaning in History*. Edited by H. P. Rickman. New York: Harper Torchbooks, 1962.

Dodd, C. H. *The Founder of Christianity*. New York: Macmillan and Co., 1970.

Donagan, Alan. *The Later Philosophy of R. G. Collingwood*. Oxford: Clarendon Press, 1962.

Doty, William G. *Contemporary New Testament Interpretation*. Englewood Cliffs, N.J.: Prentice-Hall Inc., 1972.

Dray, W. H. *Laws and Explanation in History*. London: Oxford University Press, 1957.

Dyson, A. O. *The Immortality of the Past*. London: SCM Press, 1974.

Ebeling, Gerhard. *God and Word*. Translator James W. Leitch. Philadelphia: Fortress Press, 1967.

———. *The Nature of Faith*. Translator Ronald Gregor Smith. Philadelphia: Fortress Press, 1961.

———. *The Problem of Historicity in the Church and its Proclamation*. Translator Grover Foley. Philadelphia: Fortress Press, 1967.

———. *Word and Faith*. Translator James W. Leitch. Philadelphia: Fortress Press, 1963.

Encyclopedia of Philosophy, 1967ed. S. V. "Collingwood, Robin George," by Alan Donagan.

Fackenheim, Emil L. *Metaphysics and Historicity*. Aquinas Lecture. Milwaukee: Marquette University Press, 1961.

Fuchs, Ernst. *Ermeneutica*. Translator Carmelo Vigna. Milano: Celuc, 1974 (German edition: *Hermeneutik*. Tübingen: J. C. B. Mohr (Paul Siebeck), 1970).

———. *Studies of the Historical Jesus*. Translator Andrew Scobie. London: SCM Press, 1964.

Fuller, Daniel P. *Easter Faith and History*. Grand Rapids: Eerdmans, 1964.

Funk, Robert W. *Language, Hermeneutic, and Word of God*. New York: Harper & Row, 1966.

Gadamer, Hans-Georg. *Le problème de la conscience historique*. Louvain: Publications Universitaires de Louvain, 1963.

Gadamer, Hans-Georg. *Truth and Method*. Translators Garrett Barden and John Cumming. New York: Seabury Press, 1975 (German edition: *Wahrheit und Methode*. 2nd. ed. Tübingen: J. C. B. Mohr (Paul Siebeck), 1965.

Gallie, W. B. *Philosophy and The Historical Understanding*. 2nd. ed. New York: Schocken Books, 1968.

Galloway, Allan D. *Wolfhart Pannenberg*. London: Allen & Unwin, 1973.

Gardiner, Patrick. *The Nature of Historical Explanation*. London: Oxford University Press, 1952.

———. *The Philosophy of History*. London: Oxford University Press, 1974.

———. editor. *Theories of History*. New York: Free Press, 1959.

Gibbs, Lee W. and Stevenson, W. Taylor. *Myth and Crisis of Historical Consciousness*. Missoula: Scholars Press, 1975.

Gilkey, Langdon. *Reaping the Whirlwind: A Christian Interpretation of History*. New York: Seabury Press, 1976.

Goldstein, Leon J. *Historical Knowing*. Austin: University of Texas Press, 1976.

Haight, Roger, *An Alternative Vision: An Interpretation of Liberation Theology*. New York: Paulist Press, 1985.

Hart, Ray L. *Unfinished Man and the Imagination*. New York: Herder & Herder, 1968.

Harvey, Van Austin. *The Historian and the Believer*. New York: Macmillan, 1966.

Heidegger, Martin. *Being and Time*. Translators John Macquarrie and Edward Robinson. New York: Harper & Row, 1962.

Herberg, Will. *Faith Enacted as History: Essays in Biblical Theology*. Edited by Bernhard W. Anderson. Philadelphia: Westminster Press, 1976.

Hirsch, Eric D., Jr. *Validity in Interpretation*. New Haven: Yale University Press, 1967.

Hodges, H. A. *The Philosophy of Wilhelm Dilthey*. London: Routledge & Keegan Paul, 1952.

———. *Wilhelm Dilthey: An Introduction*. London: Routledge & Keegan Paul, 1944. Reprinted New York: Howard Fertig, 1969.

Jeremias, Joachim. *The Problem of the Historical Jesus*. Translator Norman

Perrin. Facet Books, Biblical Series, No. 13. Philadelphia: Fortress Press, 1964.

Johnston, William M. *The Formative Years of R. G. Collingwood.* The Hague: Martinus Nijhoff, 1967.

Kähler, Martin. *The So-Called Historical Jesus and the Historical Biblical Christ.* Translated and edited by Carl E. Braaten. Foreward Paul Tillich. Philadelphia: Fortress Press, 1964.

Käseman, Ernst. *Essays on New Testament Themes.* Translator W. J. Montague. Naperville, Ill.: A. R. Allenson, 1964.

―――. *New Testament Questions of Today.* Translator W. J. Montague. Philadelphia: Fortress Press, 1969.

Kaufman, Gordan D. *God and the Problem.* Cambridge: Harvard University Press, 1972.

―――. *Relativism, Knowledge and Faith.* Chicago: University of Chicago Press, 1960.

―――. *Systematic Theology: A Historicist Perspective.* New York: Charles Scribner, 1968.

Ketner, Kenneth Laine. *An Emendation of R. G. Collingwood's Doctrine of Absolute Presuppositions.* Lubbock: Texas Tech Press, 1973.

Kuhn, Thomas S. *The Structure of Scientific Revolutions.* Chicago: University of Chicago Press, 1962.

Kümmel, Werner Georg. *The New Testament: The History of the Investigation of its Problems.* Translators S. MacLean Gilmour and Howard Clark Kee. Nashville: Abingdon Press, 1972.

Küng, Hans. *On Being a Christian.* Translator Edward Quinn. New York: Doubleday, 1976.

Krausz, Michael, editor. *Critical Essays on the Philosophy of R. G. Collingwood.* Oxford: Clarendon Press, 1972.

Langer, Susanne. *Feeling and Form.* New York: Scribner, 1953.

Lightfoot, R. H. *History and Interpretation in the Gospel.* London: Hodder & Stoughton, 1935.

Linge, David. "Historicity and Hermeneutic: A Study of Contemporary Hermeneutical Theory." Ph.D. dissertation, Vanderbilt University, 1969.

Lonergan, Bernard J. F. *Insight: A Study of Human Understanding.* 3rd ed. New York: Philosophical Library, 1970.

———. *Method in Theology.* New York: Herder & Herder, 1972.

Long, Eugene Thomas, editor. *God, Secularization and History: Essays in Memory of Ronald Gregor Smith.* Columbia: University of South Carolina Press, 1974.

Löwith, Karl. *Meaning in History.* Chicago: University of Chicago Press, 1949.

McCabe, Herbert. *What is Ethics All About?* Washington, D.C.: Corpus Books, 1969.

McIntire, C. T., editor. *God, History and Historians: Modern Christian Views of History.* New York: Oxford University Press, 1977.

Macquarrie, John. *An Existentialist Theology: A Comparison of Heidegger and Bultmann.* New York: Macmillan, 1955.

———. *The Scope of Demythologizing: Bultmann and His Critics.* London: SCM Press, 1960.

Maier, Gerhard, *The End of the Historical-Critical Method.* Translators Edward W. Leverenz and Rudolph F. Norden. St. Louis: Concordia, 1977.

Malet, André. *The Thought of Rudolf Bultmann.* Translator Richard Strachan. Preface Rudolf Bultmann. Garden City: Doubleday, 1971.

Marrou, Henri-Irénée. *The Meaning of History.* Translator Robert J. Olsen. Baltimore: Helicon, 1966.

Meinecke, Friedrich. *Historism: The Rise of a New Historical Outlook.* New York: Herder & Herder, 1972.

Meyerhoff, Hans, editor. *The Philosophy of History in Our Time.* Garden City: Doubleday, 1959.

Meynell, Hugo A. *An Introduction to the Philosophy of Bernard Lonergan.* New York: Barnes & Noble, 1976.

Michalson, Carl. *The Hinge of History: An Existential Approach to the Christian Faith.* New York: Scribner, 1959.

───. *Worldly Theology: The Hermeneutical Focus of an Historical Faith.* New York: Charles Scribner, 1967.

Mink, Louis O. *Mind, History and Dialectic: The Philosophy of R. G. Collingwood.* Bloomington: Indiana University Press, 1969.

Navone, John. *History and Faith in the Thought of Alan Richardson.* London: SCM Press, 1966.

New Catholic Encyclopedia, 1967 ed. S. V. "Dilthey, Wilheim," by P. L. Hug.

Newman, F. D. *Explanation by Description.* The Hague: Mouton, 1968.

Niebuhr, H. Richard. *The Meaning of Revelation.* New York: Macmillan, 1962.

Niebuhr, Richard R. *Resurrection and Historical Reason: A Study of Theological Method.* New York: Scribner, 1957.

Nygren, Anders. *Meaning and Method: Prolegomena to a Scientific Philosophy of Religion and a Scientific Theology.* Philadelphia: Fortress Press, 1972.

Ogden, Schubert M. *Christ Without Myth.* New York: Harper & Row, 1961.

───. *The Reality of God.* New York: Harper & Row, 1963. O'Meara, Thomas and Weisser, Donald, editors. *Rudolf Bultmann in Catholic Thought.* New York: Herder & Herder, 1968.

Ommen, Thomas B. *The Hermeneutic of Dogma.* American Academy of Religion Dissertation Series No. 11. Missoula: Scholars Press, 1975.

Palmer, Richard E. *Hermeneutics: Interpretation Theory in Schleiermacher, Dilthey, Heidegger, and Gadamer.* Evanston: Northwestern University Press, 1969.

Pannenberg, Wolfhart. *Basic Questions in Theology.* 2 vols. Translator George H. Kehm. Philadelphia: Fortress Press, 1970–71.

───. *Faith and Reality.* Translator John Maxwell. Philadelphia: Westminster Press, 1977.

───. *Jesus-God and Man.* Translators Lewis L. Wilkens and Duane A. Priebe. Philadelphia: Westminster Press, 1968.

───. editor. *Revelation as History.* Translator David Granskow. London: Macmillan, 1968.

———. *Theology and The Kingdom of God*. Philadelphia: Westminster Press, 1969.

———. *Theology and the Philosophy of Science*. Philadelphia: Westminster Press, 1976.

———. *What is Man?* Translator Duane A. Priebe. Philadelphia: Fortress Press, 1972.

Passmore, J. B. *A Hundred Years of Philosophy*. London: Gerald Duckworth, 1957.

Patrick, James, *The Magelalen Metaphysicals: Idealism and Orthodoxy at Oxford, 1901–1915*. Mercer University Press, 1985.

Peters, Theodore F. "Method and Truth: An Inquiry into the Philosophical Hermeneutics of Hans-Georg Gadamer and the Theology of History of Wolfhart Pannenberg." Ph.D. dissertation, University of Chicago Divinity School, 1973.

Popper, Karl. *The Poverty of Historicism*. New York: Harper Torchbooks, 1969.

Preston, Ronald H., editor. *Theology and Change: Essays in Memory of Alan Richardson*. London: SCM Press, 1975.

Reese, James M. *Experiencing the Good News: The New Testament as Communication*. Wilmington: Glazier, 1984.

Renier, G. J. *History: Its Purpose and Method*. London: Allen & Unwin, 1950.

Richardson, Alan. *Christian Apologetics*. New York: Harper, 1947.

———. *History Sacred and Profane*. Philadelphia: Westminster Press, 1964.

Ricoeur, Paul. *Freedom and Nature: The Voluntary and the Involuntary*. Translation and Introduction Erazim V. Kohak. Evanston: Northwestern University Press, 1966.

———. *Interpretation Theory: Discourse and the Surplus of Meaning*. Fort Worth: Texas Christian University Press, 1976.

Roberts, T. A. *History and Christian Apologetic*. London: SPCK, 1960.

Robinson, James M. *A New Quest for the Historical Jesus*. Studies in Biblical Theology No. 25. London: SCM Press, 1959.

Robinson, James M. and Cobb, John B., editors. *New Frontiers in Theology.* Vol. I. *The Later Heidegger and Theology.* New York: Harper & Row, 1963.

———. *New Frontiers in Theology.* Vol. II. *The New Hermeneutic.* New York: Harper & Row, 1964.

———. *New Frontiers in Theology.* Vol. III. *Theology as History.* New York: Harper & Row, 1967.

Rubinoff, Lionel. *Collingwood and the Reform of Metaphysics: A Study in the Philosophy of Mind.* Toronto: University of Toronto Press, 1970.

Russell, Anthony F. *Logic, Philosophy and History: A Study Based on the Work of R. G. Collingwood.* Lanham, MD: University Press of America, 1984.

Rust, Eric C. *Evolutionary Philosophies and Contemporary Theology.* Philadelphia: Westminster Press, 1969.

———. *Towards a Theological Understanding of History.* New York: Oxford University Press, 1963.

Schleiermacher, F. D. E. *Hermeneutics: The Handwritten Documents.* Edited by Heinz Kimmerle. Translators James Duke and Jack Forstman. Texts and Translation Series, No. 1 Missoula: Scholars Press, 1977.

Schillebeeckx, E. *God the Future of Man.* Translator N. D. Smith. New York: Sheed & Ward, 1968.

———. *Jesus: An Experiment in Christology.* Translator Hubert Hoskins. New York: Seabury Press, 1979.

———. *The Understanding of Faith: Interpretation and Criticism.* New York: Seabury Press, 1974.

Schmithals, Walter. *An Introduction to the Theology of Rudolf Bultmann.* Translator John Bowden. London: SCM Press, 1968.

Shalom, Albert. *R. G. Collingwood: Philosophe et historien.* Paris: Presses Universitaires de France, 1967.

Shea, John. *Stories of God: An Unauthorized Biography.* Chicago: Thomas More Press, 1978.

Smart, Harold R. *Philosophy and its History.* LaSalle, Ill.: Open Court, 1962.

Smith, Page. *The Historian and History.* New York: Vintage Books, 1964.

Sobrino, Jon. *Christology at the Crossroads.* Translator John Drury. Maryknoll: Orbis Books, 1978.

Sokolowski, Robert. *The Formation of Husserl's Concept of Constitution.* The Hague: Martinus Nijhoff, 1964.

Stevenson, W. Taylor. *History as Myth: The Import for Contemporary Theology.* New York: Seabury Press, 1969.

Stendahl, Krister, *Meanings: The Bible as Document and as Guide.* Philadelphia: Fortress Press, 1984.

Streeter, Burnett Hillman. *The Four Gospels: A Study of Origins.* London: Macmillan, 1930.

Stuhlmacher, Peter. *Historical Criticism and Theological Interpretation of Scripture.* Translation and Introduction by Roy A. Harrisville. Philadelphia: Fortress Press, 1977.

Thiselton, Anthony C. *The Two Horizons: New Testament Hermeneutics and Philosophical Description.* Grand Rapids: Eerdmans, 1980.

Tomlin, E. W. F. *R. G. Collingwood.* Writers and their Work No. 42. London: Longmans, Green, 1953. New edition 1961.

Toulmin, Stephen. *Human Understanding.* Vol. I: *Concepts: Their Collective Use and Evolution.* Princeton: Princeton University Press, 1972.

Tracy, David. *The Analogical Imagination: Christian Theology and the Culture of Pluralism.* New York: Crossroads, 1981.

———. *Blessed Rage for Order: The New Pluralism in Theology.* New York: Seabury Press, 1975.

———. *Plurality and Ambiguity: Hermeneutics, Religion and Hope.* New York: Seabury Press, 1986.

Tupper, E. Frank. *The Theology of Wolfhart Pannenberg.* Philadelphia: Westminster Press, 1973.

Tyson, Joseph B. *A Study of Early Christianity.* New York: Macmillan, 1973.

Van Buren, Paul M. *The Secular Meaning of the Gospel.* New York: Macmillan, 1963.

Walsh, W. H. *Introduction to the Philosophy of History.* 3rd. rev. ed. London: Hutchinson's University Press, 1967.

Wiggins, James B. editor. *Religion as Story.* New York: Harper & Row, 1975.

Williams, Bernard and Montefiore, Alan, editors. *British Analytical Philosophy.* New York: The Humanities Press, 1966.

Young, Norman J. *History and Existential Theology.* Philadelphia: Westminster Press, 1969.

Articles and Reviews

Abel, Theodore. "The Operation Called Verstehen." *American Journal of Sociology* 54 (1948–49): 211–218.

Agassi, Joseph. "Questions of Science and Metaphysics." *The Philosophical Forum* n.s. 5 (1974): 529–556.

Arthur, Christopher E. "Gadamer and Hirsch: The Canonical Work and the Interpreter's Intention." *Cultural Hermeneutics* 4 (1977): 183–197.

Beer, S. "Causal Explanation and Imaginative Re-enactment." *History and Theory* 3 (1969): 6–29.

Biehl, Peter. "Zur Frage nach dem historischen Jesus." *Theologische Rundschau* n.s. 24 (1957–58): 54–76.

Bradley, James. "Gadamer's *Truth and Method:* Some Questions and English Applications." *Heythrop Journal* 18 (1977): 420–435.

Brandon, S. G. F. "Modern Interpretations of History and their Challenge." *Modern Churchmen* 39 (1949): 238–252.

Brodie, Louis. Review of Thiselton's *Two Horizons. Thomist* 45 (1981): 480–486.

Buchdahl, G. "Has Collingwood been Unfortunate in his Critics?" *Australasian Journal of Philosophy* 36 (1958): 327–339.

———. "Logic and History: An Assessment of R. G. Collingwood's *Idea of History.*" *Australasian Journal of Philosophy* 26 (1948): 94–113.

Burhenn, Herbert. "Pannenberg's Argument for the Historicity of the

Resurrection." *Journal of the American Academy of Religion* 40 (1972): 368–379.

Cebik, L. B. "Collingwood: Action, Re-enactment, and Evidence." *The Philosophical Forum* n.s. 2 (1970): 68–69.

Coady, C. A. J. "Collingwood and Historical Testimony." *Philosophy* 50 (1975): 409–424.

Cohen, L. J. "Has Collingwood been Misrepresented?" *Philosophical Quarterly* 7 (1959): 149–150.

De Waelhens, Alphonse. "Sur une herméneutique de l'herméneutique." *Revue Philosophique de Louvain* 60 (1962): 573–591.

Dobbin, Edmund J. "Seminar on Foundations: Pannenberg on Theological Method." CTSA, *Proceedings of the 32nd Annual Convention* 32 (1977): 202–220.

Donagan, Alan. "The Croce-Collingwood Theory of Art." *Philosophy* 33 (1958): 162–167.

———. "Explanation in History." *Mind* 66 (1957): 145–164.

———. "The Verification of Historical Theses." *Philosophical Quarterly* 6 (1956): 193–208.

Dray, W. H. "Historical Understanding As Re-Thinking." *University of Toronto Quarterly* 27 (1958): 200–215.

———. "R. G. Collingwood on Reflective Thought." *Journal of Philosophy* 57 (1960): 157–163.

Ducasse, D. J. "Mr. Collingwood on Philosophical Method." *Journal of Philosophy* 33 (1936): 95–106.

Dulles, Avery. "Response to Krister Stendahl's Method in the Study of Biblical Theology." *The Bible in Modern Scholarship*. Edited by J. Philip Hyatt. Nashville: Abingdon Press, 1965, pp. 210–216.

Dykstra, Vergil H. "Philosophers and Presuppositions." *Mind* 69 (1960): 63–68.

Eliot, T. S. Review of *Religion and Philosophy*. *International Journal of Ethics* 27 (1917): 543.

Fitzmyer, Joseph A. "Belief in Jesus Today." *Commonweal* 101 (Nov. 1974): 140–141.

Fruchon, P. "Signification de l'historie de la philosophie selon l'autobiographie de Collingwood." *Les Etudes Philosophiques* 13 (1958): 143–160.

Fuller, Daniel P. "The Resurrection of Jesus and the Historical Method." *Journal of Bible and Religion* 34 (1966): 18–24.

Gadamer, Hans-Georg. "The Continuity of History and the Existential Moment." *Philosophy Today* 16 (1972): 230–240.

―――. "Intendimento e rischio." *Il Problem della Demitizzazione. Archivo di Filosofia.* 1–2. Padova: Cedam, 1961, pp. 75–82.

―――. "On the Scope and Function of Hermeneutical Reflection." *Continuum* 8 (1970): 77–95.

―――. "The Power of Reason." *Man and World* 3 (1970): 5–15.

―――. "Le problème herméneutique." *Archives de Philosophie* 33 (1970): 3–27.

Goldstein, Leon J. "Collingwood's Theory of Historical Knowing." *History and Theory* 9 (1970): 3–36.

―――. "Evidence and Events in History." *Philosophy of Science* 29 (1962): 175–194.

Greig, James C. G. "Some Aspects of Hermeneutics: A Brief Survey." *Religion* 1 (1971): 131–151.

Harris, Errol E. "Collingwood on Eternal Problems." *Philosophical Quarterly* 1 (1951): 228–241.

―――. "Collingwood's Theory of History." *Philosophical Quarterly* 7 (1957): 35–49.

―――. "Mr. Ryle and the Ontological Argument." *Mind* 45 (1936): 474–480.

Hartshorne, C. Review of *An Essay on Philosophical Method. International Journal of Ethics* 44 (1934): 357–358.

Hartt, Julian N. "Metaphysics, History and Civilization: Collingwood's

Account of their Interrelationships." *Journal of Religion* 33 (1953): 198–211.

———. Review of *Faith and Reason: Essays in the Philosophy of Religion* by R. G. Collingwood. Editor Lionel Rubinoff. *Journal of Religion* 49 (1969): 280–294.

Harvey, Van, "New Testament Scholarship and Christian Belief." *Free Inquiry* 5 (1985): 36–39.

Harvey, Van A. and Ogden, Schubert M. "How New is the 'New Quest' of the Historical Jesus?" *The Historical Jesus and the Kerygmatic Christ.* Translated and edited by Carl E. Braaten and Roy A. Harrisville. New York: Abingdon Press, 1964, pp. 197–242.

Hennelly, Alfred T. "Theological Method: The Southern Exposure." *Theological Studies* 38 (1977): 709–735.

Hirsch, Eric D. Jr. "Truth and Method in Interpretation." *Review of Metaphysics* 18 (1965): 488–507.

Hogan, John. "Gadamer and the Hermeneutical Experience," *Philosophy Today* 20 (1976): 3–12.

Hopkins, Jasper. "Bultmann on Collingwood's Philosophy of History." *Harvard Theological Review* 58 (1965): 227–233.

Illanes, Felipe Pardines. "Dilthey y Collingwood." *Filosofía y letras: Revista de la facultad de filosofía y letras* 19 (1950): 87–105.

Innis, Robert E. "Hans-Georg Gadamer's Truth and Method: A Review Article." *Thomist* 40 (1976): 311–321.

Kennedy, D. E. "The Wood and the Trees: The Philosophical Development of R. G. Collingwood." *Australian Journal of Politics and History* 10 (1964): 245–248.

Kimmerle, Heinz. "Hermeneutical Theory or Ontological Hermeneutics." *Journal for Theology and the Church.* Vol. 4 *History and Hermeneutic.* Editor Robert W. Funk. New York: Harper Torchbooks, 1967, pp. 107–121.

Kisiel, Theodore. "The Happening of Tradition: The Hermeneutics of Gadamer and Heidegger." *Man and World* 2 (1969): 358–385.

Knox, T. M. "Notes on Collingwood's Philosophical Work with a Bibliography." *Proceedings of the British Academy* 29 (1943): 469–475.

Linge, David. "Dilthey and Gadamer: Two Theories of Historical Understanding." *Journal of the American Academy of Religion* 41 (1973): 536–553.

Llewelyn, J. "Collingwood's Doctrine of Absolute Presuppositions." *Philosophical Quarterly* 11 (1961): 49–60.

McCallum, R. B. "Robin George Collingwood: 1889–1943." *Proceedings of the British Academy* 29 (1943): 463–468.

MacIver, A. M. "The Character of an Historical Explanation." *Proceedings of the Aristotelian Society,* Supplementary Volume, 21 (1947): 33–50.

MacKay, Donald S. "On Supposing and Presupposing." *Review of Metaphysics* 2 (1948): 1–20.

MacKinnon, D. M. Review of *The Idea of History. Journal of Theological Studies* 47 (1946): 249–253.

Merkley, Paul. "New Quests for Old: One Historian's Observations on a Bad Bargain." *Canadian Journal of Theology* 16 (1970): 203–218.

North, Robert. "Pannenberg's Historicizing Exegesis." *The Heythrop Journal* 12 (1971): 377–400.

Nicol, Iain. "History and Transcendence." *God, Secularization and History: Essays in Memory of Ronald Gregor Smith.* Edited by Eugene Thomas Long. Columbia University of South Carolina Press, 1974, pp. 76–91.

O'Malley, John W. "Reform, Historical Consciousness, and Vatican II's Aggiornamento." *Theological Studies* 32 (1971): 573–601.

Pannenberg, Wolfhart. "Did Jesus Really Rise from the Dead?" *Dialog* 4 (1965): 128–135.

Peters, Ted. "The Nature and Role of Presuppositions: An Inquiry into Contemporary Hermeneutics." *International Philosophical Quarterly* 14 (1974): 209–222.

———. "Truth in History: Gadamer's Hermeneutics and Pannenberg's Apologetic Method." *Journal of Religion* 55 (1975): 36–56.

———. "The Use of Analogy in Historical Method." *Catholic Biblical Quarterly* 35 (1973): 475–482.

Post, John. "A Defense of Collingwood's Theory of Presuppositions." *Inquiry* 8 (1965): 332–354.

Rescher, Nicholas. "On the Logic of Presuppositions." *Philosophy and Phenomenological Research* 21 (1961): 521–527.

Richmond, I. A. "Appreciation of R. G. Collingwood as an Archaeologist." *Proceedings of the British Academy* 29 (1943): 476–480.

Ricoeur, Paul. "The Model of the Text: Meaningful Action Considered as a Text." *New Literary History* 5 (1973): 91–117.

———. "Philosophical Hermeneutics and Theological Hermeneutics." *Studies in Religion/Science Religieuses* 5 (1975–76): 14–33.

Ritchie, A. D. "The Logic of Question and Answer." *Mind* 52 (1943): 24–38.

Rotenstreich, N. "From Facts to Thoughts: Collingwood's Views on the Nature of History." *Philosophy* 35 (1960): 122–137.

Rubinoff, Lionel. "Collingwood's Theory of the Relation between Philosophy and History: A New Interpretation." *Journal of the History of Philosophy* 6 (1968): 363–380.

———. "Collingwood and the Radical Conversion Hypothesis." *Dialogue: Canadian Philosophical Review* 5 (1966): 71–83.

———. "History and Perception: Reflections on R. G. Collingwood's Theory of History." *Philosophical Forum* 2 (1970): 91–107.

Ryle, Gilbert. "Back to the Ontological Argument." *Mind* 46 (1937): 53–57.

———. "Mr. Collingwood and the Ontological Argument." *Mind* 44 (1935): 137–151.

Rynin, David. "Donagan on Collingwood: Absolute Presuppositions, Truth and Metaphysics." *Review of Métaphysics* 18 (1964): 301–333.

Sclafani, Richard. "Wollheim on Collingwood." *Philosophy* 51 (1976): 353–359.

Shalom, Albert. "R. G. Collingwood et la metaphysique." *Les Etudes Philosophiques* 10 (1955): 693–711.

Shea, John. "Theology and Autobiography." *Commonweal* 105 (June 1978): 358–362.

Simonds, A. P. "Mannheim's Sociology of Knowledge as a Hermeneutic Method." *Cultural Hermeneutics* 3 (1975): 81–105.

Skinner, Quentin. "Conventions and the Understanding of Speech Acts." *Philosophical Quarterly* 20 (1970): 118–138.

———. "Meaning and Understanding in the History of Ideas." *History and Theory* 8 (1969): 3–53.

Stek, John H. "The Modern Problem of the Old Testament in the Light of Reformation Perspective." *Calvin Theological Journal* 2 (1967): 202–225.

Stendahl, K. S. V. "Biblical Theology, Contemporary." *Interpreter's Dictionary of the Bible.* Vol. 1. Editor George Arthur Buttrick. New York: Abingdon Press, 1962. pp. 418–432.

———. "The Bible as Classic and the Bible as Holy Scripture." *Journal of Biblical Literature* 103 (1984): 3–10.

———. "Method in the Study of Biblical Theology." *The Bible in Modern Scholarship.* Editor Philip Hyatt. Nashville: Abingdon Press, 1965, pp. 196–209.

Strauss, Leo. "On Collingwood's Philosophy of History." *Review of Metaphysics* 5 (1952): 559–586.

Sykes, Norman. "Some Current Conceptions of Historiography and Their Significance for Christian Apologetic." *Journal of Theological Studies* 50 (1949): 24–37.

Templeton, Douglas. "Kerygma: A Definition." *God, Secularization and History: Essays in Memory of Ronald Gregor Smith.* Edited by Eugene Thomas Long. Columbia: University of South Carolina Press, 1974, pp. 92–106.

Tjalve, Niels. "Collingwood og Theologerne: Historie og forstaelse." *Dansk Teologisk Tidsskrift* 35 (1971): 145–185.

Tomlin, E. W. F. "The Philosophy of R. G. Collingwood." *Ratio* 1 (1958): 116–135.

Turner, Geoffrey. "Wolfhart Pannenberg and the Hermeneutical Problem." *Irish Theological Quarterly* 39 (1972): 107–129.

Walpole, Hugh. "R. G. Collingwood and the Idea of Language." University Studies No. 55. *University of Wichita Bulletin* 38 (1963): 1–8.

Walsh, W. H. "The Character of an Historical Explanation." *Proceedings of the Aristotelian Society*, Supplementary Volume, 21 (1947): 33–50.

———. "Historical Causation." *Proceedings of the Aristotelian Society* 43 (1962–63): 217–236.

———. "The Limits of Scientific History." *Historical Studies* 3 (1961): 45–47.

———. "R. G. Collingwood's Philosophy of History." *Philosophy* 22 (1947): 153–160.

INDEX OF NAMES

Please note: n. indicates citation in a note. Author might be cited in subsequent notes on same page.

Abel, T., 67n., 165n.
Achtemeier, P., 35n.
Agassi, J., 44, 66n.
Anderson, H., 200n.
Anselm, St., 96n.
Antoninus Pius, 61–62
Archimedes, 147
Aristotle, 32–33, 84–85
Arthur, C., 68n.
Augustine, St., 38n., 96n., 118n., 194
Ayer, A., 18, 94n.

Bacon, F., 45, 47
Balducelli, R., 4
Barth, K. T., 7, 94n., 167
Bartsch, H. W., 198n.
Bateson, G., 118n., 140n.
Becker, C., 120n.
Beer, S., 165n.
Betti, E., 121n.
Bianchi, E., 95n.
Biehl, P., 39n., 201n.
Bornkamm, G., 179, 201n.
Bosanquet, B., 14
Braaten, C., 200n., 201n., 203n.
Bradley, F. H., 10, 14, 36n., 104, 109
Brandon, S. G. F., 198n.
Brodie, L., 199n.
Brutus, 134
Buchdahl, G., 37n., 39n., 67n., 119n., 141n., 162n.
Bultmann, R., 1, 4, 7–8, 34, 35n., 39n., 90–91, 97n., 114, 120n., 137, 142n., 156, 164n., 167–183, 190, 195–196, 198n., 199n., 200n., 202n., 208
Burhenn, H., 193, 203n., 204n., 205n.
Buri, J., 180–181

Caesar, 109, 133–134, 150–151
Cassirer, E., 20
Cebik, L. B., 140n., 162n.
Childs, B., 120n.
Coady, C., 111–112, 119n., 120n., 141n.
Cobb, J., 35n., 203n.
Cohen, L. J., 37n., 69n.
Collingwood, W. G., 12
Cook, Wilson, J., 14
Coreth, E., 4, 88, 97n., 159–160, 165n.
Croce, B., 9–10, 15–16, 26, 32, 36n., 94n., 171

Debbins, W., 37n., 40n., 67n., 118n., 119n., 120n., 121n., 140n., 141n., 162n.
de Ruggiero, G., 38n.
Descartes, R., 12, 45, 76
DeWaelhens, A., 67n.
Dilthey, W., 7, 9–10, 22, 34, 36n., 67n., 94n., 118n., 125, 164n., 167, 169, 171, 180, 183, 196, 202n., 205n.
Dobbin, E., 205n.
Dodd, C. H., 142n., 198n.

Donagan, A., 17–18, 33, 37n., 38n., 40n., 41n., 66n., 69n., 95n., 118n., 119n., 140n., 141n., 144, 162n., 163n.
Doty, W., 199n.
Dray, W. H., 69n., 141n.
Dulles, A., 142n.
Dykstra, V., 93n., 95n.
Dyson, A. O., 200n.

Ebeling, G., 179, 201n.
Edwards, K., 14
Eliade, M., 142n.
Epicurus, 146
Erikson, E., 87
Euclid, 145

Fackenheim, E., 39n., 94n., 97n., 118n.
Fichte, J. G., 104–105
Fitzmyer, J., 105n.
Florovsky, G., 142n.
Fuchs, E., 179, 201n.
Fuller, D., 203n., 204n.
Fuller, R. H., 198n.
Funk, R., 39n.

Gabler, J. P., 142n.
Gadamer, H. G., 1, 4–5, 7, 22–23, 28, 32, 35n., 36n., 39n., 40n., 41n., 44, 47–48, 51–58, 60–61, 63–65, 66n., 67n., 68n., 69n., 71–73, 89–91, 93n., 97n., 121n., 125, 136, 142n., 144, 147, 151, 156, 158–160, 162n., 164n., 165n., 168, 183–184, 196, 205n., 209, 211n.
Galloway, A., 191, 204n.
Gardiner, P., 69n., 141n., 158, 162n., 165n.
Gibbon, E., 96n.
Gibbs, L., 142n.
Goldstein, L., 61, 69n., 97n., 112, 119n., 120n., 121n., 140n., 141n., 144, 162n., 163n.
Graham, E., 13

Green, T. H., 14
Greig, J., 198n.

Hadrian, 148–149
Haight, R., 2, 6n., 95n.
Hanson, A., 205n.
Harris, E., 38n., 39n., 41n., 93n., 120n., 141n.
Harrisville, R., 200n., 201n., 211n.
Hart, R., 35n., 68n.
Hartt, J., 4, 6n., 93n., 96n., 198n.
Harvey, V., 4, 35n., 119n., 141n., 142n., 157–158, 165n., 178, 200n., 201n., 206n.
Hegel, G. W. F., 9, 11, 15, 20, 28, 56–57, 104–106, 160
Heidegger, M., 7, 20, 23, 34, 55, 91, 97n., 167n., 170, 182, 202n.
Hennelly, A., 95n.
Herakles, 181
Herodotus, 186
Hirsch, E., 121n.
Hodges, H., 36n., 67n., 140n.
Hogan, J., 41n.
Hopkins, J., 164n., 173, 200n.
Hug, P. L., 205n.
Husserl, E., 20

Innis, R., 70n.

Jaspers, K., 171
Jesus, 2–3, 25–26, 136–137, 169, 171, 177–181, 184, 191–192, 196
Johnston, W., 35n., 36n., 37n., 94n.

Kähler, M., 199n.
Kant, I., 10–11, 47, 76, 102, 104–106
Käsemann, E., 179, 201n.
Kaufmann, G., 4, 35n., 87, 96n., 137–138, 142n., 199n., 206n.
Kennedy, D. E., 69n.
Ketner, K. L., 93n.
Kierkegaard, S., 94n.
Kimmerle, H., 22, 39n.
Kisiel, T., 68n., 97n.

Knox, T. M., 16–18, 28–29, 36n., 37n., 38n., 40n., 93n., 95n.
Krausz, M., 37n., 38n., 93n., 95n.
Kuhn, T., 94n.
Kümmel, W. G., 142n.
Küng, H., 2, 87, 96n.

Lightfoot, R. H., 198n.
Linge, D., 67n.
Llewelyn, J., 93n., 96n.
Lonergan, B. J. F., 1, 4, 7, 39n., 42n., 67n., 83, 90–91, 97n., 114, 118n., 120n., 121n., 141n., 156, 163n., 164n., 211n.
Long, E. T., 165n.
Luther, M., 176, 201n.

Mackay, D., 93n.
Macquarrie, J., 137, 142n., 200n.
Maier, G., 2, 6n.
Malet, A., 171–172, 199n.
Marius, 147
Marx, K., 209
Masson, R., 4
McCabe, H., 164n.
McCallum, R., 37n.
Merkley, P., 39n., 142, 179, 201n.
Meyerhoff, H., 120n.
Meynell, H., 67n.
Michalson, C., 142n.
Mink, L., 18–19, 24, 36n., 38n., 39n., 40n., 44, 66n., 69n., 95n., 102, 104, 118n., 119n., 121n., 141n., 162n., 200n., 202n.
Montefiore, A., 162n.
Myers, J. N., 97n., 164n.

Navone, J., 198n.
Nelson, H., 54, 154–155
New Questers, 142n., 179, 198n., 201n.
Newman, F. D., 162n.
Nicol, I., 164n., 165n., 201n., 211n.
Niebuhr, H. R., 142n.
Niebuhr, R., 142n.
Nietzsche, F., 146

North, R., 203n., 204n.
Nygren, A., 93n.

Ogden, S., 87, 96n., 97n., 178, 180–181, 200n., 201n., 202n.
O'Meara, T., 211n.
Ommen, T., 69n., 211n.

Palmer, R., 35n., 140n.
Pannenberg, W., 1, 3–5, 7, 35n., 141n., 142n., 168, 182–196, 198n., 202n., 203n., 204n., 205n., 206n., 208
Passmore, J., 38n., 41n.
Patrick, J., 37n., 40n., 198n.
Paul, St., 190–191, 201n.
Peters, T., 68n., 72, 88, 93n., 97n., 198n., 203n., 204n., 205n.
Plato, 11, 32, 47, 51, 53, 78, 105
Polanyi, M., 93n.
Popper, K., 141n., 195–196
Post, J., 93n.

Reuther, R., 95n.
Richardson, A., 198n., 205n.
Richmond, I. A., 36n., 37n.
Rickman, H., 67n.
Ricoeur, P., 7, 142n., 164n.
Roberts, T. A., 198n.
Robinson, J., 35n., 39n., 67n., 164n., 179, 200n., 201n., 203n.
Rothenstreich, N., 38n.
Rubinoff, L., 18–21, 36n., 37n., 38n., 39n., 40n., 41n., 94n., 95n., 96n., 97n., 118n., 119n., 141n., 155, 162n., 164n., 165n., 175, 200n., 211n.
Ruskin, J., 12, 26, 76
Russell, A., 66n.
Ryle, G., 96n.
Rynin, D., 93n.

Schillebeeckx, E., 2, 35n., 68n.
Schleiermacher, F., 7, 22, 54, 183
Schmithals, W., 198n., 199n.
Segundo, J. L., 95n.

Shalom, A., 37n., 38n., 120n.
Shea, J., 211n.
Simonds, A., 66n., 164n.
Skinner, Q., 66n., 68n., 164n.
Sobrino, J., 2
Socrates, 29, 51–52
Sokolowski, R., 140n.
Spengler, O., 194
Stendahl, K., 4, 6n., 138–139, 142n., 207, 211n.
Stevenson, W. T., 142n., 200n., 201n., 203n.
Strauss, L., 38n.
Streeter, B. H., 13, 37n., 198n.
Stuhlmacher, P., 211n.
Sykes, N., 198n.

Thales, 84
Thiselton, A., 199n.
Thomas, Aquinas, St., 163n.

Tillich, P., 87, 96n.
Tjalve, N., 39n., 204n.
Tomlin, E., 38n., 96n.
Toulmin, S., 37n., 83, 94n., 95n., 96n.
Toynbee, A., 194
Tracy, D., 2, 6n., 7, 35n.
Troeltsch, E., 7
Tupper, E. F., 202n., 203n.
Turner, G., 202n., 203n.
Tyson, J., 141n.

Van Buren, P., 198n.
Villeneuve, P. C. J., 54

Walsh, W. H., 141n., 143–144, 162n.
Weisser, D., 211n.
Wiggins, J., 211n.
Williams, B., 162n.

Young, N., 202n.